THE UPPER SILESIAN INDUSTRIAL REGION

THE

UPPER SILESIAN

INDUSTRIAL REGION

Norman J. G. Pounds

Professor of Geography,
Chairman, Institute of East European Studies
Indiana University

INDIANA UNIVERSITY PUBLICATIONS

GRADUATE SCHOOL

SLAVIC AND EAST EUROPEAN SERIES, VOL. 11

1958

9967

Composed At The

INDIANA UNIVERSITY

RESEARCH CENTER IN

ANTHROPOLOGY, FOLKLORE, AND LINGUISTICS

Swoim Przyjaciołom z Towarzystwa Geograficznego w Katowicach, z wyraznami wdzięczności poświęca Autor.

FOREWORD

The forms of place-names employed in this book are those currently used in the countries concerned. To this rule there are only two exceptions. Where there is an essentially English form, as in the case of Warsaw and the names of the countries themselves, this is used. Secondly, when a place-name occurs in an essentially historical context, a different form may be used. Thus, the greatest of the territorial magnates of Upper Silesia is referred to as the Prince of Pless, though elsewhere the little town which was his seat is known as Pszczyna. To assist in understanding the place-names of this region the Polish, Czech, German and conventional English forms, if they exist, are given in the appendix. All measures of weight are quoted in metric tons.

The author desires to thank the Social Science Research Council and the Graduate School of Indiana University for their financial help in studying the Upper Silesian area; his colleagues, Professors V. L. Benes, N. Spulber and P. S. Wandycz, for their assistance, and many friends in both Poland and America.

Bloomington, Indiana   Norman J. G. Pounds
May, 1958

TABLE OF CONTENTS

LIST OF MAPS AND DIAGRAMS

LIST OF ABBREVIATIONS

The following abbreviations are used for the more frequently cited serial publications:

A.d.M.	Annales des Mines.
B.u.H.J.	Berg- und Hüttenmannisches Jahrbuch.
B.u.H.R.	Berg - und Hüttenmannische Rundshau.
B.u.H.Z.	Berg- und Hüttenmannische Zeitung.
D.O.T.	Department of Overseas Trade, Report on Economic and Commercial Conditions.
G.	Glückauf.
G.P.	Gospodarka Planowa.
H.	Hutnik.
J.d.M.	Journal des Mines.
J.d.S.V.f.B.u.H.	Jahrbuch des Schlesischen Vereins fur Berg- und Hüttenwesen.
M.B.	Metal Bulletin.
M.R.	Montanistische Rundschau.
O.Z.f.B.u.H.	Oesterreichische Zeitschrift für Berg- und Hüttenwesen.
P.G-H.	Przegląd Górniczo-Hutniczy.
R.d.l'I.M.	Revue de l'Industrie Minérale.
R.d.M.M.	Revue de Minéralogie: Mémoires.
R.U.d.M.	Revue Universelle des Mines.
S.u.E.	Stahl und Eisen.
W.G.	Wiadomości Górnicze.
W.H.	Wiadomości Hutnicze.
Z.d.O.B.u.H.V.	Zeitschrift des Oberschlesischen Berg- und Hüttenmannischen Vereins.
Z.f.d.B.H.u.S.	Zeitschrift für das Berg-, Hütten- und Salinenwesen im Preussischen Staate.
Z.G.	Życie Gospodarcze.

CHAPTER I

SILESIA IN THE EIGHTEENTH CENTURY

Fern von gebildeten Menschen,
am Ende des Reiches, wer hilft euch
Schatze finden ünd sie glucklich
Zu bringen ans Licht?
J. W. Goethe, at Tarnowskie Góry, 1790.

In the last month of the year 1740 the armies of King
Frederick II of Prussia invaded the province of Silesia. For
a generation or more the Prussian rulers had asserted a
vague claim to this territory, and, shadowy though it was, this
had served to give a cloak of legality to this act of agression.[1]

Silesia lay on both sides of the river Odra, and stretched
from near the source of the river north-westward for nearly
250 miles to the borders of Brandenburg. In the earlier middle ages it had formed part of the realm of the Piast Kings of
Poland, but in the thirteenth century it was ceded to the Bohemian crown. Four centuries later, along with Bohemia, the
province of Silesia passed to the Austrain house of Hapsburg,
and at the time of Frederick II's invasion, it formed part of
the lands of Duchess Maria Theresa of Austria.

The province which the Prussians conquered differed in
several respects from that which the Polish King Casimir had
ceded to Bohemia some four centuries earlier. In the intervening years there had been numerous small territorial
changes. Among these the most important were the cession
to Silesia in 1462 of the County of Glatz (Kłodzko), in the Sudeten Mountains, and the loss by Silesia of the Counties of Cieszyn, Oświęcim and Zator. The former brought to Silesia the
small but important coalfield of Wałbrzych; the latter deprived Silesia of the southernmost part of the hitherto undis-
covered coalfield of Upper Silesia.[2]

For almost five years the Prussians fought to preserve
their conquest. Frederick was quick to set up administrative
machinery in Silesia, but it was not until after peace eventually came to Europe in 1763 that he was able to do much toward developing its resources.[3] Silesia was a poor and

1

backward province. Its cities were few and small, and much
of its soil was both of little value and badly cultivated. The
mineral resources of Silesia were extensive and varied, but
the most valuable of them, the coal of Upper Silesia, had not
yet been exploited and its true extent was quite unknown.

The Land: The river Odra, rising within the hills of Bohemia, beyond the southern boundary of Silesia, formed an
artery for the province.[4] It was an unruly river; little attempt
had been made to tame it, and in springtime it often flooded
with great violence. Below Wrocław it was used regularly
for navigation, but upstream from this point to Racibórz navigation was attended with considerable difficulty and hazard.[5]
The Odra was fed by numerous tributaries from the south-
west. These rose in the Sudeten Mountains of Bohemia and
dropped steeply to the Silesian plain. By contrast, the right
bank tributaries were few, and their contribution to the Odra,
small. Most important of them were the Kłodnica and the
Małapanew, whose current was used to power the first iron-
works built by the Prussian government.

Most of Silesia is occupied by the plain of the river Odra.
Along its western margin the Sudeten Mountains rise steeply;
to the east are the less spectacular uplands of Małopolska, or
Little Poland. A belt of alluvium follows the course of the
Odra and of each of its larger tributaries, but away from the
river and at a rather higher level lay vast areas of infertile
sand and gravel. To west and south of Wrocław the less fertile deposits had been covered by a mantel of loess, and here
the land was more thickly settled and more intensively cultivated than in most other parts of Silesia.[6]

To the south-east, in the area that has come to be called
Upper Silesia, the soil again deteriorates. The plain of the
Odra is interrupted by hills, formed generally by the outcrop-
ping of harder rocks, which yield a soil even less fertile than
that of Lower Silesia.

The area of hills and rolling plateaus, which made up Upper Silesia, merge westward into the Sudeten Mountains of
Bohemia and southward into the Beskid Mountains. Between
the Sudeten and the Beskid Mountains is the Moravian Gate,
one of the few openings in that belt of highlands which stretches
across Europe from the Rhineland almost to the Black Sea.[7]

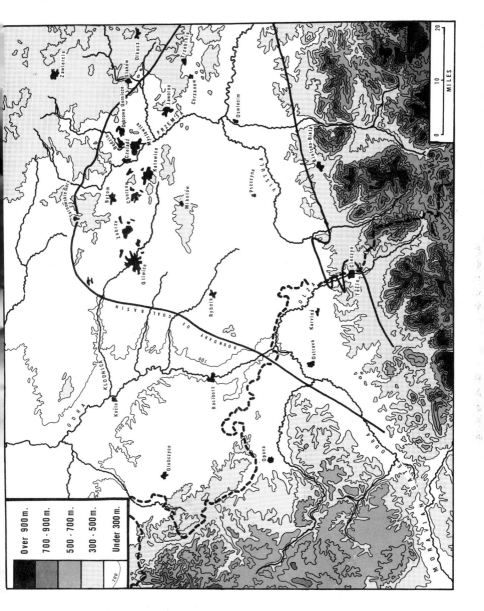

Figure 1:   Upper Silesia and the Moravian Gate.

The Moravian Gate had been of incalculable historical importance. The prehistoric amber trade between the Mediterranean and the shores of the Baltic Sea had passed through it. Medieval merchants travelling between the Italian and the East German cities had used it. It had guided military campaigns, and control of its northern approaches was to be of no small strategic value to Prussia.

Thus the plateau of Upper Silesia lay at the convergence of three routes. To the south-west the route through the Moravian Gate followed first the Upper Odra, no longer a navigable river, and then the Morava to its junction with the Danube. Northwestward the Odra guided the traveller to Wrocław, to Brandenburg and to the Baltic coast, while to the east the infant Vistula had carved a valley between the Beskids and the hills of Małopolska. There, where the river had acquired at least the semblance of navigability, had grown up the ancient Polish capital of Kraków.

But in Upper Silesia itself no city of size and importance had developed. Opole, Głubczyce and Racibórz were little more than large villages, and in the future industrial area the only urban settlements were the very small walled towns of Gliwice, Bytom, Będzin and Czeladź.[8]

The climate of Silesia is one of the most extreme in Europe. Winters are long and severe, and average temperatures may be below freezing point for three months of the year. Snow lies long, and navigation is brought to a standstill by ice. Spring is usually a time of flood, as the last snows melt away and the sodden land absorbs little of the rainfall. Summers are hot, and the rainfall comes in violent storms. But this, nevertheless, is the season when the level of rivers is lowest and navigation most difficult, as the rainfall is quickly evaporated into the hot air. At this time of the year the mill-wheels were stilled and the hammer-works silenced, because the small streams on which they relied, no longer had the strength to move them.

The loess-covered lands of Silesia and of neighboring parts of Moravia and Małopolska were mostly under cultivation at the time of the Prussian conquest. They were dotted with villages, sometimes tightly built and surrounded by the patchwork quilt of open-fields; more often long and streetlike,

with farmholdings reaching back behind the houses to the distant forest edge or to the limits of the next village.

Agricultural land was less extensive in Upper than in
Lower Silesia. Forest covered the valley of the little Małapanew river, and a further belt of forest stretched between the
Odra and the Vistula. Only in the extreme south, where Silesia bordered Moravia and the county of Cieszyn, did cropland
predominate. Elsewhere, cultivation was practiced only on
small, rounded clearings made in the woodland.[9]

The People: The population of Silesia soon after the Prussian conquest, was about 1,162,000.[10] During the Seven Years'
War, the area was fought over, and the population suffered
greatly. By 1764 it had been reduced to 1,112,000. Silesia
had recovered quickly from the destruction of the Silesian
Wars; its recovery after 1763 was no less rapid, and aroused
the admiration of Mirabeau.[11]

The only settlement in Silesia with pretensions to size
and importance was Wrocław. Its population was about
50,000,[12] but no other city exceeded one-tenth of this. In Upper Silesia the largest cities had no more than 3000, and, in
the future industrial area, Bytom and Gliwice were little towns
of only about 2000 inhabitants.[13] All cities, except Wrocław,
were predominantly agricultural in character and function.
In the midst of each was a large open square, the Rynek, or
Ring, where the weekly market was held. Manufacturing industries were restricted to the domestic crafts of the weaver and
blacksmith, the woodworker and tanner.

At the time of the Prussian conquest, the German language was spoken in no more than half the Province of Silesia.
According to Mirabeau,[14] the river Odra separated a German-
speaking area, west of the river, from the area to the east in
which he found a "corrupt Polish." The line of the Odra was
only an approximate language boundary. North of Wrocław
German was widely spoken at this date to the east of the river,
while Upper Silesia was almost entirely Polish, only the cities
forming islands of German speech.[15]

The language boundary in Silesia was in large measure
also a religious boundary. Protestants—mainly Lutheran—
predominated in the German speaking areas of the north and
west. There they were said to make up five-eights of the

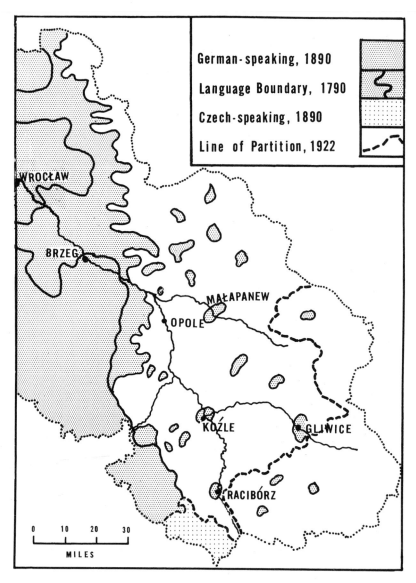

German-speaking, 1890

Language Boundary, 1790

Czech-speaking, 1890

Line of Partition, 1922

WROCŁAW

BRZEG

MAŁAPANEW

OPOLE

KOŹLE

GLIWICE

RACIBÓRZ

0   10   20   30

MILES

Figure 2: The language boundary in Upper Silesia (based on J. Partsch).

population. In Polish-speaking Silesia, Roman Catholics out-
numbered all others by eighteen to one.

The line which separated Pole from German and, though
less distinctly, Roman Catholic from Lutheran, served also to
divide a region of lower from one of higher material culture.
Mirabeau stigmatized the ignorance and coarseness which he
found in the Polish villages and praised the "civilising" work
of Frederick II in establishing colonies of Germans amid the
Poles.[16] The course of German penetration and settlement of
Silesia had been guided very largely by the soil conditions.
The loess-covered plains west of the Odra had been settled in
the thirteenth century. German settlers spread along the fertile margin of the Sudetes and Beskid Mountains, and converted the Slavs around them to German methods of land tenure and land cultivation.[17] To what extent this region was
"germanized" in a cultural sense is uncertain, for their work
was in part undone by a subsequent Slav resurgence.[18] At the
time of the Prussian conquest the population of all Upper Silesia and of parts of Lower was in the main Polish in language
and Catholic in religion.

Regions of Upper Silesia: Silesia as a whole was a poor
and backward province, and the least progressive part of it
was Upper Silesia.[19] As usually defined, Upper Silesia consists of the most south-easterly part of the province, and is
limited on the north-west by a line drawn roughly from the
Bohemian border near Otmuchów to the ancient Polish border,
near Byczyna.[20] The whole area was divisible into four con-
trasted regions.

Most distinctive of these was the plain of the river Odra
itself, a narrow belt of alluvial land which stretched from
south to north across the area.[21] West of the river the ancient rocks which made up this part of Upper Silesia were
deeply covered with loess, making it the most extensive and
best settled part of the area. Nevertheless, toward the northwest, the loess gave place to the sands and gravels near Niemodlin. West of both the loess and the sand regions lay the
Sudetes.

East of the Odra river there was greater variety in the
terrain. The most conspicuous feature was a limestone ridge,
known as the Chełm which stretched from east to west and

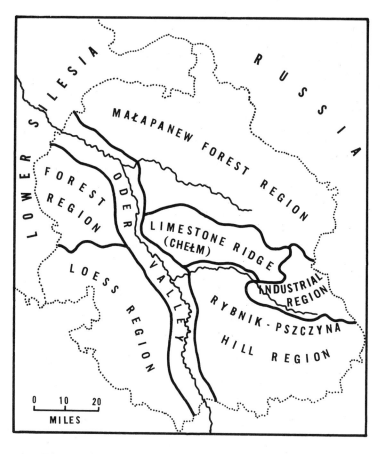

Figure 3: The geographical regions of Upper Silesia (after J. Partsch).

overlooked the Odra in a steep bluff, called the Góra Swiętej Anny, or Annaberg.[22] The ridge is composed of Triassic limestone, a soft and porous deposit, already known at the time of the Frederician conquest for its deposits of the ores of lead, zinc and iron. To the north of Chełm, the limestone dipped beneath a wide and deep spread of sand and gravel, which covered almost continuously the valleys of the Małapanew and the Chełm supported a soil of no high fertility, but its woodland cover was thin and easy to clear. The Małapanew and Stobrawa valleys, by contrast, were densely wooded, and the slight value of the soil offered little inducement to clear the land for cultivation.

A low escarpment marked the southern edge of this limestone region. From its foot there stretched southward a rolling plateau. It was built of rocks lower in the geological scale than the Triassic limestone; amongst these were the coal measures which actually rose to the surface over parts of this area.

It was over this undulating plateau that the industrial area was to develop. It lay on the watershed between the Vistula and the Odra. Westward the Kłodnica and Ruda flowed to the Odra; to the east, the river Przemsza, formed by the confluence at Mysłowice of the Czarna (Black) and Biała (White) Przemsza, flows south to join the Vistula, gathering the waters of the small streams, Brynica and Rawa, which rise within the industrial area (see figure 4). The prevailing direction of the drainage is east-west, and the moderate relief of the area is also marked by low east to west ridges. South of the gentle escarpment formed by the Muschelkalk, lies a strip of rolling country, with the Bytomka flowing to the west and the Brynica to the east. A ridge of higher ground, on the crest of which sits the present city of Chorzów, separates this from the Rawa valley. It is this low ridge, only some eight miles long from near Zabrze in the west to a point near Siemianowice in the east, which has always been the heart of the industrial region.

From the Chorzów ridge the land drops more steeply than is usual in this area into the Rawa valley, in which lies Katowice. To the south of the Rawa another ridge at present sets a limit to the industrial area. Much of this line of low hills is

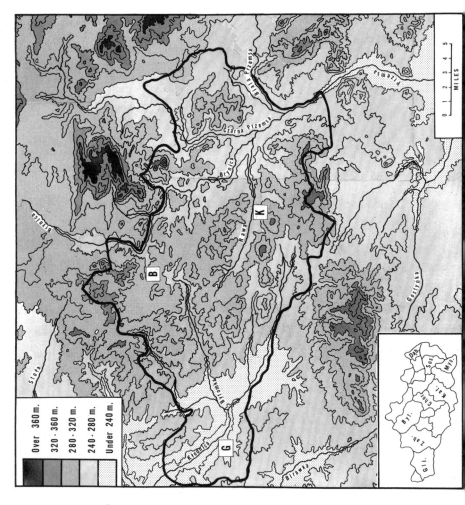

Figure 4: The Relief of the Upper Silesian Industrial Region.

still under forest. Coal mines have been opened here, but its
surface is generally too steep for factory development. From
here the land drops to an almost level plain which stretches,
beyond Mikołów, Rybnik and Pszczyna, to the marshy, lake-
strewn valley of the Vistula.

The pattern of settlement and land-use in Upper Silesia
in the mid-eighteenth century accorded closely with those of
terrain and soil. The sand and gravel lands of Niemodlin and
of the Małapanew and Stobrawa valleys were covered with almost continuous forests, amid which agricultural settlements
were infrequent. The loess-covered lands west of the Odra
and in the extreme south were well settled and mostly under
cultivation. The Chełm ridge was also partly cleared and cultivated, more probably on account of the thinness of its woodland cover than of the merits of its soil. But south of this the
less fertile parts of the hilly land of Rybnik and Pszczyna remained under dense woodland.

Most of Upper Silesia was made up then, as it continued
to be until after the First World War, of the great estates of
the landed nobility. These had been built up over a period of
several centuries. War, famine and all that contributed to the
misery of the peasantry enabled the landowners to strengthen
their hold and extend their possessions.[23] The map (figure 5)
shows the extent of these great estates towards the end of the
nineteenth. But most of the families whose lands are shown
here, Henckel von Donnersmarck, Hohenlohe, the Prince of
Pless (Pszczyna), and Schaffgötsch, already ruled much the
same area a century and a half earlier. At the time of the
Prussian conquest, serfdom prevailed throughout this area.
The free population was small, and was made up of townsfolk,
merchants and gentry. The tillers of the soil, who formed the
bulk of the population, were bound to the land, and, unless the
exigencies of war drove them afield, they spent their lives in
or near their native villages at a level but little above that of
starvation.[24]

Manufacturing industries were but little developed. Flax
was grown and woven into linen, and woolen cloth was made.[25]
Though Silesia as a whole exported cloth in not inconsiderable
quantities, Upper Silesia enjoyed none of the benefits of this

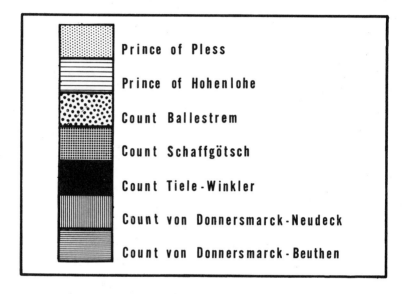

Prince of Pless

Prince of Hohenlohe

Count Ballestrem

Count Schaffgötsch

Count Tiele-Winkler

Count von Donnersmarck-Neudeck

Count von Donnersmarck-Beuthen

trade. Such manufactures as it possessed were to satisfy the simple needs of its own peasantry.

Minerals and Mining: The backwardness and proverty of Upper Silesia were relieved only by its mining. The mineral wealth of Silesia was abundant and varied.[26] Gold, silver, copper and lead had long been mined in the Sudeten Mountains. In the plain there were deposits of brown coal and concretionary masses of iron-ore which could be recovered from the bogs and swamps. In Upper Silesia, the Triassic limestone beds were a rich source of metals, and yielded lead, silver and iron and, though no one at this time suspected its true nature, calamine, the ore of zinc, was dug and used to make brass. But the greatest resource of Upper Silesia was its coal, and this was in the mid-eighteenth century little known and almost completely unused.

Iron-ore was probably the most widely mined of these minerals. Though the ores were not of particularly high quality, the abundant charcoal from the forests made smelting

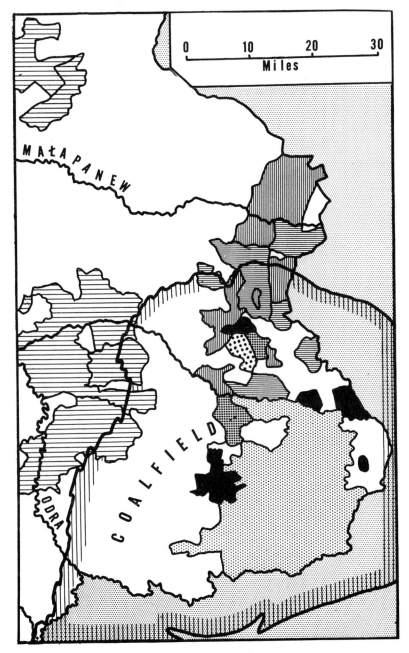

Figure 5: The Great Estates in Upper Silesia.

and iron-working relatively cheap.[27] Bog-ores were obtained
from the marshes that lined the courses of many of the rivers
of Upper Silesia. The blast furnace had been introduced about
twenty years before, and at the time of the Prussian conquest
there were no less than twelve blast furnace works in Upper
Silesia.[28] Refineries, were more numerous. They either produced a soft iron directly from the ore in a single process or
refined the high-carbon metal that came from the blast furnaces.

At this time also iron-working was widely spread throughout southern Poland.[29] Ironworks were established in some instances by the monasteries; in others, by master craftsmen
who had been brought into the area by the great landowners,
but in many instances the works had passed under the control
of the landowners.[30] The latter operated mines and furnaces
just as they did the rest of their estates, using the unfree labour of their serfs.[31] Nevertheless, the quantity of iron made
must have been very small. There was no appreciable trade
in iron, and the output sufficed only for the modest needs of
the local population.

Lead mining was almost as old as iron-working in Upper
Silesia.[32] Ore was obtained from the Triassic limestone as
early as the thirteenth century, and later medieval records
suggest that lead continued to be worked profitably in this area.
Lead could be smelted with relative ease; it had many commercial uses, and its refining yielded a small quantity of silver as
a byproduct. In the sixteenth and seventeenth centuries, mining reached its apogee in the Tarnowskie Góry and Bytom
areas, but already the mines had reached the water-table, and
further mining was conditional upon discovering some effective
means of removing water from the pits.[33] About 1652, Graf
Henckel von Donnersmarck, who owned large areas of lead-
bearing land, had an adit cut to drain his pits. Other adits
were cut in the following years, but these only postponed the
problem. Mines were, one by one, obliged to close as they
reached the water-table. In the lead-bearing region there had
once been hundreds of small pits, but by 1741 their number
had been reduced to fifteen, with an average employment of
probably no more than four. In 1754-5 the mining of lead
ceased.

Closely associated with the lead ores were those of zinc, but, unlike lead, zinc was a particularly intractable metal.[34] The ore mined at this time was the carbonate of zinc, or calamine. It was not until early in the eighteenth century that this ore was first smelted in Europe, and metallic zinc obtained. Until this time the metal was unknown, and calamine was considered to be an 'earth' rather than mineral, a fact which was to have a very significant bearing on mining law as it related to zinc. It had, however, long been known that calamine, added to copper, produced a hard metal of considerable tensile strength, known as brass,[35] and at this time calamine was chiefly used for this purpose.

In the sixteenth century calamine from the Triassic beds of Upper Silesia was used for this purpose. Calamine from Bytom was shipped down the Odra, some of it to be alloyed with Swedish copper. Calamine working continued and early in the eighteenth century, Georg von Giesche, a Wrocław merchant who had dealt in calamine, obtained from the Emperor Leopold of Hapsburg the exclusive right to mine calamine in Silesia for twenty years.[36] Von Giesche opened mines at Scharlej and Bobrek. His early attempts to send his calamine down the Vistula to the port of Gdańsk for export were defeated by the rivalry of Polish producers, and von Giesche was obliged to rely on the Odra for transport. His concession was in due course renewed by the Emperor and, after the Prussian conquest, was extended by Frederick II in 1743 and again in 1762.

All this while no attempt was made in Silesia to extract metallic zinc from the calamine, and the fiction was maintained that calamine was not metalliferous and was thus outside the law relating to metals. But already metallic zinc had been produced in Western Europe by the distillation of calamine.[37] Despite attempts to keep details of the new process a secret, news of it spread, and it became increasingly difficult for the heirs of Georg von Giesche to maintain their privileged position both against trade rivals and against landowners, eager to establish their claim to participate in a lucrative mining business. However, the firm of Georg von Giesches Erben succeeded in keeping its monopoly until the end of the century.

Coal did not at this time count among the mineral assets of Upper Silesia. It had long been known and worked in the Kłodzko and Wałbrzych districts of Lower Silesia. Even in Upper Silesia, people could hardly have been ignorant of its existence. But it was not at this time used in smelting any of the minerals mined there, and for the needs of brickworks and glass furnaces and for the domestic uses of castle and cottage there was an abundance of lumber.

Mining Law: Mining law is one of the strongest influences on the development of any metal industry. It imposes conditions which are often as rigorous as those dictated by the natural conditions in which the minerals occur. Georg von Giesche owed his success in part to the fact that calamine, not being recognized as the ore of a metal, was excluded from the regalian law. By the regalian law the king could concede the right to mine anywhere within his realm, without reference to the surface owner, receiving as his "royalty" a porportion of the metal obtained. The regalian law once applied to the tin mining of Cornwall, [38] but has since disappeared from England. It was, however, strongly entrenched in Germany, where the privileges which it conferred devolved upon the German princes. [39] Both the Duke of Hapsburg and the King of Prussia exercised regalian rights in their respective lands, so little change in this respect could be expected from the change in sovereignty in Silesia. [40]

But the Hapsburgs had alienated the right to concede mining privileges and to receive a tithe of the minerals obtained for certain areas. It was claimed, for example, that in 1618 the Emperor Ferdinand II conferred this "Bergbau-Privilegium" on the family of Henckel von Donnersmarck in respect of the lands which the family owned. [41] The grant of similar privileges to the Prince of Pless was made in the fifteenth century. The lands both of von Donnersmarck and of Pless, were divided, the former into the Tarnowitz-Neudeck and the Beuthen–Siemianowitz lands; the latter into Pless, Myslowitz-Kattowitz and several lesser estates. [42] Each of these fragmented units claimed to inherit the bergregal privileges which had been granted long before to its parent estate.

At the time of the Prussian conquest, these privileges extended only to a narrow range of ores, and, as far as Upper

Silesia was concerned, these were gold, silver and lead. Both calamine (zinc) and iron, as well as coal, were excluded. It may be that in the popular mind at this time the Bergregal metals were associated with deep mines, which caused little disturbance to the surface of the land, and might thus be worked without consulting the local landowner.[43] On the other hand, coal, iron-ore, brick-clay, building stone, as well as calamine, were thought of as being obtained from shallow, open workings which could play havoc with surface rights. It does not follow that mining law was particularly solicitous at this time of the rights of the landowner (as distinct from the King or owner of regalian rights), but this circumstance may help to explain an otherwise anamalous classification of minerals.

Closely linked with the regalian right to concede mining rights and to receive tithe, was the Bergbaufreiheit, the right of any holder of a concession to search for and work minerals anywhere.[44] To this general right, the Henckels and the Princes of Pless opposed the "lex excludendi alios", the right to forbid prospecting and mining on their lands. In effect, these great princes claimed quasi-sovereign powers over their lands in respect of regalian minerals.

Some of their claims, however, were open to dispute, but a settlement of outstanding legal problems was never pressed under the Hapsburgs. It was clear, however, that calamine was not a regalian mineral and that the great landowners were in no privileged position regarding it. The right to mine it could be conceded, as in fact the Emperor Leopold, in 1704, granted it to von Giesche, irrespective of the rights of Henckel and Pless.

Mining law in Upper Silesia was in a sad state of confusion when the Prussians came. It was not many years before a smoother administrative machine, coupled with Frederick II's penchant for economy, began to straighten out this legal muddle. Two trends became manifest: the list of regalian minerals was extended by the inclusion of, among others, coal and calamine, and the Prussian State began to prune the regalian privileges of the local princes.

Notes

1. Upper Silesia, Foreign Office (Peace) Handbooks, no. 40, London, 1920, 10-13. For contemporary accounts see: Historische und Geographische Beschreibung des Herzogthums Schlesien, Freystadt, 1741, and Gesammelte Nachrichten und Dokumente den gegenwärtigen Zustand des Herzogthums Schlesiens, 1741.

2. Louis Eisenmann, "Les Silésies dans l'Histoire," in La Silésie Polonaise, II, Paris, 1932, 1-14.

3. Klemens Lorenz, Friedrich der Grosse und Schlesien, Breslau, 1936; Hermann Fechner, Geschichte des Schlesischen Berg- und Hüttenwesens, Z.f.d.B.H.u.S., XLVIII, 1900, 357-401.

4. J. Partsch, Schlesien: eine Landeskunde für das deutsche Volk, Breslau, 1896-1911, I, 173-204.

5. Comte de Mirabeau, De la Monarchie prussienne sous Frédéric le Grand, London, 1788, I, 350.

6. Walter Geisler, Wirtschafts- und verkehrsgeographisches Atlas von Schlesien. Breslau, 1932, Platter 3,4.

7. Géographie Universelle, IV, i, 257-263; IV, ii, 582-4, 651-5.

8. Alfred Hornig, "Rozwój górno-śląskiego zespołu miejskiego," Czasopismo Geograficzne, XXV, 1954, 126-145; Tadeusz Ladogórski," Ludność Śląska i jej struktura społeczna w drugiej połowie XVIII wieku," Przegląd Zachodni, VI, 1950, ii, 31-48.

9. Gesichichtlicher Atlas von Schlesien, Stück I, Friderizianische Siedlungen rechts der Oder bis 1800, 3 Blätter.

10. R. Koser, Zur Bevölkerungsstatistik des preussischen Staates von 1756-1786, Forschungen zur Brandenburgischen und Preussischen Geschichte, XVI, 1903, 583-589; Mirabeau, op.cit., I, 349.

11. Mirabeau, op.cit., I, 346-348; see also T. Ladogórski, op.cit.

12. ibid., I, 345-346.

13. Stefan Gołochowski, "Gliwice u progu industrializacji, " Studia Śląskie, 266-309; Przegląd Zachodni, VIII, 1952.

14. Mirabeau, op.cit., I, 369.

15. Partsch, op, cit., I, 364; La Silésie Polonaise, Paris, 1932, 15-35.

16. Mirabeau, op.cit., I, 347-8; 369.

17. Hermann Aubin in Cambridge Economic History, I, 364-397.

18. W. Kuhn, Siedlungsgeschichte Oberschlesiens, Würzburg, 1954, 141 ff.

19. John Quincy Adams, Letters on Silesia, written during a Tour through that Country in the Years 1800, 1801, London, 1804, 28 ff.

20. W. Geisler, Oberschlesien-Atlas, Breslau, 1938.

21. J. Partsch, op.cit., I, 30-31; E. de Martonne, "La Géographie humaine de la Haute Silésie, " La Silésie Polonaise, Paris, 1932, 15-35.

22. H. Dubowy, "Der Chelm, Oberschlesiens Muschelkalkrücken, " Veröffentlichungen der Schlesischen Gesellschaft für Erdkunde, Heft 8, Breslau, 1928.

23. Jan Rutkowski, Historia Gospodarcza Polski, Warsaw 1953, esp. 197 et seq; "Poland, Lithuania and Hungary, " Cambridge Economic History, I, 398-402; Histoire Economique de la Pologne, Paris, 1927, 101 et seq; J. Partsch, op.cit., II, 8-11.

24. Mirabeau, op.cit., I, 352-353.

25. K. Olbricht, Schlesien: Grundriss einer Landeskunde, Breslau, 1933, 76; Mirabeau, op.cit., I, 74-109; J. Q. Adams, op.cit., 60, 127.

26. G. A. Stenzel, Geschichte Schlesiens, Breslau, 1853. 291-300; G. Grünhagen, Geschichte Schlesiens, Gotha, 1886, II, 383 ff; A. O. Meyer, "The Development of Silesia, " in Germany and Poland in their Historical Relations, ed. A. Brackmann, Munich, 1934, 158-166. See also "Schlesiens Bergbau und Hüttenwesen, Urkunden und Akten, " in Codex Diplomaticus Silesiae,

XX, XXI, Verein für Geschichte und Alterthum Schlesiens, 1900-1.

27. Jan Rutkowski, "Sauneries et mines de fer dans l'Ancienne Pologne," Annales d'Histoire économique et sociale, VI, 1934, 387-389.

28. L. Beck, Geschichte des Eisens, III, 919; Hermann Fechner, "Geschichte des Schlesischen Berg- und Hüttenwesens in der Zeit Friedrichs des Grossen, Friedrich Wilhelms II und Friedrich Wilhelm III," Z.f.d.B.H.u.S., XLVIII, 1900, 279-290; Kuhn, op.cit., Karte 6.

29. Studia z Dziejów Górnictwa i Hutnictwa, Instytut Historii Kultury Materialnej, vol. I, Wrocław, 1957; see especially "Stan Badań nad dziejami górnictwa i hutnictwa w Polsce," 9-128; J. Pazdur, "Materiały do dziejów hutnictwa zelaza w Polsce w XVIII wieku," 319-359.

30. W. Ozieblowski, "Erzbergbau in Polen," Z.d.O.B.u.H.V., LXVIII, 1929, 518-527.

31. Wacław Długoborski, "Początki kształtowania się klasy robotniczej na Górnym Śląsku," Kwartalnik Historyczny, LXI, i, 1954, 150-77; also, "Rekrutacja górników w zagłębiu górnośląskim w okresie przed zniesieniem poddaństwa," Przegląd Zachodni, VI, 1950, ii, 49-88.

32. G. A. Stentzel, op.cit., 299; "Schlesiens Bergbau und Hüttenwesen, Urkunden," ed. K. Wutke, Codex Diplomaticus Silesiae, XX, 1900 and XXI, 1901.

33. A. Steinbeck, Geschichte des Schlesischen Bergbaues, seiner Verfassung, seines Betriebes, 2 vols, Breslau, 1857, II, 137-231; Handbuch des Oberschlesischen Industriebezirks, Band II of Festschriften zum XII Allgemeinen Deutschen Bergmannstage zu Breslau, 1913, 62-74.

34. F. Krantz, Die Entwicklung der oberschlesischen Zinkindustrie, Kattowitz, 1911, 2-3; L. von Wiese, Beiträge zur Geschichte der wirtschaftlichen Entwicklung der Rohzinkfabrikation, Jena, 1903, 21-30; A. Steinbeck, op.cit., 235-244; K. Wutke, Geschichte der Bergweksgesellschaft Georg v. Giesche's Erben, Breslau, 1904, I, 33-41.

35. See notes by H. C. and L. H. Hoover in Georgius Agricola, De Re Metallica, (1556), trans. and ed. H. C. and L. H. Hoover,

London, 1912, 408-410; E. A. Smith, The Zinc Industry, London, 1918, 8-12.

36. K. Wutke, Geschichte der Bergwerksgesellschaft Georg v. Giesche's Erben, vol. I,; Die Allgemeine Geschichte der Gesellschaft bis zum Jahre 1851, Breslau, 1904.

37. Walter R. Ingalls, The Metallurgy of Zinc and Cadmium, New York, 1906, I et seq.

38. G. R. Lewis, The Stannaries, London, 1908, 69-70.

39. Handwörterbuch der Staatswissenschaften, sub. "Bergbau," Jena, 1924, II, 472-483.

40. E. Zivier, Geschichte des Bergregals in Schlesien, Kattowitz, 1898.

41. Dziegiecki, "Das Bergweks-Privilegium der Standesherrschaft Beuthen-Tarnowitz in Oberschlesien," Z.d.O.B.u.H.V., XXXV, 1896, 409-419.

42. Gedike, "Geschichte der schlesischen Bergbau- Privilegien," Zeitschrift für Bergrecht, XIII, 1872, 234-256, 359-395; XIV, 1873, 475-482; XV, 1874, 219-259.

43. H. Fechner, op.cit., XLVIII, 1900, 357-401.

44. Handbuch des Oberschlsischen Industriebezirks, II, 125-129; J. Partsch, op.cit., II, 56-60.

CHAPTER II

THE PRUSSIAN ADMINISTRATION: 1741-1800

Ich finde ein unbeschreibliches Vergnügen in
der Vorstellung dieser vielleicht noch sehr entfern-
ten Zukunft und freue mich im voraus der Zeiten,
wo belebte Industrie, schnellere Circulation und
Cultur diesen ungeachteten Winkel zur Perle der
preussischen Krone erheben und dessen Bewohner
aus armen gedruckten Sklaven zu gebildeten und
glücklichen Menschen umschaffen werden.
Graf von Reden to Frederick II, 1787.

The Prussia of Frederick II was a congeries of territories which had been acquired under differing pretexts by the
Hohenzollerns over a period of many centuries. Its nucleus
lay in Brandenburg, but around this area the Prussian rulers
grouped an extensive though scattered domain. Prussia, itself, formerly in the hands of the Teutonic Knights, was acquired in 1618. At about the same time, a group of territories
was inherited in the Rhineland. With the expulsion of the
Swedes from Germany, lands were gained along the north
coast, and fragments of land in Saxony and South Germany
were also added to the Prussian realm.[1]

Such were the Prussian lands when, by the Treaty of Berlin in 1743, they received the further addition of Silesia. They
were yet further enlarged in 1772, when the Hohenzollerns received West Prussia as their share of the first despoliation of
Poland. By the Second Partitition in 1793, she added the territory, sometimes known as South Prussia, which included Poznań, Gniezno and Częstochowa. The Third and last Partition
of 1795 gave Prussia not only lands along the Narew and middle Vistula rivers but also the so-called New Silesia, which
adjoined the Silesian lands acquired half a century earlier.

But the political map was soon to be changed again. In
1807 Napoleon created the Grand Ducy of Warsaw, allocating
to it most of the Polish territory that had gone to Prussia and
Austria in the Third Partition. In this way Prussia lost

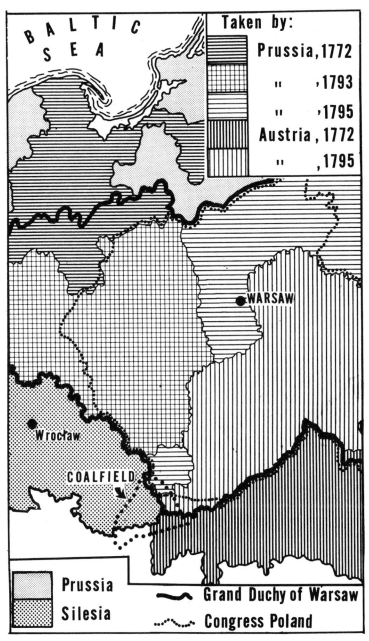

Figure 6: The Partitions of Poland, in relation to her coalfield.

possession of New Silesia. Her occupation of it, lasting only
twelve years, had been too short a period for Prussian institutions to have made much impression.

A fresh pattern of boundaries emerged after the defeat of
Napoleon. Polish hopes that the Grand Duchy of Warsaw was
to be the nucleus of a recreated Poland were disappointed. Instead, Prussia took back much of the territory she had lost in
1807. Austria regained a small area to the south of Kraków,
and the rest was constituted the Kingdom of Poland, but with
the Russian Tsar as its monarch. After 1830 the fiction of an
independent Polish kingdom was abandoned, and the so-called
"Congress" Poland was absorbed into the Russian Empire.

In this way Upper Silesia came to be divided between Prussia, Russia and Austria. Prussia gained the lion's share of
the coalfield and most of the ore deposits. But the resources
of the region were at this time too little known to have influenced
in any way the delimitation of boundaries in the area. Prussia also
possessed most of the developed iron-works as well as the lead and
zinc smelters. For over half a century the further development of
the mineral and industrial resources took place mainly on Prussian
soil, though late in the 19th century considerable advances were
made in both Austrian and Russian territory. The interrelations of
Austrian and Russian industry with that of German-held Upper Silesia is the theme of chapter seven of this book.

The Prussian Administration: Frederick II inherited from
his father not only a well trained army but a full treasury and
at least the framework of an effective civil administration.[2]
The latter he made more effective and extended to the newly
acquired province of Silesia.[3]

Frederick II was not slow in introducing Prussian civil
administration to Silesia.[4] In 1741, two Kriegs-und Domanen-
kammern were established, with their seats respectively in
Głogówek and Wrocław.[5] These bodies were charged, not only
with the collection of revenue and the administration of royal
estates in Silesia, but also with the control of iron-works and
mines and the supervision of forests and waterways. Frederick
was strenuous in encouraging industry and domestic trade and
in reducing Prussia's dependence on other countries, but in
Silesia progress was slow.[6] Constructive work had mostly to
wait until Frederick's wars were over. In 1768 he established

a Bergwerks-und Hüttendepartment of the Prussian government, and at its head he placed von Hagen.[7] One of the first
acts of the new chief was to intitute an enquiry into the conduct of mines in Silesia. A few months later he reported to
the king that "in the Silesian Chambers no one had any real
knowledge of mines and iron-works" and proposed the creation
of an Oberbergamt, responsible to his own department.[8]

In 1769, this office was established with jurisdiction over
Silesia, and at the same time a new code of mining law was
promulgated. Yet there remained many obstacles to the
smooth development of mining and industry. The older Chambers resented this new department which they were powerless
to control. They did nothing, however, to assist it, and, as
the boundary separating their respective functions was far
from clearly drawn, disputes between them were not infrequent.[9]

The seat of the Oberbergamt was at Reichenstein, on the
Bohemian border, in an area of which Frederick entertained
great hopes. But these hopes were ill-founded and in 1778, the
office was moved to Reichenbach and a year later to Wrocław.
There was already in Upper Silesia a mining administration,
or Bergamt, responsible to the family of Henckel von Donnersmarck, and supervising the works on the Henckel estates.
Nothing illustrates more clearly the confusion in Upper Silesia
than the quasi-royal rights which this family had arrogated to
itself. The Prussian mines administration denied the rights
claimed by Henckel's Bergamt, but, as a sop to the family's
pride, nominated Count Henckel to be president of the local
Bergamt of Tarnowskie Góry. This was one of four Bergamte
which were set up under the Oberbergamt to supervise mining
affairs in Upper Silesia. As the mining industry developed in
the 19th century, and concentrated more heavily in Upper Silesia, further changes in the structure of the Oberbergamt and
of its dependent Amte became necessary.

Mining brought a considerable income to the Treasury,
chiefly in the form of tithe, and it became the duty of the Silesian Chamber after 1741 to insist more vigorously on the pay-
ments due to it. After long debate the government made good
its claim to a tithe of the coal produced from the Lower Silesian coalfields, but this additional obligation led to the closing

of some mines.[10] At Tarnowskie Góry, in Upper Silesia, silver was obtained along with the lead. There the miners at
first refused to pay tithe; then paid, and finally compromised
with the authorities, undertaking to exploit their mines more
effectively if excused payment. Tin miners in the Sudeten
mountains evaded the tithe, but copper miners were less fortunate. The Chambers made good their claim to a tithe of arsenic and saltpetre, but, strangely enough, the tithe was not
exacted of iron ore and of the zinc ore, calamine. The authorities were clearly unhappy about these exceptions, and surely
cannot have accepted the reasons they gave, that iron-ore was
not a mineral but an "earth" and that it was not obtained "auf
bergmannische Weise." It is likely that a tithe of a mineral
produced as widely and sometimes as secretly as iron-ore
was almost impossible to collect.[11]

Along with the uncertainty regarding tithe there went
doubts as to other fiscal and social obligations. In 1769 a code
of mining law was introduced to Silesia. Most of its regulations were already known in Germany and were observed at
least locally, but the codification had the merit of removing
doubts and uncertainties. It maintained the ancient Bergbaufreiheit, the right of any person to prospect for the regalian
minerals and to obtain a concession to work them on payment
of tithe. On the other hand, it safeguarded the interests of the
landowner by making provision for him to hold half the shares
in the undertaking.[12]

The mining law also provided for contributions to the
Knappschaftskasse, a kind of welfare fund for the miners, and
also, though from coal mines alone, to the Bergbauhülfskasse
which was charged with the building of roads, the cutting of
adits and similar works of general value.

These provisions derived from Roman law, but were subject to great local variation.[13] Similar regulations governed
the medieval tin-mining industry in England.[14]

The new mining code also enshrined the Direktionsprinzip.
This also derived from the regalian principle, that certain
minerals belong to the King. If he conceded the right to work
the minerals, he nevertheless retained an interest in the effi-
cent operation of the mine. With this end in view the technical
direction of the mine had to be entrusted to a public official,

nominated by and responsible to the local Bergamt. It can
readily be seen how important a factor in the development of
industry was the Obergergamt and its subordinate Bergamte,
especially when it is remembered that the smelting and metal
fabricating industries were also subject to the Direktionsprinzip.

Feudal Privileges and Immunities: The Prussian bureaucracy had little difficulty in enforcing the new law in most of
Silesia. In the extreme southeast, however, regalian rights
were claimed by certain of the landed magnates. It is true
that in Germany the regalian right had belonged in theory to
the emperors, but had passed, either by prescriptive right or
direct grant, to the princes of the Empire. With the extinction
of most of the duchies, the privilege was transmitted to the
humbler local nobility.

We have seen already how Henckel von Donnersmarck was
obligated to abate his claims. Subsequently, however, the Henckel claims were revived and upheld by a Prussian court, but
only in so far as they related to silver and lead. This permitted the family to grant concessions and to exact tithe of the
silver and lead obtained from its lands, without reference to
the Bergamt. The exclusion of iron-ore and zinc derived, of
course, from the fact that they were not regarded by Prussian
law as regalian minerals. The case of coal concessions on
Henckel lands was raised in the 19th century, and also settled
in favour of the Henckel family.[15]

More important than the privileges claimed by the Henckel
family were those of the Prince of Pless. The Standesherrschaft Pless covered a large area near the Russian and Austrian borders, and, from the point of view of mining law;
formed "a state within a state."[16] Its privileges, deriving
from the 15th century, were more extensive than those of any
other territory. The Prince of Pless could open mines and establish smelting works without reference to any higher authority
or payment of tithe. Furthermore, he possessed the jus excludendi alios, the right to forbid others to prospect for minerals on his land.[17] The Bergbaufreiheit, which was affirmed
in the mining code of 1769, did not extend to the lands of Pless.
The Princes of Pless establised their own mining administration, or Bergamt, with its seat in Mikołów, and continued to

exercise their regalian rights until these were terminated by
Germany's defeat in 1918 and the transfer to Poland of most
of the lands of Pless.

The territories of Mysłowice and Katowice were separated
from Pless early in the 16th century, and passed into the possession of the Mieroszewski family. This family's claim to
share in the bergregal privileges had lain dormat for three
centuries because no significant mineral deposits had been
found. But the opening of coal mines and the discovery of lead
and zinc ores led to their revival. In 1805 Graf von Mieroszewski claimed the same privileges as those held by the Prince
of Pless. When, in the 1830's, these lands passed to Franz
Winkler, he too claimed the regailian right, but was denied by
order of the Prussian government. After a protracted legal
dispute Winckler's claim was upheld, and it was allowed that
regalian rights belonged also to a number of other fragments
of territory which at one time or another had been separated
from the Standesherrschaft Pless.

By the mid-19th century mining law and administration
had become only a degree less complex than before the reforms of Frederick II. The time was ripe for a further re-
form of Prussian mining law, and this is discussed in chapter
four.

The great landowners had thus a large measure of control
over the use of the minerals that occurred on their lands.
They exercised also a similar control over the labour of the
peasants who lived there. Serfdom was not abolished in Prussia until 1810. Before this date peasants were directed by
their masters to the tasks of making charcoal, extracting ore
and carting the raw materials to the furnaces.[19] In these ways
they performed their labour dues when their services were not
needed in the fields. Długoborski has shown that on the great
estates free labour was employed only at the level of managers
and technicians; the rest was forced service of the peasants.
By contrast, the fiscal works, established by the Prussian
government, was obliged to rely mainly on free labour and also
to recruit it in central Germany.

Heinitz and Reden: The legal and administrative reforms
in Silesia might have been a great deal less successful but for
the work of two of Frederick II's leading officials. In 1777

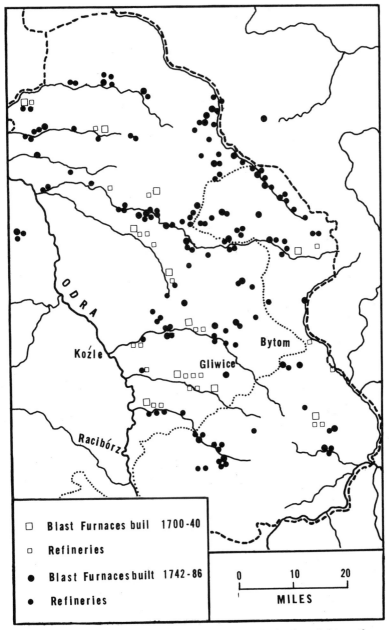

Figure 7: Ironworks in Upper Silesia in the eighteenth century (after W. Kuhn).

Frederick appointed to the presidency of the Bergwerks-und
Hüttendepartement of the Prussian State Friedrich Anton, Freiherr von Heinitz. He had been born in Saxony in 1725, and
later was in service of the Duke of Brunswick as a mines in-
spector. He had visited the mines of Central Europe, Scandi-
navia and England, and he brought to his new task not only energy and an administrative capacity of a high order, but also
an intimate knowledge of mining practice and of the refining
of metals.[20] His field, however, was the whole of Prussia.
In 1779 he appointed Friedrich Wilhelm, Graf von Reden to be
director of the Silesian Oberbergamt. Von Reden was a much
younger man. He was born at Hameln, in Lower Saxony, in
1752, studied at Göttingen and, though still under thirty, had
travelled widely in the mining districts of Western Europe.[21]
He resembled von Heinitz, whom he was to succeed as head of
the Prussian mines department, in character and training, and
the two worked closely together to further the ends of the Prussian government.

The se objectives were defined in instructions sent by von
Heinitz to the Upper Silesian Oberbergamt[22]; efforts were to
be made to increase the output of certain minerals hitherto
imported from abroad; a strict supervision was enjoined of the
conduct of all privately owned mines and works; the Oberbergamt was to see to it that only skilled and efficient miners and
furnacemen were employed, and that everything possible was
done to improve the efficiency and increase the output of the
mines and factories. Lastly, the Oberbergamt was to show dili-
gence in collecting the tithe and all other taxes due to the Prussian government.

The following pages will show how well the office of Oberbergamt, directed by von Reden, fulfilled the instructions it received. We must not, however, underrate the achievement of
the years which preceded the appointment of von Heinitz and
von Reden. The number of blast furnaces and iron refineries
had increased considerably since 1741[23]; the work of prospecting
had been intensified, but the discoveries made were certainly
not commensurate with the great expenditure of effort. Furthermore, the Silesian Chambers had themselves established fiscal
iron-works, and their example led a number of individuals to
establish privately operated works.

In the interval between the Silesian Wars and the Seven Years' War, the Prussian government was particularly active in establishing iron-works.[24] Its motive was strategic and sprang from the need to increase the supply of guns and munitions. In 1753 a site was chosen for such a blast furnace and refinery in the Krasiejów Forest in Upper Silesia. By the end of 1754 two blast furnaces were in production on the bank of the Małapanew river, which supplied power for the bellows and hammers.[25] Bog ore was obtained from the neighboring valleys, and charcoal from the surrounding forests.

In 1755 a third blast furnace was built on the Budkowiczanka stream, near Kluczbork and refineries and a wire-drawing plant were established in the vicinity.

Such was the state of affairs when the Silesian Oberbergamt was established. In 1780 control of these works was transferred from the Silesian Chambers to the Oberbergamt, and thus for over twenty years they were under the direct supervision of von Reden.

The work of von Reden in Upper Silesia can be divided into: (a) his efforts to improve and extend the iron industry, (b) his contribution to the revival of lead and zinc mining, (c) his encouragement of coal-mining, and (d) his efforts to improve and develop such ancilliary services as roads and canals. This work in each of these fields was however closely dependent upon that in the other three.

Upper Silesian iron-works: Von Reden further extended the fiscal iron-works, establishing a refinery and cannon-foundry at Dębska Kuźnica, and at Königshuld a steel works for the purpose of making agricultural tools.[26] But already the supply of charcoal was presenting difficulties; not that it was difficult to come by in so forested a country, but it was mostly of poor quality and made from soft woods.[27]

In 1786, von Reden again visited England, ostensibly to negotiate the purchase of a steam-engine for the Friedrichsgrube lead mine, but it is likely that it was on this occasion that he took with him specimens of Upper Silesian coal and consulted the English ironmaster, William Wilkinson, on their use.

In 1789 coke, made from coal taken from a pit at Zabrze, was used in one of the Małapanew furnaces. The experiment was not successful, but, after a blast-furnace had been rebuilt and its height and the strength of its blast increased, greater success was achieved.[28] It is generally held that Wilkinson himself visited Upper Silesia at this time, and that it was on his advice that changes were made in the construction of the furnace.[29] In any case, the quality of pig-iron produced with coke was improved, and the output of the Małapanew works was much increased. Indeed the partial success of coke—smelting was such as to encourage von Reden to build another furnace more conveniently placed with regard to the coal mines than was Małapanew.

The result was the Gliwice works, begun in 1794 and brought into production in 1796.[30] The construction of the furnace and its operation at least during its early years was supervised by the Scottish iron-master, John Baildon, who had learned his craft at the Carron Works of Falkirk.[31] It would appear, from Daubuisson's description of the works in 1801,[32] that Baildon was not the only English employee of the Prussian State to be found at Gliwice. Nevertheless, in spite of this expert guidance, the new furnace was at first a failure and part of its wall had to be taken down in order to remove a partially fused mass of iron and slag, evidence perhaps that an English pattern of furnace was not necessarily suited to the Upper Silesian materials.[33]

The Gliwice furnace stood 40 feet high, and was probably the largest on the continent of Europe at this time. It smelted at first a rather limy ore that was found near Tarnowskie Góry; local limestone was used as flux, and coal brought from Zabrze was converted to coke in mounds at the works. Gliwice was probably chosen as the site of the works because the possibility offered of using water power and because the Kłodnicki Canal, then under construction, would link it with the river Odra. The Royal Ironworks consisted of a single blast-furnace, with a number of cupolas and reverberatory furnaces which were used to melt down the pig-iron for casting. Castings were the only product: in time of peace, stoves, cooking pots and ornamental ironwork; at other times, cannon, which were both cast and bored at Gliwice.

The ultimate success of the Gliwice foundry led von Reden to plan another works that could produce iron of suitable quality for the refinery.[34] King Frederick William III did not favor

this further extension of the State's participation in industry,
and would have preferred to leave the undertaking to private
enterprise. It was still, however, a little premature to ex-
pect this of the Silesian landowners. Von Reden had his way,
and a site was chosen adjoining a fiscal coal mine, the Königsgrube, that had recently been opened near Chorzów.[35] The
works were to be called the Königshütte and were to consist
of two large, coke-fired blast furnaces together with refineries
and finishing works. The first blast furnace was blown in 1802.
It exceeded the Gliwice furnace in size, and was named the
"Redenofen." The second, called the "Heinitzofen," began production a few months later. In 1805, a third furnace was added.

It must not be supposed that in this period of twenty-five
years all developments in the field of ferrous metallurgy were
inspired by von Reden and financed by the Prussian State. The
number of blast furnaces in Upper Silesia alone had increased
from 37 to 59 in the period of Prussian rule, and of refineries
of all kinds from 132 to 219.[36] Only a small fraction of this
increase was due directly to governmental action. Most of
these works were small; some were destined to be quite
ephemeral, and all produced the simple goods—iron castings,
scythes and other agricultural implements and ornamental
iron-work—required by a rather poor and predominantly
rural society. If most of the works established owed little to
the Prussian State, it was nevertheless in the fiscal works that
all significant innovations and technical advances were made.
Foremost amongst these was of course the use of coke in the
blast furnace; of scarcely less importance was the building of
the tall blast-furnace, the introduction of cylinder-blast and of
the steam-engine for creating it. In the next century the local
people continued to construct little blast-furnaces and small
refineries, no more complex than a blacksmith's shop, but a
few amongst them built on a larger scale, used coke, puddled
their iron and kept abreast of recent developments. The leaven
introduced by von Reden into Upper Silesia was beginning to
work.

The non-ferrous metals: We have seen already how the
mining of lead dwindled in importance, until production ceased
in the early years of Prussian rule. The reason was a mechanical one; the depth of the mines was increasing, and no means

had been found of ridding them of water. The ore of lead was a regalian mineral; there was nothing to prevent von Reden from taking over the abandoned mines in the name of the State and developing them with the aid of the most up-to-date technical aids of his day. Only the steam engine, it seemed, could solve the basic problem of ridding the mines of water, and it was in part to arrange the purchase of such a machine that von Reden went to England in 1786.

A Watt pattern steam engine was ordered from Samuel Homphray of Penydarren. This was brought by sea from South Wales to Szczecin, then by barge up the Odra to Opole and thence overland to Tarnowskie Góry.[37] The assembling of the machine was a matter of very considerable difficulty for the miners, unskilled in the ways of steam engines. Ultimately a local mechanic succeeded not only in discovering what was wrong with the mechanism but also in remedying the deficency.[38]

The steam engine was installed a few miles to the north of Tarnowskie Góry, in an area previously much worked for lead. Here von Reden had opened the Friedrichsgrube and, in a valley nearby had built a lead smelter.[39] Expansion of the lead mines was rapid and by 1802 no less than six steam engines had been set up near Tarnowskie Góry.

The mining of the mineral, calamine, had not, like that of lead, been interrupted, and the von Giesche family continued to exercise its monopolistic privilege of mining and marketing it. By the mining law of 1769 calamine was assimilated to the regalian minerals, but the von Giesche'sche Erben continued to be protected by their patent until it expired in 1782. Von Heinitz and von Reden were opposed to any extension of the privilege. Most of the von Giesche workings lay on the land of Henckel von Donnersmarck, and the latter was clearly eager to take part himself in the lucrative business of working the calamine. It is possible furthermore that von Reden was anxious to conciliate the Henckels if this could be done without cost to the Oberbergamt.[40] In the end the von Giesche privilege was renewed for a further twenty years, but the concern was obliged to compromise with the Henckels, undertaking to pay them a royalty and to make good all damage done to their lands. When the privilege again lapsed in 1802, the Prussian government refused to renew it, and the monopolistic role of von Giesche'schen Erben ended.

The beginning of the 19th century saw another and more fundamental change in the zinc industry of Upper Silesia. It was noted in the previous chapter that zinc is an unusually difficult mineral to smelt because the temperature at which it dissociates itself from its carbonate is higher than its own boiling point.[41] It is thus smelted as a vapor, which has to be condensed to a liquid form. Zinc smelting was first practiced successfully in England about 1720, but throughout the 18th century the calamine mined in Upper Silesia was used in its crude state to add to copper in brass-making. About 1798 zinc was first distilled in Upper Silesia by Johann Christian Ruhberg.[42] He had learned of the process in England and applied it at a glass furnace which he managed at Wesoła on the lands of the Prince of Pless. But there was little demand for metallic zinc, and it was not until 1809 that the first zinc smelter was built.[43]

Coal mining: The coal deposits which today form the chief wealth of Upper Silesia, were strangely late in being opened up. The coal seams outcrop at many places in Upper Silesia, and there can be little doubt that coal was dug from shallow pits many years before the Prussian conquest of Silesia.[44] But there was little demand for coal at this time in a region as densely forested as Upper Silesia. The first coal mines to be formerly conceded were the Emanuelssegensgrube, on the lands of the Prince of Pless, in 1769, and the Brandenburggrube, near Ruda, in 1771. It is probable, however, that in both cases the actual concession was merely the legalization of a state of affairs that may have existed for several years. In his memoire, addressed to Frederick II, on the mineral wealth of Prussia,[45] von Heinitz commented: "The abundance of coal in the Principality of Pless and the difficulty of selling it owing to the abundance of wood, has led to the manufacture there of lampblack." It probably served also to burn bricks and lime, and, when Heinitz wrote, von Reden had already experimented with coke in the blast furnace.

It was, however, the steam-engine which von Reden had installed at the royal lead mine that contributed most at this time to the development of coal-mining. Its rapacious demand

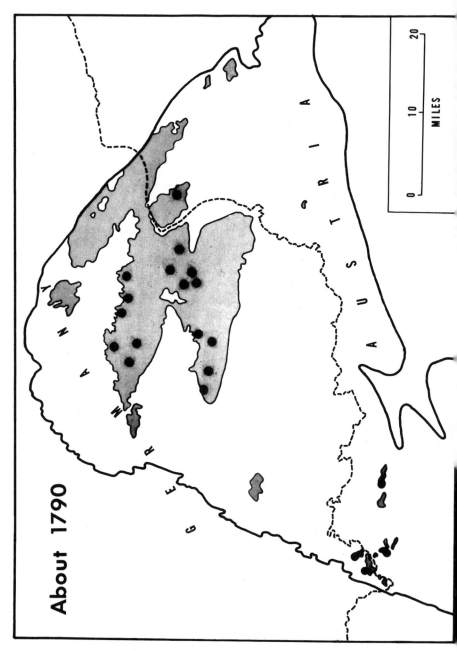

Figure 8: Coal mines in Upper Silesia, about 1790.

for fuel, supplemented a year or two later by that of the Gliwice blast-furnace, led von Reden to open the two fiscal mines
of Königsgrube and Königinluisengrube. Within a short time
these had become the largest, best equipped and most efficient
in Upper Silesia, and by 1799 they contributed nearly half the
coal mined.[46] There were at this time nineteen productive
mines, producing together 38,546 tons.[47] At the same time
there were no less than 54 active mines in Lower Silesia, with
an output of 116,190 tons.

The growth of mining, under the leadership of von Reden,
necessitated improved means of transport. Lead, calamine
and iron goods had to be exported to other parts of Germany,
for it was part of the economic policy of Frederick II to make
Prussia as nearly as possible a self-contained unit. Foremost
amongst his tasks was the improvement of navigation on the
river Odra,[48] to be followed by the cutting of a canal to link
the river with the coalfield area of Upper Silesia. The canal
was proposed in 1788 as a means whereby Berlin could be supplied cheaply with coal, and elaborate plans were prepared for
a canal to join the Odra with the Vistula. Work was begun in
1792, and within ten years very considerable progress had
been made. By 1806 a length of canal was in use between Gliwice and the coal mines of Zabrze, but damage by flooding de-
layed the completion of the rest until 1812.[49] The new canal
left the Odra near Koźle and followed the valley of the Kłodnica
river to Gliwice.

The high hopes that were entertained of the new canal
were not fulfilled, chiefly because of recurring difficulties
along the Odra itself. But water transport did give a considerable impetus to mining and factory development in Upper Silesia, and widened greatly the scope of its market.

Notes

1. J. A. R. Marriott and C. Grant Robertson, The Evolution of Prussia, Oxford 1946, 58-70.

2. J. A. R. Marriott and C. G. Robertson, op.cit., 128.

3. For a rather biased comparison of Austrian and Prussian

rule in Silesia see Gustav Freytag, "Bildern aus der deutschen Vergangenheit," Gesammelte Schriften, VIII, 299 ff.

4. Emil Wolff, Grundriss der preussisch-deutschen socialpolitischen und Volkswirtschaftsgeschichte, Berlin, 1899, 30-33.

5. H. Fechner, op.cit., XLVIII, 1900, 295 ff.

6. Reinhold Koser, König Friedrich der Grosse, Stuttgart 1893-1903, I, 423-456; H. Fechner, "Die Fabrikengründungen in Schlesien nach dem siebenjährigen Kriege unter Friedrich dem Grossen," Zeitschrift für die gesamte Staatswissenschaft, LVII, 1901, (Tübingen) 618-652; Anton Zoltmann, "Die Wirtschaftspolitik Friedrichs des Grossen," Gesellschaftswissenschaftliche Abhandlungen, VIII, 1937.

7. H. Fechner, ibid., 307 ff.

8. Forneberg, "Beiträge zur Geschichte der schlesischen Bergbehorden unter Friedrich dem Grossen," Z.d.O.B.u.H.V., LII, 1913, 499-503.

9. Handbuch des Oberschlesischen Industriebezirks, Band II of Festschrift zum XII Allgemeinem Deutschen Bergmannstage, Kattowitz, 1913, 120 ff; H. Fechner, op.cit., 312 ff.

10. H. Fechner, op.cit., XLVIII, 358-361.

11. See K. T. von Inama-Sternegg, Deutsche Wirtschaftsgeschichte, Leipzig, 1901, III, part 2, 143.

12. E. Zivier, Geschichte des Bergregals in Schlesien, Kattowitz, 1898; H. Fechner, op.cit., XLVIII, 367-70; Handbuch des Ober schlesischen Industriebezirks, II, 94 ff.

13. Handwörterbuch der Staatswissenschaften, Jena, 1924, Band II, sub Bergbau.

14. G. R. Lewis, The Stannaries, London, 1908, 65-84.

15. Dziegiecki, "Das Bergswerks-Privilegium der Standesherrschaft Beuthen-Tarnowitz in Oberschlesien," Z.d.O.B.u.H.V., XXXV, 1896, 409-419; see also Wilhelm Szewczyk, Skarb Donnersmarcków, Warsaw, 1956.

16. J. Partsch, Schlesien, Breslau, 1896-1911, II, 60.

17. Gedike, "Geschichte der schlesischen Bergbau–Privilegien," Zeitschrift für Bergrecht, XIII, 1872, 234-256; Handbuch des Oberschlesischen Industriebezirks, II, 124-125.

18. Gedike, op.cit., XIII, 1872, 359-395; Handbuch des Oberschlesischen Industriebezirks, II, 125-127.

19. W. Długoborski, Początki kształtowania się klasy robotniczej na Górnym Śląsku, Kwartalnik Historyczny, LXI, i, 1954, 150-177.

20. K. Wutke, Aus der Vergangenheit des Schlesischen Berg-und-Hüttenlebens, Breslau, 1913, 25-90.

21. K. Wutke, op.cit., 91-185; article on von Reden by Grunhagen in Allgemeine deutsche Biographie, XXVII, 510-3.

22. Quoted by H. Fechner, op.cit., XLVIII, 1900, 318-320.

23. H. Fechner, op.cit., IL, 1901, 1-86.

24. ibid., 14.

25. Gentzen, "Denkschrift zur Feier des hundertfünfzigjährigen Bestehens der Königlichen Hütte zu Malapane," Z.f.B.H.u.S., LII, 1904, 201-228; L. Wachler, Geschichte des ersten Jahrhunderts der Königlichen Eisenhütten-Werke Malapane vom Jahre 1753 bis 1854, Glogau, 1856; Oskar Simmersbach, "Die Begründung der oberschlesischen Eisenindustrie unter Preussens Königen," S.u.E., XXXI, i, 1911, 213-217, and Sammlung Berg-und Hüttenmännischer Abhandlungen, Heft 74, Kattowitz 1911, 8-18; H. Fechner, Die Königlichen Eisenhüttenwerke Malapane und Kreuzburgerhütte, 1753 bis 1780, Z.f.d.B.H.u.S., XLIII, 1895, 75-102.

26. Karl Jürgens, 150 Jahre Werk Königshuld, S.u.E., LV, ii, 1935, 977-81.

27. Journal des Mines, XIV, An XI, 156; see also von Heinitz, Mémoire sur les produits du règne mineral de la Monarchie Prussienne, Berlin, 1786, 21-2.

28. "Vom Schmelzen der Eisenerze im Hohenofen bey abgeschwefelten Steinkohlen," Schlesische Provinzialblätter, XI, 1790, 141-5; Fritz Redlich, History of American Business Leaders, Ann Arbor, 1940, 35-39.

29. Ludwig Wachler, Geschichte des Ersten Jahrhunderts

der Königlichen Eisenhütten-Werke Malapane vom Jahre 1753 bis 1854, Glogau, 1856.

30. F. W. Lürmann, "Ein Jahrhundert deutschen Koshocho-fenbetriebes," S.u.E., XVI, 1896, ii, 801-824; "Die 100jährige Jubelfeier der Königl. Hütte zu Gleiwitz," S.u.E., XVI, 1896, ii, 701-3.

31. W. Paley Baildon, Baildon and the Baildons, 3 vols., no date, II, 491-492.

32. J. F. Daubuisson, "Notice sur la Fonderie de Fer de Gleiwitz, dans la Haute Silésie," J.d.M., XIV, An XI (1801), 455-468.

33. R. Seidel, "Die Königliche Eisengiesserei zu Gleiwitz," Z.f.d.B.H.u.S., XLIV, 1896, 373-386.

34. O. Simmersbach, S.u.E., XXXI, i, 1911, 213-217.

35. "Die Gründung und Inbetriebsetzung der Königshütte," Z.d.O.B.u.H.V., XLI, 1902, 397-406; H. Fechner, op.cit., L, 1902, 757-760; L. Beck, op.cit., III.

36. H. Fechner, op.cit., IL, 503.

37. J. F. Daubisson, "Notice sur les Machines à vapeur des mines de Tarnowitz en Silésie," J.d.M., XIV, An XI (1801), 37-41.

38. This is a striking parallel to the achievement of Franz Dinnendahl when the first steam engine was brought to the Ruhr area; see Rheinisch-Westfälische Wirtschaftsbiographien, I, Münster, 1932, 357-372.

39. J. F. Daubuisson, "Du gisement et de l'exploitation d'une couche de Galène, près de Tarnowitz en Silésie," J.d.M. XVII, An XIII (1803), 325-344; "Exposé des travaux en usage à la Fonderie de plomb de Frederickshütte, près Tarnowitz," ibid., 437-454.

40. K. Wutke, Geschichte der Bergwekesegesellschaft Georg von Giesche's Erben, Breslau, 1904, vol. I., 91-125.

41. J. Percy, The Metallurgy of Lead, London, 1870; W. R. Ingalls, The Metallurgy of Zinc and Cadmium, New York, 1906, 1-4.

42. A. Rzehulka, "Zum hundertjährigen Bestehen der
oberschlesischen Zinkindustrie," Z.f.d.B.H.u.S., LVII, 1909,
342-8; Allgemeine Deutsche Biographie, XXIX, 429-431.

43. Sabass, "Beitrag zur Gründungsgeschichte der Lydognia
Zinkhütte zu Königshütte," Z.d.O.B.u.H.V., IL, 1910, 534-549;
K. Wutke, op.cit., I, 165-169.

44. C. Gaebler, Das oberschlesische Steinkohlenbecken,
Kattowitz, 1909, 4.

45. M. de Heinitz, Mémoire sur les produits du règne
minéral de la Monarchie prussienne, Berlin, 1786, 19; this
memoire is also printed in Comte de Mirabeau, De la Monarchie Prussienne, London, 1788, II, 213-303.

46. Gaebler, op.cit., 5-6; "Schlesiens Steinkohlenwerke
vor 60 Jahren," J.d.S.V.f.B.u.H., I, 1859, 371-373; H. Fechner,
op.cit., L, 1900, 415-499.

47. Figures in metric tons, are from T. Schulz, Die Entwicklung des deutschen Steinkohlenhandels, Waldenburg, 1911.

48. Julius Neugebauer, "Zur Geschichte der Oderschiffahrt," Schlesische Provinzialblätter, Neue Folge, I, 1862,
208-217; 261-272.

49. Kurt Schroth, "Zur Geschichte des Klodnitz-Kanals,"
Z.d.O.B.u.H.V., LIII, 1914, 116-122; J. Partsch, op.cit., I,
199-200; Alfred Hornig, "Kanał Kłodnicki i Gliwicki," Geografia w Szkole, VII, 1954, 66-72.

CHAPTER III

THE MINERAL DEPOSITS OF UPPER SILESIA

"... on peut dire qu'il n'y a pas de pays plus propre aux establissements des mines et de leurs ateliers. Aussi les fours et les forges de fer, les martinets de cuivre, les fabriques de laiton, de tales, fer blanc et cuillers... y ont déjà beaucoup prospère, et si l'on veille à une bonne administration des bois... si l'exploitation des mines de fer et de la pierre calcaire se fait dorenavant en règle... on verra bientot ces éstablissements se multiplier..."
Frederich Anton Freiherr von Heinitz, 1786.

In the previous chapters we have passed in review the developments that took place in the 18th century in the mining of iron, lead, zinc and coal. Some account is necessary of the geological circumstances which had brought together this remarkable concentration of mineral wealth. This is due, in the first place, to the occurrence in Upper Silesia of two quite separate series of mineral-bearing rocks, belonging to different geological ages. The older of the two is the Carboniferous series, which contains the whole of the coal reserves and also certain types of iron ore sometimes associated with coal. The other, consisting of nearly level beds of sandstone, limestone and shale, contains the ores of lead, zinc and iron, as well as of other minerals such as cadmium and silver.

The Upper Silesian Coalfield: The coalfield of Upper Silesia is one of a series of coal basins which lies along the southern margin of the North European Plain between northern France and the Ukraine. The coalfields of Belgium, the Netherlands and of Germany are links in this chain. To the south of the coalfields are hills, built of rocks of greater age than the coal measures. Towards the north the coal seams, as a general rule, dip away from view beneath a cover of younger deposits.

The outcrop of the coal measures, that is the area over which the coal-bearing rocks rise to the light of day, is small

42

in each case. The greater part of every coalfield is hidden
beneath a mantle of later deposits. It is thus in several instances difficult to define precisely the extent of the coalfield.
The Ruhr coalfield of northwest Germany, for instance, extends at an ever increasing depth for an indefinite distance
northward beneath the German Plain. The coalfields of Saxony and Lower Silesia are more clearly finite in area. They
occupy small basins within the folds of the older rocks which
surround and enclose them.

The Upper Silesian coalfield approximates to the pattern
of the latter.[1] It is a basin of roughly triangular shape. Along
its edges the lowest and oldest rocks in the coal series rise to
the surface. Around it is the barren limestone of the lower
carboniferous. This coal basin is, by European standards, of
exceptional size. Along its northwest and southeast-facing
sides it measures no less than 75 miles, and its shortest side,
that towards the northeast, is over 50 miles in length. The
total area of the coalfield is over 2000 square miles, larger
than the known area of the Ruhr coalfield.[2]

In structure the Upper Silesian coalfield may be said to
resemble a series of triangular dishes, set one inside the
other, each dish representing a group of coal seams. Around
the sides the seams dip towards the center of the basin. The
uppermost, or younger seams occupy the middle of the basin;
the older and lower seams rise around the margins. This far
from complex structure is illustrated in figure 11.

The simplicity of this structure is, however, obscured by
the occurrence of a number of upfolds or "saddles," trending
in general from west to east. The amplitude of most of these
folds is small; they introduce complexities into the coal mining and bring some of the lower seams close to the surface of
the ground, without, however, destroying the basin-structure
of the region as a whole (fig. 12). Across the northern corner
of the basin is developed such a saddle, not only of vastly
larger dimensions than the others but also of greater historical
and economic importance. Over a distance of some 20 miles,
from Zabrze eastwards to Mysłowice, this upfold has brought
an intermediate range of the coal series to the surface.[3]
These beds, known appropriately as the Saddle Beds (Grupa
Siodłowa, Sattelflöze) are economically the most important in

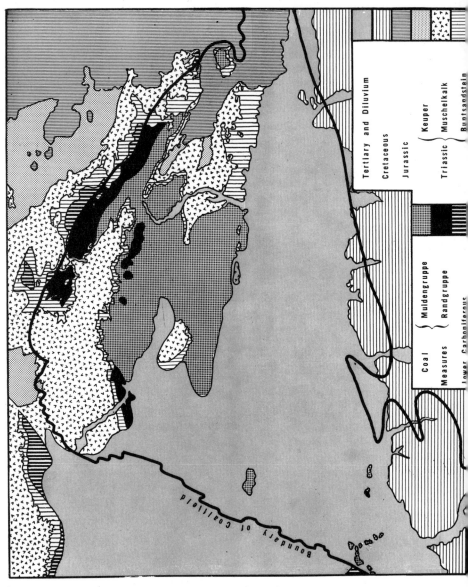

Figure 9: The Geology of the Upper Silesian Coal Basin (after R. Michael).

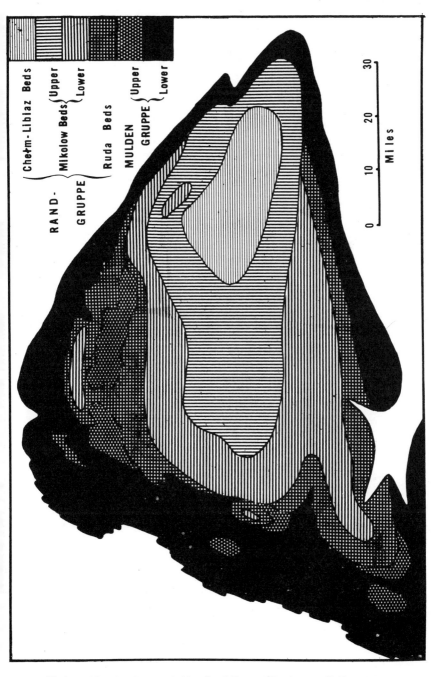

Figure 10: Geology of the Coal Deposits (after K. Kukuk)

the whole series, and their occurrence here has been the chief
factor in the growth of the Upper Silesian industrial area beneath which they lie.

The coal seams themselves are grouped, on palaeontologi-
cal and petrographic evidence, into groups[4]: the older seams,
which outcrop only around the margins of the coalbasin, form
the Grupa brzeźna or Randgruppe, while the younger beds,
which occupy the interior of the basin, are the Gruppa łękowa or
Muldengruppe. The Saddle Beds are the lowest division of the
Basin Group. Each of these groups if further subdivided on
geological evidence.

Margin Group	Basin Group
2 Ostrava beds-upper	7 Chelm-Libiąz beds
1 Ostrava beds-lower	6 Mikołów beds-upper
	5 Mikołów beds-lower
	4 Ruda beds
	3 Saddle beds

The seams of the Margin Group are presumed to underlie
the basin as a whole, though at a depth which puts them beyond
the range of mining, even beyond the range of prospecting. In
estimating the total coal reserves of the basin no account is
taken of these deep deposits.

The coal-bearing series is unusually thick and the coal
seams are very numerous. As is to be expected, however, in
a coalfield of such extent, there are considerable changes as
the seams are traced across the basin. In general, the series
becomes thinner and the seams less numerous as they are
traced toward the east. The following table illustrates this
contraction eastwards in the deposits[5]:

	West		East	
	Thickness of workable coal	Total thick-ness of beds	Thickness of workable coal	Total thick-ness of beds
Basin Group	91.57 m.	2960.06 m.	40.67 m.	1646.12 m.
Saddle Group	27.32 m.	270.24 m.	12.03 m.	15.75 m.
Margin Group	51.97 m.	3530.29 m.	8.20 m.	904.53 m.
Total	170.86 m.	6760.59 m.	60.90 m.	2566.40 m.

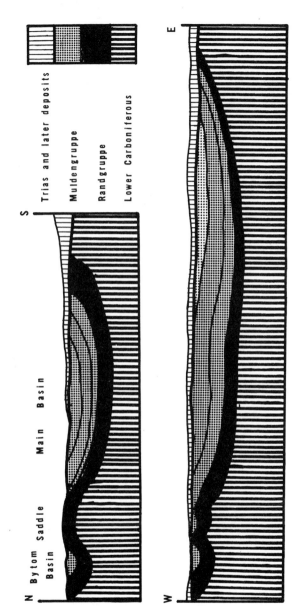

Figure 11: Generalized cross-sections through the Upper Silesian-Moravian coal basin.

Legend:
- Trias and later deposits
- Muldengruppe
- Randgruppe
- Lower Carboniferous

N — Bytom Basin — Saddle — Main Basin — S

W — E

The best of the workable seams are of exceptional thickness. At Zabrze the six seams of the Saddle Beds have a combined thickness of 28.2 meters, and the largest seam (Schuckmannflöz) is 8.6 meters and the next (Pochhammerflöz), 6.5 metres.[6] The thinning-out toward the east of these particular beds is marked by the disappearance of the sandstone and shale which separate them. The result is the appearance near Mysłowice of a single seam, the Redenflöz, with a thickness of over 12 meters.[7]

It is difficult to generalize about the seams of the Margin Group because they appear only around the margins of the coal basin, and their continuity beneath the Basin Group is not proven. The seams in the latter group, however, can be examined over a large area by means of numerous mines and bores. There the same characteristics are displayed as in the Saddle Beds, thick seams diminishing eastwards both in number and in size.

It is commonly said that the Upper Silesian coalfield is unusual in the smoothness and regularity of its seams, and in the ease with which they can be worked. In general this is true. The seams which comprise the Basin Group are more level and free from interruption than the seams of most other coalfields, but even here the seams are more faulted than is sometimes recognized. In the "Saddle," for example, are some quite complex structures. Between the lowermost of the Saddle Beds and the underlying Margin Group is a discordance. The lower series is extensively faulted, but these particular disturbances do not in general extend upwards into the upper series. The Orłowa fault, however, which lies parallel with the northwest margin of the coalfield, is a very extensive dislocation and brings the Basin Group up against the Margin Group along a distance of 67 miles.

The structure of the margins of the coal basin is not fully understood. While its intricacies have been unravelled in the extreme north, along parts of the western margin and in the extreme southwest, where mines and boreholes have not laid it open, its details are imperfectly known. This is especially true of the southeastern margin, where deposits associated with the up-lift of the Carpathian Mountains have deeply covered the margin of the coalfield. Where, however, the Margin Group has

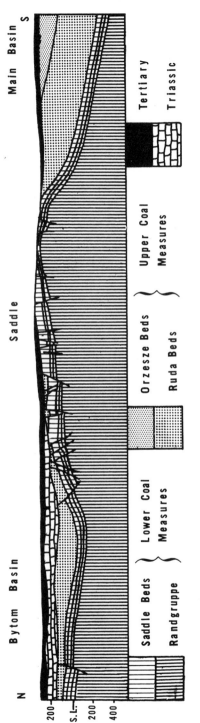

Figure 12: Section through the Saddle between the Bytom and the Main Coal Basins (after R. Michael).

been extensively studied, its structure has often been found to
be unusually complex. In many places the coal seams rise almost vertically towards the surface; in some places they have
been overfolded or thrust-faulted.

The Zabrze-Mysłowice "Saddle," which has already been
described, divides the coal basin into two unequal parts. North
of the "Saddle" is the small Bytom Basin, from which the
seams rise relatively steeply outwards in most directions.
South of the "Saddle" is the main coal basin (Hauptmulde) of
the Upper Silesian field. It covers at least three-quarters of
the whole coalfield, and its seams, though steeply inclined
around its margin, are fairly level over the whole interior of
the basin.

Very early in the history of its development, it was found
that the Upper Silesian coal was not in general of coking quality.
Most was unsuitable for coking. That obtained from the "Saddle" beds near Zabrze was the least unsuited, but even here
the coke obtained was soft and friable, and could not be used
easily in large blast furnaces. Only in the Ostrava-Karvinná
region of the coal basin, within the present boundary of Czechoslovakia, was a good coking coal to be found.

Beds of iron-ore are widely distributed through the Upper
Silesian coal measures,[8] as indeed they are in many other
European coalfields. The deposits are irregular in thickness
and individually they extend over only short distances. They
were mined whenever encountered in the course of coal-mining,
but they were poor in quality and were rarely themselves the
objective of prospecting. In the upper measures of the coal
series the quality of the ore improves and it was more eagerly
sought for at these levels. During the middle years of the 19th
century the coal-measures ore made an appreciable contribution to the needs of the Upper Silesian blast-furnaces.[9] But
accessible beds were gradually exhausted, and the ore-supply
from this source was by the end of the century of negligible
importance.

POST-CARBONIFEROUS DEPOSITS

In previous pages we have spoken of the upper surface of
the coal-bearing rocks as if it were the surface of the earth.
In reality, however, this is not so. The deposition of the

coal-measures was accompanied by faulting and folding, and after they had been laid down further folding produced the basin as we know it today. Very extensive denudation followed in post-Carboniferous times. The coalfield area was reduced to a peneplain, and the upturned beds of the coal series were truncated. The land surface that emerged is represented by the heavy line in figures 11 and 12. It is this surface which represents the upper surface of the coal series of the foregoing discussion. This surface, produced during the post-Carboniferous cycle of denudation, was then submerged beneath the sea, and a fresh series of marine and lacustrine deposits was laid down. These are the Permian, Triassic, Jurassic, Cretaceous and Tertiary beds, which with a greater or lesser thickness cover most of the coal basin. It is in this series of deposits, notably in the Trias, that the second group of minerals, the ores of lead, zinc and iron, were chiefly formed.

The Ore-bearing Triassic Deposits: The Permian deposits, which directly overlie the coal-bearing beds, are of feeble thickness, outcrop over a very small area and contain no mineral deposits of economic value. But above them are the very important Triassic beds.[10] These can be divided into three parts: at their base is the rather thin deposit of Bunter Sandstone (Buntsandstein); above there are the rather thicker deposits of the Shelly Limestone (Muschelkalk), and finally the Keuper beds. The whole group nowhere exceeds 360 metres in thickness, so that, compared with the coal measures, it is a very thin deposit. The most important part of the Triassic series is undoubtedly the Shelly Limestone. This is for the most part, as its name implies, a shelly limestone. Its middle portions have been dolomitzied, that is, part of its calcium has been replaced by magnesium. Near the base of the Middle Shelly Limestone occur ore deposits of lead, zinc, and iron.

There ores occur as masses of irregular shape and varying size, filling cavities left by the solution of the dolomite (fig. 14). The ores were undoubtedly brought upwards in a fluid form, and attempts have been made to associate their occurrence with the distribution of faults in the underlying Carboniferous, through which the liquids and gas could have passed. The sketch on this page shows how the ore-bodies commonly occur.

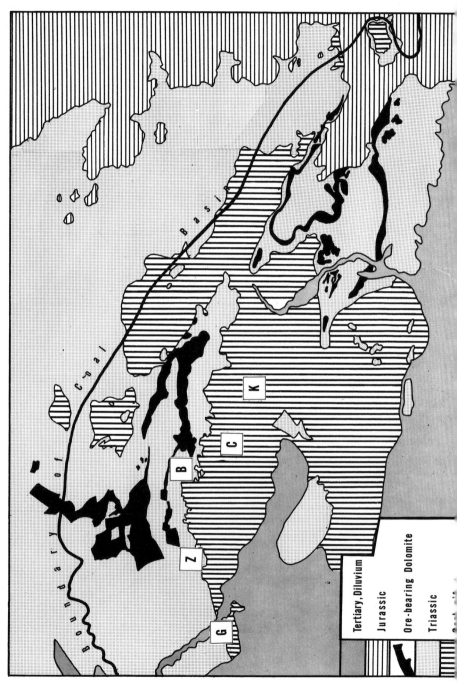

Figure 13: Geology of the Lead - Zinc Deposits. Letters represent: Gliwice (G), Zabrze (Z), Bytom (B), Chorzów (C), Katowice (K).

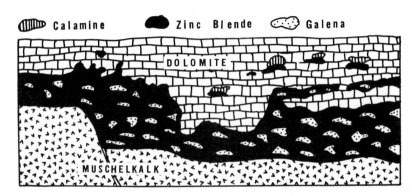

Figure 14: Section through typical lead-zinc deposit.

The zinc ores commonly present are the sulphide-blende
(ZnS.), and the carbonate-calamine ($ZnCO_3$). Lead is represented most often by its sulphide, galena (PbS). With these
are associated certain other economic minerals. A little silver occurs with the lead, and the blende is usually accompanied by cadmium. Sometimes the galena is scattered in small
masses through large deposits of blende; sometimes masses
of calamine and blende are in close juxtaposition; sometimes
there is an even scattering of all three minerals in small con-
cretions through the dolomite.

The iron-ores which are found as irregular, lenticular
masses are probably of a quite different origin from the non-
ferrous metals. They occur on ancient surfaces of the Shelly
Limestone, and were probably left behind after the solution
and removal of the limestone.[11] This iron is mostly brown ore
($Fe_2O_3.3H_2O$), with about 30 per cent iron. It provided one of
the main sources of ore in the early days of the Silesian iron
industry,[12] but the trace of zinc that was commonly present in
the iron created difficulties in the blast furnace, and the iron-
workers turned away readily to other sources of ore.

Quite apart from their significance as ore-bearing rocks, the Triassic limestones have in more recent times come to be used as a source of water for the industrial area. The pervious limestone, with its numerous solution cavities, is an admirable water-bearing rock, and it was the abundance of water in the workings that led in the 18th century to the temporary abandonment of lead-mining. Until late in the 19th century springs arising naturally in the Trias sufficed for water-supply, but the growing population density and scale of industry led to the sinking of wells in the Trias and the use of abandoned mines which tapped the water-bearing beds (see page 152).

Above the Triassic beds were laid down the Jurassic and Cretaceous series, made up mainly of limestone. A long period of erosion followed during which the Jurassic and Cretaceous were stripped from the coalfield area of Upper Silesia. Today the westerly edge of these deposits forms a scarp 30 miles away to the north-east of the industrial area (fig. 9). In the Jurassic beds of Poland, just as in those of southern Germany, of Lorraine and of the English Midlands, bedded iron-ore is found, considerable in amount but generally poor in quality. These ores were too remote to have been used in the early days of the Upper Silesian industry, but in recent years the ores of Częstochowa and Kielce have been of considerable importance.

The Tertiary and Later Deposits: The Tertiary period which followed was marked by the building of the Carpathian Mountains. Shallow seas formed over Upper Silesia, while the mountains were being folded to the south. Beds of sand, clay and limestone, with sometimes beds of rock salt and of other minerals left behind as the seas dried up, were laid down. Scattered deposits of bog iron-ore (limonite) were also formed in the Tertiary deposits and have been worked sporadically along the Odra valley.[13]

The last phase in the evolution of Upper Silesia was the Ice Age. The northern ice-sheet just reached the coalfield area, and the whole region was covered by the sands and gravels left by the floods of melt-water that escaped from it. These deposits are locally very thick, and their extreme infertility is largely responsible for the great extent of the land that remains under forest in Upper Silesia. Marshes formed in depressions in the land-surface, and nodular masses of bog iron-ore formed amid the peaty deposits.

But after the Ice Age and even at intervals during it strong winds spread a fine, fertile dust, or loess, over parts of the area, sometimes hiding the sterile sands and gravels and raising greatly the level of fertility. Most agricultural settlements are on patches of loess, while the sands and gravels support forests and yielded the bog-ores, both so important in the early days of the iron industry.

The map (fig. 10), shows the extent of the coal basin of Upper Silesia, but the coal measures outcrop over only about 15 per cent of this area. Most important by far is the outcrop of the "saddle" beds between Zabrze and Dąbrowa. Southwards from here is an extensive area where the seams of the Muldengruppe reach the surface (fig. 9). Elsewhere the outcrops are very small in area, but have in all cases given rise to mining: Rybnik, Hlucin, Moravska Ostrava and Karvinná in Moravia, and Tenczynek in West Galicia. For its first hundred years the coal-mining industry was confined to these outcrops of the coal-measures, and even today few mines have been sunk through the later deposits to work the "hidden" parts of the coalfield.

The Triassic and later deposits must formerly have stretched across the whole area, but today they are found extensively only over the northern and north-eastern parts of the coalfield with only a few small occurrences in other parts (fig. 9). The Triassic beds begin along the northern margin of the Zabrze-Mysłowice saddle and, with but little interruption, stretch northwards over the Beuthen coal basin, until they are in Nurn hidden by the Jurassic. From near Tarnowskie Góry a belt of Triassic deposits stretches south-eastwards towards the Vistula, expanding to cover a large area near Chrzanów.

The ore-bearing dolomite covers only a small part of this area (fig. 13). Though it forms irregular and confusing shapes on the ground, its occurrences may be said to form three distinct groups. The largest and most important lies around Tarnowskie Góry, stretching southwards from here to Bytom. The second, covering a much more restricted area, lies to the east of Bytom, and the third, completely detached from these two,

is near Chrzanów and lay through the 19th century in Russian
Poland.

CREATION OF THE GEOLOGICAL MAP

These complexities of geological structure were unravelled
at a very early date. The earliest specifically geological description of this region is contained in the memoir of von
Heinitz (1786).[14] But, as might be expected of a writing as
early as this, no true picture emerges of the structure of the
coal basin and of the relation to it of the later deposits. But,
in a series of publications spread through the 19th century,[15]
we can see our present body of geological knowledge slowly
taking shape. Already, in the first decade of the century Leopold von Buch had discerned the elements of the geological picture.[16] By 1822, von Oeynhausen had worked out the broad
structure of the coal-basin and the relation to it of later deposits, and published a geological map of the region.[17] Later,
the writings of von Carnall[18] and Krug von Nidda[19] intensified
the knowledge of the area, and prepared the way for Ferdinand
Roemer's comprehensive study.[20] In 1860 Carl Mauve published a geological map[21] of the conceded area of the coalfield
(fig. 16). This was followed by the ambitious and accurate
maps of Roemer. From this time onwards publications on the
geology of the Upper Silesian coalfield and mineral deposits
become very numerous.[22] They are, however, in general restricted to local stratigraphical or mineralogical problems
and to establishing the connections between the[23] outcrops and
defining the hidden margin of the basin.[24] Noteworthy exceptions, however, are the long and detailed studies of the region
as a whole by R. Michael[25] and S. Czarnocki.[26]

Notes

1. R. Michael, Die Geologie des oberschlesischen Steinkohlenbezirkes, Abhandlungen der Königlichen Preussischen Geologischen Landesanstalt, Neue Folge, LXXI, 1913; K. Patteisky
and J. Folprecht, "Der Rumpf des oberschlesischen Steinkoh-
lengebirges, " Z.d.O.B.u.H.V., LXX, 1931, 558-565. Stefan
Czarnocki, Polskie Zagłębie Węglowe, Warsaw, 1935, is the
best available study of the geology of the coalfield.

2. S. Czarnocki in Livret-Guide du II Congrès de Géographes et Ethnographes slaves en Pologne 1927, ed. L. Sawicki, Kraków, 1927, 83-9; Z.d.O.B.u.H.V., LXV, 1926, 739-745.

3. F. Tornau, "Der Flötzberg bei Zabrze," Jahrbuch der Königlichen Preussischen Geologischen Landesanstalt und Bergakademie, XXIII, 1902, 368-524.

4. R. Michael, "Die Gliederung der oberschlesischen Steinkohlenformation," Jahrbuch der Königlich Preussischen Geologischen Landesanstalt und Bergakademie, XXII, 1904, 317-340.

5. C. Gaebler, Das oberschlesische Steinkohlenbecken, Kattowitz, 1909, 41 ff.

6. R. Michael, "Die Geologie des oberschlesischen Steinkohlenbezirkes," Abhandlungen der Königlich Preussischen Geologischen Landesanstalt, LXXI, 1913.

7. ibid., 192.

8. R. Michael, op.cit., 85-87.

9. A. Sachs, op.cit., 112-113.

10. R. Althaus, "Die Erzformation des Muschelkalks in Oberschlesien," Jahrbuch der Königlichen Preussischen Geologischen Landesanstalt, XII, 1891, 37-98.

11. R. Michael, op.cit., 374-376.

12. F. Raefler, "Die Brauneisenerzlagerstätten Oberschlesiens," B.u.H.R., XI, 1914-15, 67-75; XII, 1915-16, 1-9, 11-8; Pologne 1918-1939, Neuchâtel, n.d., II, 78-9.

13. A. Sachs, op.cit., 114-115.

14. von Heinitz, Mémoire sur les produits du Règne minéral de la Monarchie prussienne, Berlin, 1786, 16-25; in Comte de Mirabeau, De la Monarchie Prussienne, London, 1788, II, 247-270.

15. Bibliography in Jahrbuch der Königlichen Preussischen Geologischen Landesanstalt und Bergakademie, XXIII, 1905, 409-410.

16. Leopold von Buch, "Geognostische Uebersicht von Neu-Schlesien," Gesammelte Schriften, I, 1867, 719-739.

17. Carl von Oeynhausen, Versuch einer geognostischen Beschreibung von Oberschlesien, Essen, 1822.

18. von Carnall, "Ueber die Lagerung und Verbreitung der Steinkohlenflötze," Jahresbericht der Oberschlesischen Gesellschaft für vaterlandische Kultur, XXXVIII, 1860, 28-30.

19. Krug von Nidda, "Ueber das oberschlesische Steinkohlenbecken," Jahresbericht der Schlesischen Gesellschaft für vaterlandische Kultur, XXXII, 1854, 28-34.

20. F. Roemer, Geologie von Oberschlesien, Breslau, 1870.

21. C. Mauve, Flötz-Karte des Steinkohlen-Gebirges bei Beuthen, Gleiwitz, Myslowitz und Nicolai in Ober-Schlesien, 1860.

22. For bibliography, see F. Tornau in Jahrbücher der Königlichen Preussischen Geologischen Landesanstalt und Bergakademie, XXIII, 1905, 409-410.

23. W. Jičinsky, "Der Zusammenhang der mahrisch-schlesischen und der preussisch-schlesischen Kohlenformation," O.Z.f.B.u.H., XXV, 1877, 255-7; 267-9; 280-1; K. Patteisky, in M.R., XVII, 1925, 621-9.

24. Significant studies of the limits of the coal basin are by R. Michael, Z.d.O.B.u.H.V., LI, 1912, 394-414; M.R., IV, 1912, 1197-1205, 1241-4; Jahrbuch der Königlichen preussischen Geologischen Landesanstalt zu Berlin, XXXIII, i, 1914, 159-304; H. Folprecht, M.R., VII, 1915, 393-400, 441-7; K. Patteisky, B.u.H.J., LXXII, 1924, 49-64, and M.R., XVII, 1926, 557-9; Grzybowski, M.R., IV, 1912, 918-925. The extent of current knowledge is summarized by P. Kukuk, "Die geologischen Grundlagen des Oberschlesischen Steinkohlenbeckens," G., LXXVI, 1940, 1-13; 30-2.

25. R. Michael, op.cit.

26. S. Czarnocki, op.cit., 1935.

CHAPTER IV

UPPER SILESIA: 1800-1918: COAL MINING

"Der Kohlenreichlum dieser Gegenden, die
Anzahl und Machtigkeit der Flötze, Welche
in selten unterbrochener Regelmassigkeit auf
weite Erstreckungen gelagert sind, ist aus-
serordentlich, und ubertrifft die übrigen Nie-
derlagen des Steinkohlen-Gebirges beiweitem."
Carl von Oeynhausen (1822).

The departure of von Reden marked the end of an epoch
during which the officials of the Prussian State had by their
vigor and foresight created a mining and manufacturing industry amid the forests and wastes of Upper Silesia. Four
years after von Reden left Silesia for Berlin, the Prussian
armies were defeated at Jena, and Prussia became a depend-
ency of the French. The mines and industries of Upper Silesia suffered severely both from neglect and from the ravages
of war.[1] But the lessons of von Reden's administration were
not lost. A memorandum prepared by the Oberbergamt in
1804, after recounting the success of experiments in smelting
with coke, went on to say that two private furnace-owners "had
already followed the example of the State, and more would
doubtless follow."[2] Upper Silesia played a part in the rebuilding of Prussia after the Treaty of Tilsit, and, following the
loss of her Rhineland provinces, Prussia turned more to Silesia for metal goods. It is said that the Prussian guns which
helped to defeat the French at Leipzig in 1813 had been cast at
Gliwice the foundry.[3]

THE COAL-MINING INDUSTRY

At the beginning of the 19th century the few mines that
were worked lay on the outcrop of the coal measures (fig. 8),
and it was many years before mines were sunk through the
Triassic and later deposits to reach the hidden coalfield.

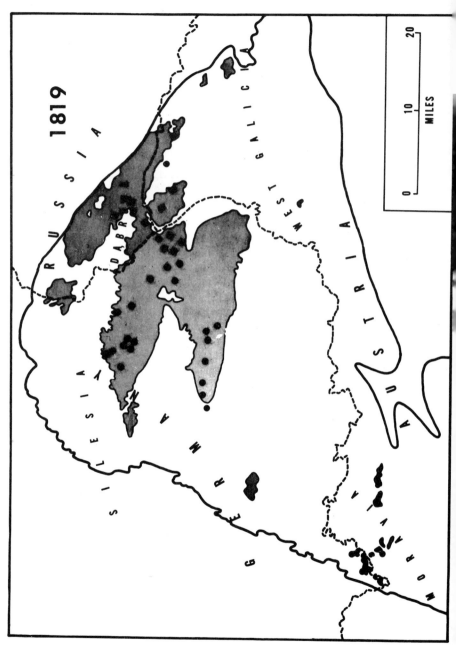

Figure 15: Coal mines in Upper Silesia and adjoining areas in 1819.

von Oeynhausen's map of 1819[4] showed merely a closer sprink-
ling of mines in those areas that had already been worked for
several decades (fig. 15). Indeed, for the first half of the century mining was virtually confined to three small areas of the
coalfield: (1) the outcrop of the "saddle" beds between Ruda
and Mysłowice, with an extension southwards into the forests
of Pszczyna, (2) the outcrop of the Basin Group stretching
from Mikołów westward through Orzesze to Dębiensko, and
(3) the small outcrops at Hlucin in the south-west of the field.
    The more northerly of these outcrops stretched eastwards
into Russian or "Congress" Poland and into Austrian Galicia.
The Hlucin outcrop was virtually continuous with that of Ostrava and Karvinná in Moravia. On each of these extensions
of the Prussian-held field mining began early in the 19th century.
    By the middle years of the century the whole of the out-
crop had been conceded, though not all concessions were ac-
tively worked. Carl Mauve's map of 1860[5] (fig. 16) shows that
concessions and even mines were beginning to fill in the empty
area between the more northerly and southerly extensions of
the main outcrop, and to spread over the hidden Bytom basin,
north of the "saddle." By the end of the century almost the
whole coalfield, except its little explored southern extremity
and south-eastern margin, had been marked out in concessions.[6]
    The unusually complete statistics that were published by
the Prussian government[7] permit one to trace the geographical spread of mining over the German part of the field. It is
unfortunate that comparable figures are not available for the
Russian-and Austrian-held portions of the coalfield. The maps,
figures 17 to 20, show graphically this outward movement of
mining from the older centers of activity.
    Throughout the century the largest units of production
were those operated by the Prussian State. In 1799, the two
fiscal mines, Königsgrube and Königinluisengrube, produced
about 45 per cent of the Upper Silesian output. This proportion declined during the century, but in 1912 still amounted to
17 per cent of the total.
    Most of Upper Silesia belonged, as we have already seen,
to a handfull of families.[8] By far the most significant landowners in the coalfield region, were the Prince of Pless, who,

exercised quasi-regal powers over his vast domains; the two
branches of both the Henckel von Donnersmarck and the Hohenlohe families, who owned coal-bearing lands near Bytom,
as well as much of the lead and zinc producing area; Count
Tiele-Winkler, who during the century succeeded to the Katowice-Mysłowice lordship; Count Schaffgötsch and Count Ballestrem.

The problem was to induce these great landowners to exercise their privilege of developing the vast resources that
lay ready to their land. But demand for coal was small and
they were slow to avail themselves of this opportunity. As
the needs of the smelting industries grew and more steam engines were installed in the mines, however, the need for coal
increased. Demand from these sources was supplemented by
the requirements of brick-kilns and limeworks, as construction industries began to expand in the wake of the mining and
metallurgical. The Kłodnicki Canal allowed coal to be sent
to the Odra river and thus to Berlin. But the small size of
the canal and difficulties of navigation on the Odra severely
handicapped this traffic. The volume of trade on the canal
grew slowly, but in its peak year 1852 amounted altogether to
only 88,100 tons—at least half ot it coal.[9] After this date the
importance of canal and river declined steadily as that of the
railways grew.

The first railway line into Upper Silesia was from Wrocław, through Opole, Gliwice and Katowice to Mysłowice. It
was begun in 1842, but not completed until 1846. In the following year the line was continued in the direction of Kraków. In
1848 the line from Warsaw made connection with this railway
(see fig. 17). In the next ten years great progress was made.
The net began to thicken within the industrial area, and lines
were completed through Rybnik to Racibórz and through Oświęcim to Moravia and Vienna. Later a line was laid down
northwards through Tarnowskie Góry in the direction of Poznań and connections with Moravia and the Odra towns was improved.

The expansion of coal production and distribution went in
step with the extension of the railway net. Dr. Marian Frank
has traced this connection, and has shown that as the coal-mining industry grew, it relied increasingly on distant markets.[10]

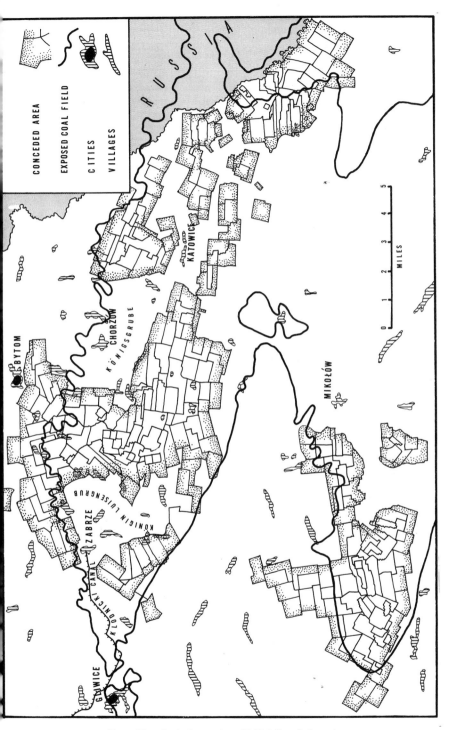

Figure 16: Coal Concessions, 1860 (after C. Mauve).

It soon became apparent that the Prussian State was no
longer willing to take the initiative in opening mines and establishing works, as it had done during von Reden's tenure of
office. In 1822, the vague but extensive mining rights enjoyed
by the State were narrowed and defined, leaving the landowners
greater freedom to develop the resources that lay beneath
their own soil.[11] The State at this time acquiesced more
readily than Frederick II and his ministers would have done
in the private exercise by the land owners of bergregal rights.
Thus it came about that the landed families were themselves
the operating mine companies. At first the coal mines were
managed in much the same way as the forests or other exploit-
able resources. This had certain advantages; there could not
easily be any conflict of interest between the landowner as
owner of mines and as proprietor of agricultural land and forest. Labor supply was more easily manipulated, when the
mines were merely an appendage of a great feudal estate. On
the other hand, there was a shortage of capital, except in the
fiscal mines. When, with the increasing depth and mechanization of the mines, this shortage of capital became severe,
many of the landowners converted their coal mining—or, for
that matter, their lead, zinc, iron and steel—businesses
into Aktiengesellschaften, and raised capital in the money markets of Wrocław and Berlin. The banks and syndicates of merchants made loans to or actually took over some of the mining
and industrial assets of Upper Silesia. But the banks never
played in eastern Germany as important a role as they did in
western in the actual establishment of mining and industrial
firms. The nucleus of almost every one of these was the hered-
itary estates of one of the great landed families of the region.

Foremost amongst those families which, early in the 19th
century, exploited their own coal resources, was the Prince of
Pless. He owned a large part of the main coal basin (fig. 5),
where the seams were too thickly covered by later deposits to
be worked, but he held also the outcrop near Mikołów. Here
was established the Plessische Bergamt, charged with direct-
ing mining on the Prince's lands. Henckel von Donnersmarck,
Schaftgötsch and Ballestrem owned between them much of the
"saddle" area between Gliwice and Katowice, and after the re-
striction of the State's sphere of activities, they also began to

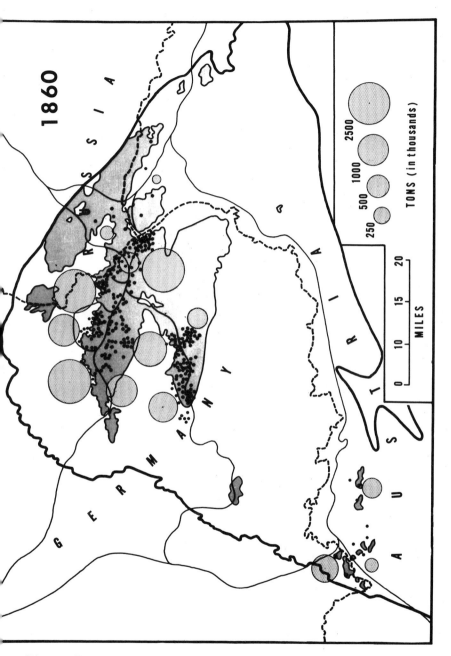

Figure 17: Coal mines and coal output in the Upper Silesian-Moravian
coal basin, in 1860.

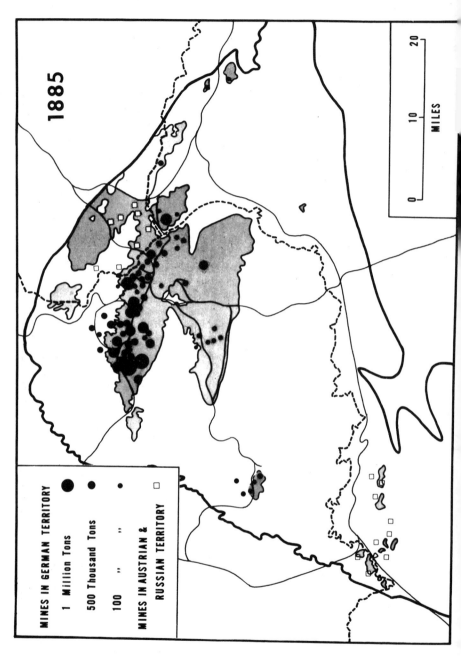

1885

MINES IN GERMAN TERRITORY
● 1 Million Tons
● 500 Thousand Tons
· 100 " "
□ MINES IN AUSTRIAN & RUSSIAN TERRITORY

20
10
MILES
0

Figure 18: Coal mines in the coal basin of Upper Silesia-Moravia, in 1885.

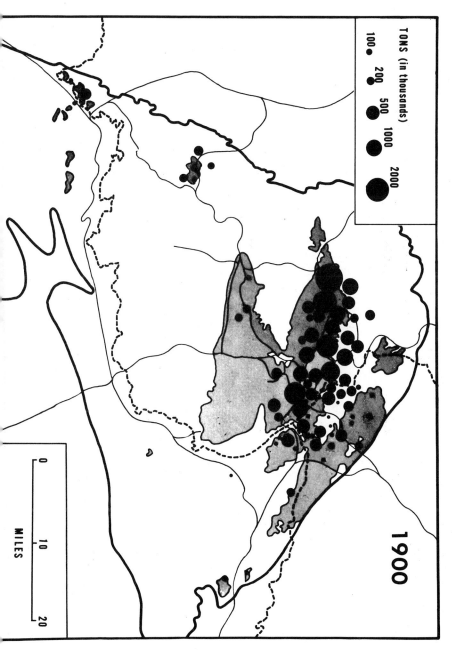

TONS (in thousands)

100 •
200
500
1000
2000

1900

0
10
20

MILES

Figure 19: Coal Mines and coal output in Upper Silesia and adjoining areas, in 1900.

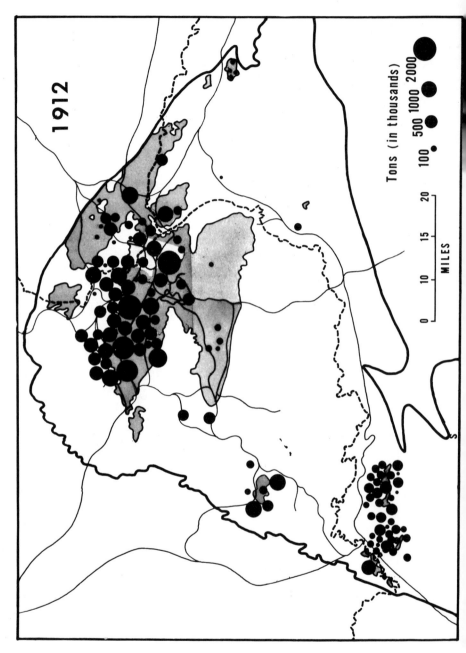

Figure 20: Coal mines and coal output in the coal basin of
Upper Silesia-Moravia, in 1912.

develop their own resources. The Katowice-Mysłowice lordship lay along the Przemsza river, in the extreme east of Upper Silesia. The known coal resources were large, and, in the northern part of the lordship, were easily mined. The assurance to Tiele-Winkler of bergregal rights on his lands was followed by a more active development of his coal resources. The maps, figures 17 to 20, showing the distribution of coal mining at intervals through the century, need little comment. Mining spread from the area of the exposed coalfield to neighboring areas of the hidden field.[12] The opening of mines was due quite as much to the initiative of the local landowner as to favorable local geological and economic conditions.

It was fortunate for a coal-mining industry with as little investment capital as the Upper Silesian that, from the technical point of view, the coalfield was probably the easiest in Europe to develop. Not only were the seams unusually thick as well as less disturbed than those of most other European coalfields; they actually outcropped over a considerable area and dipped beneath other beds at a shallow angle.[13] The result was that mines were generally very shallow. In the 1860's, the highly productive Königsgrube had penetrated only 64·75 meters below the surface, and the average depth of coal working was only between 80 and 100 meters.[14]

A method of mining was evolved to suit the thick and regular seams. Galleries were excavated through the seams, cutting the latter into rectangular masses. These were then extracted by a kind of longwall method and the roof allowed to collapse.[15] The mining of thick seams in this fashion at only shallow depths led of course to superficial subsidences. This would have been a matter of serious importance in any area more densely settled and highly cultivated Upper Silesia. But here little damage could be done to heath and forest, and the common ownership of mineral and surface rights obviated most difficulties. At the end of the 19th century attempts were made to check roof-fall by filling the excavated space with sand, "flushed" in by water. But little progress was made in using this method until recent years (see page 211).

Attempts had been made in the 18th century to cut adits to drain the zinc and lead mines. In 1794, another adit was

begun at Zabrze, near the Kłodnica river.[16] Its purpose was
to drain water from the Königinluisengrube, but it was extended to the Königsgrube by 1863. This Hauptschlüsselstol-
len drained effectively those mines which lay along its ten
mile length, and along the lower part of its course the adit
served also the needs of navigation, allowing coal from Köni-
gin Luise to be shipped by this route down to the valley of the
Kłodnica. Elsewhere, pumps were used to keep the mines dry,
but their shallow depth and relatively small influx of water
made this a relatively easy task.

Fire-damp was rare in Upper Silesian mines, though in
some mines there was a certain risk of dust explosions. Only
in the southwest of the coalfield, in Hlucin and neighboring
Ostrava, had precautions normally to be taken against using
a naked flame in the workings.[17]

Upper Silesian coal had from 24 to 33 per cent of gaseous
matter, and was generally classified as "long-flame" or "gas"
coal. While making it particularly suitable for domestic purposes and for use in steam boilers, this quality diminished
its value as a coking coal.[18] Upper Silesian coke was firable,
transportable only with difficulty, and tended to be crushed to
a powder in the blast furnace.[19] It was fortunate that the earliest seams to be worked—the "saddle" beds near Zabrze—
were among the more suitable for coking. But the unsuitability of most of the others was discovered early, and writers
on Upper Silesia in the 19th century frequently lamented their
inadequacy in this respect.[20]

In reality, however, a passable coke could be made from
coal taken from the lower beds in the "saddle" group.[21] Some
half-dozen mines, lying between Zabrze and Chorzów, acquired a reputation for their coking coals, and had some influ-
ence on the location of iron-works. In a few places elsewhere
coal of coking quality could be produced in small quantities,
especially near Rybnik and in the Hlucin area.[22]

Much of the Upper Silesian coal, especially that from the
mines of Rybnik and Pszczyna, was particularly friable, and the
mines yielded little lump coal. This was undoubtedly a factor
hindering the opening of mines in these areas. Towards the
end of the century, however, the practice grew up of compress-
ing the finer coal into brickets.[23]

There was a conspicuous change during the century in ways in which the coal was used. Early in the century the smelting works—lead and zinc as well as iron—together with metal fabricating works, grew to be by far the largest users of coal. About the middle of the century, for example, the zinc and iron furnaces took 58 per cent of the coal mined in Kreis Bytom.[24] In other Kreise the demands at least of the zinc smelters would have been appreciably less. Nevertheless, it is apparent that at this time mining and metallurgy constituted by far the largest sources of demand. The consumption of fuel by the metallurgical industries increased during the century, though less rapidly than the output of metal goods.[25] This was, of course, due to an increasing efficiency in the use of fuel. But local industries took a steadily diminishing fraction of the total coal output. From 14.3 per cent in 1868, the consumption of lead and zinc smelters fell to 4.5 per cent in 1901.[26] That of the iron and steel works fell from 22.2 per cent to 6.3. On the other hand, improving means of transport permitted the coal to be distributed more widely. In 1868, only 39 per cent of the coal mined was sent away by rail; in 1901, over 70 per cent.

The Transport Problem: Upper Silesia never ceased to suffer from its distance from the chief markets of Central and Western Europe. The river Odra was extensively used in the 17th and 18 centuries, and much work was done to render it suitable for barge traffic.[27] We have already seen how the Kłodnicki Canal was constructed in order to link the river with the coalfield (page 37). Coal shipments began by this route in 1802, but the canal and river never fulfilled the high hopes that were entertained for them. The terminus of the canal at Zabrze was not easy to reach from the mines, and the navigation of the Odra itself was less easy for coal barges than it had been for the lighter craft of an earlier century. In fact, coal shipments exceeded 60,000 tons in only one year before the coming of the railways drastically reduced the importance of the canal and river.

During the middle years of the century coal despatched from the mining area tended to use the railways. But river and canal were not forgotten, and when, in Berlin, Central Germany and north German ports, the competition of English and

Ruhr coal began to be felt,[29] there were renewed demands for
improved waterways that would permit Upper Silesia to meet
this threat. Improvements were made in the Kłodnicki Canal,[30]
but it took the threat to Upper Silesian interests embodied in
the West German proposal to cut the Dortmund-Ems Canal
from the Ruhr to the North Sea, to bring about any comparable
work on the Odra itself.[31] Work on the river proceeded slowly
enough, but the volume of river traffic increased and Upper
Silesia was able for a time to maintain its position in the Berlin market, if not also in that of the North German ports,
where the English competition was more severe.[32]

Then came the proposal to construct the Mittelland Canal,
which would have the effect of putting Berlin in direct water
communication with the Ruhr. Upper Silesian interests were
determined to oppose the carrying through of this proposal,
unless commensurable improvements were made in the Kłodnicki Canal and river Odra.[33] The plan for the canal did not
in fact materialize before the First World War, but in the
closing years of the pre-war century, the Upper Silesian coal
industry was fighting a slowly losing battle against Ruhr and
English coal in the markets of Berlin and central Germany.[34]

The river Przemsza, which for part of its length formed
the eastern boundary of Upper Silesia, flows down to the Vistula. It was navigable for only very small craft, and then for
only a part of the year, but nevertheless sufficed to carry
small quantities of Upper Silesian coal downstream to markets
in Austrian Galicia and Russian Poland.

It was not until 1845 that Upper Silesia was first linked by
rail with the rest of Germany by the Oberschlesische Eisen-
bahn. This followed the river Odra and was linked with the
industrial area by a branch-line from Koźle through Katowice
into Austrian territory at Oświęcim.[35] Subsequently a line was
laid down from Tarnowskie Góry to Wrocław along the right
bank of the Odra and another running north from Tarnowskie
Góry to Poznań. Rail connections were established with Warsaw, Kraków and Vienna, and by the 1880's the network, illustrated in figure 18, had emerged.

Towards the east and south-east Upper Silesian coal met
with little competition, but also it found few markets.[36]   The
map, figure 23, shows how, blocked in the west and north by

West German and English coal, the Upper Silesian reached
far into Poland and the Danubian lands. This pattern of trade
foreshadows in an interesting fashion the commercial pattern
of the present day.[37]

This coal trade with eastern and southeastern Europe
was necessarily by rail. Coal movement on the Przemsza and
Vistula was negligible and proposals for a canal from the Odra to the Danube were still-born. Despite the high tariffs
which protected the Russian market, the Upper Silesian market was tending to increase very slowly toward the east and
south-east as it contracted to the west and north-west.

Growth of Coal Production: At the beginning of the 19th
century, coal production in Upper Silesia was little more than
a quarter of that from the Wałbrzych mines of Lower Silesia,
and there is little doubt but that the latter were thought to hold
the greater promise for the future. In fact, Daubuisson and
Héron de Villefosse regarded the Fuchsgrube, one of the Wałbrzych mines, as amongst the very best in all Germany.[38]
But after about 1790 the rate of expansion of Lower Silesian
production was slow. These mines had the initial advantages
of earlier development and greater ease of access, but the
seams were thin and highly folded, and it was not long before
the greater advantages of the Upper Silesian field became apparent. By 1822, the output of Upper Silesia had exceeded that
of Lower, and thereafter its growth was unusually rapid. The
graph shows the production of German Upper Silesia from the
late 18th century until 1920. During this period output rose
from less than 50,000 tons to a maximum of over 42,000,000
tons. High as this rate of increase was, it was in fact exceeded by that of the Ruhr, and in fact Upper Silesia only just
kept pace with the increasing output of Germany as a whole.
For half a century it ranged between 20 and 24 per cent of the
national total. During this period the output of the coalfields
of Lower Silesia and Hannover increased only slightly, while
that of the Saxon fields declined. In 1860 Upper Silesia and
the Ruhr had provided 54 per cent of Germany's coal, by 1900,
they were yielding nearly 80 per cent.

The effect of this was to intensify the sense of conflict
between these dominant coal producers of West and of East
Germany. No other coalfield was of more than local importance,

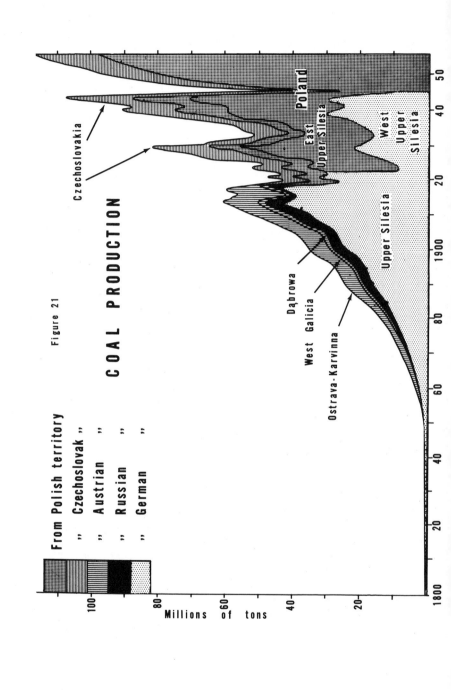

Figure 21

COAL PRODUCTION

From Polish territory
   ,,   Czechoslovak ,,
   ,,   Austrian   ,,
   ,,   Russian   ,,
   ,,   German   ,,

Millions of tons

Czechoslovakia

Poland

East Upper Silesia
West Upper Silesia
Upper Silesia

Dąbrowa
West Galicia
Ostrava-Karvinna
Upper Silesia

1800   20   40   60   80   1900   20   40

20   40   50

100

80

60

40

20

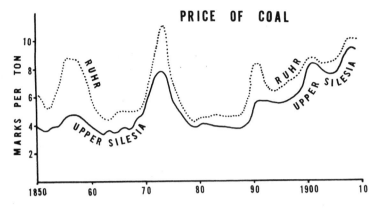

Figure 22: Price of coal in Upper Silesia and in the Ruhr.

and the line, drawn from north to south across Central Germany, where the delivered price of Ruhr coal was equal, quality for quality, to that of Upper Silesian coal, became of crucial importance. But the working out of this conflict was interrupted by the First World War and in the end prevented by the partition of the Upper Silesian coalfield in 1922.

A trading association was formed in 1890 among the coal producers of Upper Silesia. It proved to be a very loose kind of cartel; prices were fixed, but no quotas were assigned. Its operation was free from dissention, partly because, as "the mines are few and the owners intimately associated, the need for a closer organization is not felt. It has been called a 'family affair.'"[39]

In 1850 Upper Silesian coal was cheaper than any other coal in Germany, and at the pit-head was little more than half the price of Ruhr coal.[40] But during the following half century the gap began gradually to close. Improved methods cheapened, production in the Ruhr, while the deepening pits and rising labor costs increased the price of Upper Silesian coal. By 1909 the price of Upper Silesian coal was raised almost to the level of that of the Ruhr. This, combined with the superior transport facilities in West Germany, gradually reduced the area of distribution of Upper Silesian Coal.

Throughout most of the century the coal-mining industry

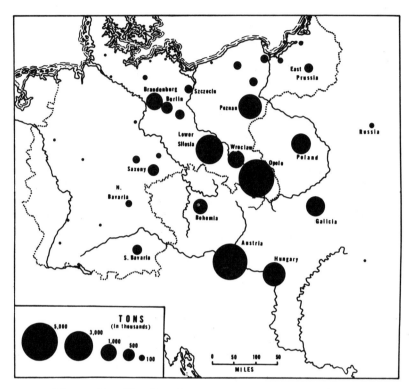

Figure 23: The distribution of coal from Upper Silesia in 1910.

was second in importance, measured by the value of its products, to iron and steel. But its contribution to the total pro-
ductivity of the industrial region was increasing. Since about
1888 the coal-mining industry has exceeded in the value of its
product both the iron and steel and the lead and zinc industries[41]:

	Coal and Iron ore	Iron and Steel	Lead and Zinc
1869-79	36.4%	42.9%	20.7%
1880-87	34.4	41.7	29.3
1888-94	38.6	35.2	26.2
1895-1902	44.0	40.0	16.0
1903-13	43.7	37.6	18.7

Notes

1. K. Wutke, Aus der Vergangenheit des Schlesischen Berg- und Hüttenbetriebs, Breslau, 1913, 279-349.

2. Quoted in K. Wutke, op.cit., 385-394.

3. W. J. Rose, The Drama of Upper Silesia, London, 1936, 38; "Upper Silesia," Baltic and Scandinavian Countries, III, 1937, 210-214.

4. Carl von Oeynhausen, Versuch einer geognostischen Beschreibung von Oberschlesien, Essen, 1822; the map appears in three folded sheets; see also "Schlesiens steinkohlenwerke vor 60 Jahren," J.d.S.V.f.B.u.H., I, 1859, 371-3.

5. Carl Mauve, Flötz-Karte des steinkohlen-Gebirges bei Beuthen, Gleiwitz, Myslowitz und Nikolai in Oberschlesien, Breslau, 1860; the map is in twelve large sheets. See also Krug von Nidda, "Ueber das oberschlesische steinkohlenbecken," Jahresbericht der Schlesischen Gesellschaft für vaterlandische Kultur, XXXII, 1854, 28-34.

6. R. Michael, "Übersichtskarte der Besitz-Verhältnisse im Oberschlesischen Steinkohlenrevier und den Nachbarbezirken," Z.d.O.B.u.H.V., Juni, 1913.

7. Published in Zeitschrift für Berg- Hütten- und Salinenwesen im Preussischen Staat, from 1853.

8. J. Partsch, Schlesien, II, 8-11.

9. Alfred Hornig, "Kanał Kłodnicki i Gliwicki," Geografia w Szkole, VII, 1954, 66-72.

10. Marian Frank, "Przyczynek do badania wydobycia węgla w Polsce na tle rozwoju sieci kolejowej w Śląsko–dąbrowsko-krakowskim Zagłębiu Węglowym do pierwszej wojny

światowej, Zeszyty Naukowe Wyższej Szkoły Ekonomicznej w Katowicach, I, 1957, 1-35.

11. J. Partsch, op.cit., II, 56; Bernhard Kosmann, Oberschlesien, sein Land und seine Industrie, Gleiwitz, 1888, 20-24.

12. R. Wachsmann, "Der Steinkohlenbergbau im Rybniker Revier," Z.d.O.B.u.H.V., LXIII, 1924, 233-238; Gerke, "Ueber den Plesser Bergbau und die Boerschachte," Z.d.O.B.u.H.V., LXVIII, 1929, 124-9.

13. Léo Gérard, "Notice sur l'exploitation de la houille," R.U.d.M., XVI, 1865, 383-426.

14. ibid., 395.

15. Lucius W. Mayer, "Advanced Methods of Mining Coal in Silesia," Engineering and Mining Journal, LXXXVI, 1908, 887-892.

16. J. Partsch, op.cit., II, 55; L. Gerard, op.cit., 419-420.

17. Handbuch der Kohlenwirtschaft, ed. K. Borchardt & K. Bonikowsky, Berlin, 1926, 223ff; K. Bonikowsky, "Die Oberschlesische Montanindustrie," Z.d.O.B.u.H.V., LI, 1912, ., 11-20.

18. J.d.S.V.f.B.u.H. I, 1859, 361.

19. M. Baumont, La Grosse Industrie Allemande et le Charbon, Paris, 1928, 68 ff.

20. Much of the coke continued to be made in heaps (Meilern) after the fashion of charcoal until the middle of the century: G. A. Lampadius, Manuel de Métallurgie Générale, Paris, 1840, I, 112-3; G. Wolf, "Darstellung der Cokes in Meilern auf die Königshütte," O.Z.f.B.u.H., XV, 1867, 173-5, 178-9.

21. B. Kosmann, op.cit., 141 ff; F. G. Bremme, "Die oberschlesische Berg- und Hüttenindustrie," S.u.E., XV, 1896, ii, 755-764. For an account of individual mines, see: H. Volz, Die Bergwerks- und Hüttenverwaltungen des Oberschlesischen Industrie-Bezirks, Kattowitz, 1892.

22. R. Wachsmann, "Der Steinkohlenbergbau im Rybniker Revier," Z.d.O.B.u.H.V., LXIII, 1924, 233-238; Kosmann, loc.cit.

23. S.u.E., XVI, 1896, ii, 757; Handbuch des Oberschlesischen Industriebezirks, Kattowitz, 1913, II, 93.

24. H. Solger, Der Kreis Beuthen in Oberschlesien, Breslau, 1860, 91-93.

25. Handbuch des Oberschlesischen Industriebezirks, II, 346 ff; B. Kosmann, op.cit., 112.

26. J. Partsch, op.cit., II, 66.

27. J. Neugebauer, "Zur Geschichte der Oderschiffahrt," Schlesische Provinzialblätter, Neue Folge, I, 1862, 208-217; 261-272.

28. K. Schroth, "Zur Geschichte des Klodnitz-Kanals," Z.d.O.B.u.H.V., LIII, 1914, 116-122.

29. J.d.S.V.f.B.u.H., I, 1859, 73-74.

30. ibid., I, 1859, 148-149.

31. Z.d.O.B.u.H.V., XXV, 1886, 28-31; and supplement. B. Kosmann, op.cit., 31-33; J. Ritter von Renauld, "Der Bergbau und die Hüttenindustrie von Oberschlesien," 1884-1897, Münchener Volkswirtschaftliche Studien, XXXVIII, 1900, 8 ff.

32. Z.d.O.B.u.H.V., XXVIII, 1889, 283-287; "Zu dem Entwurf eines Gesetzes betreffend die Verbesserung der Oderwasserstrasse unterhalb Breslau," Z.d.O.B.u.H.V., LII, 1913, 103-115.

33. Z.d.O.B.u.H.V., XXXVII, 1898, 399-410; Prinz von Pless, "Die Absatzverhältnisse des oberschlesischen Kohlenreviers," Z.d.O.B.u.H.V., LXII, 1923, 183-204.

34. "Die Frachtlage Oberschlesiens für Eisenbahn- und Wassertransport," Probleme der Weltwirtschaft, XIX, 1914.

35. J. Partsch, op.cit., II, 63; B. Kosmann, op.cit., 27-28.

36. P. Helmuth von Kulmitz, "Das Absatzgebiet der schlesischen Kohle," Probleme der Weltwirtschaft, XIX, 1914.

37. A. H. Stockder, Regulating an Industry, New York, 1932, 57.

38. J. F. Daubuisson, "Notice sur l'exploitation des Houillères de Waldenburg en Silésie," J.d.M., XV, 1803, 88-103;

A. M. Héron de Villefosse, De la Richesse Minérale, Paris, 1819, II, 514-527.

39. F. Walker, Monopolistic Combinations in the German Coal Industry, American Economic Association, New York, 1904, 120; also A. H. Stockder, History of the Trade Associations of the German Coal Industry, New York, 1924, 118-127.

40. T. Schultz, Die Entwicklung des deutschen Steinkohenhandels, Waldenburg, 1911, 87 ff.

41. Franciszek Ryszka, "Kapitał monopolistyczny na Górnym Śląsku i formy jego polityki," Studia Śląskie, 209-265, Przegląd Zachodni, VIII, 1952, (Zeszyt dodatkowy).

CHAPTER V

UPPER SILESIA 1800-1914:
THE LEAD–ZINC INDUSTRIES

Wann die Schmeltzer im schmeltzen seyn, so
samblet sich in der Vorwandt unten am Often
in den Klufften, das es nicht ausgestrichen
worden, zwischen den Schiefferstein, eine
Metall, welche von ihnen Zinck oder Conter-
feht genennet wird, und so sie an die Vorwandt
klopffen, so fleust dieselbe Metall heraus in
einen Trog, den sie untersetzen, dieselbe Metall
is weiss gleich einem Ziehn, doch harter und
ungeschmeidiger, und klinget als ein Glocklein.
G. E. von Loehneyss, Bericht vom Bergwerke, 1617.

At the beginning of the 19th century the mining of lead and
zinc was thought to hold greater promise for the future than
that of coal. Indeed, an important reason for opening the Königsgrube coal mine had been the supply of fuel to the royal
lead mines and smelters.

Zinc ores and Zinc Mining: The ores of zinc, along with
those of lead and iron, occurred in the dolomite beds in the
lower Shelly Limestone.[1] Figure 13 shows the general distribution of the ore-bearing dolomite. But the ores themselves
were spread unevenly over this area. The most extensive deposits of zinc ores were a mile or two to the north of Bytom,
where zinc ores formed an almost continuous deposit lying
west to east for four miles.[2] Smaller deposits lay to the east
and west of Bytom and near Sucha Góra. But towards the
north the proportion of lead and iron ores in the dolomite increased, while that of the zinc declined.

Zinc ore occurred in two forms, as the carbonate (calamine) and as the sulphide (blende). The blende formed by far
the larger deposits, but technical difficulties prevented it from
being used until late in the 19th century. We have seen already
that Georg von Giesche obtained at the beginning of the 18th
century an exclusive right to mine calamine in Silesia, and
that his heirs succeeded in having this patent renewed until 1802.

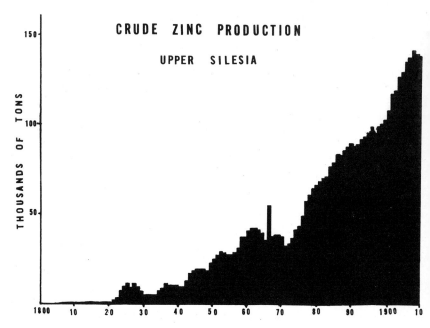

Figure 24: Crude zinc production in Upper Silesia, 1800-1910.

Thenceforward, the von Giesche concern had to sue for concessions, pay tithe and subject their works to the supervision of
the local Bergamt. The change meant also that the great landowners could also mine such zinc deposits as occurred in their
lands and either sell the calamine to the brass founders or
smelt it and sell metallic zinc.

It is doubtful whether the landowners would have concerned themselves with calamine if, at about this time, Ruhberg had not succeeded in producing metallic zinc at the Wesola glass furnace. This furnace lay on the lands of the Prince of Pless, who was not fortunate enough to possess deposits of calamine (compare figures 5 and 13). In his experiments Ruhberg had used the Schwamm which formed at the lip of those blast-furnaces which had smelted an iron-ore containing calamine.[3] Further progress was difficult on the Pless lands, but in 1806 the Prussian State built the Lydognia Hütte, close to the Königshütte ironworks.[4] Schwamm from the blast furnaces continued to be used for a year or two, but the transition was soon made to the ores themselves.

After the end of the Napoleonic Wars there followed a rapid expansion in zinc production, as the great landowners entered the field. The Henckel von Donnersmarck family, on whose lands were many of von Giesche's enterprises, were foremost. When, in 1821, the Prussian government, in the interests of conserving the ore resources, tried to restrict the building of new smelters, Henckel replied that he would establish his smelters, if necessary, beyond the Russian frontier, and the new Prussian ordinance regarding smelters was withdrawn.[5] Count Ballestrem, through his agent, Carl Godulla, was also very industrious in opening mines and building smelters, and the families of Schaffgötsch and Tiele-Winkler were only a degree less active. In 1829 pressure of the landowners secured the exclusion of zinc mines and smelters from the supervision of the Bergamte. The effect of this was to leave the conduct of the works in the unfettered control of their owners.

By 1821 there had sprung up no less then 33 zinc smelters, and the production of crude zinc had increased from about 100 tons in 1809 to over 10,000 in 1824. Great as had been the increase in demand for zinc during the previous years, the producing capacity had undoubtedly been overexpanded. In the later 1820's and early 1830's there was a recession (see figure 24), but thereafter market conditions improved and the expansion of the industry continued though at a slower rate.

Zinc Smelting: The method of smelting zinc introduced by Ruhberg continued to be used, with modifications and improvements, throughout the century. The calamine was first calcined or roasted, in order to drive off moisture and to reduce the carbonate to an oxide ($ZnCO_3 = CO_2 + ZnO$). This was a simple process, and for many years it was common to use exhaust fumes from the smelters for the purpose. But the final process of reducing ZnO to metallic zinc was much more difficult. The oxide was heated in a retort with carbon, which served as a reducing agent. Metallic zinc formed as a vapor and was condensed. The process, however, was difficult to manipulate. The zinc vapor oxidized very readily, and for this reason, it had to be kept in a reducing atmosphere of carbon monoxide. This was achieved by using muffles, long, tubelike containers, made of fire clay.[6] These were charged with a mixture of coke (carbon) and zinc oxide, and placed in a furnace so that the open end of each muffle projected through the furnace wall and terminated in a small receptacle in which the metallic zinc liquified.

Not all the zinc, however, condensed in this fashion. However much care was taken, some of the vapor became oxidized, forming minute white grains, each consisting of nucleus of zinc enclosed in a patina of oxide. Furthermore, a minute quantity of lead came off with the zinc from the muffles, and when, towards the end of the century, blende began to replace calamine, cadmium fumes were also given off from the muffles. If a very pure zinc was needed, the metal had to be melted down again in a reverberatory furnace and the lead, which had a very much higher melting point, recovered as lumps from the liquid zinc.

In the course of the century ever larger batteries of muffles were built. The furnaces, always very extravagant of coal, were adapted to burn gas, and then higher temperatures were secured by using a regenerative furnace.

Towards the middle of the 19th century the local production of calamine failed to keep pace with the growing demand for zinc.[7] It was discovered quite early in the century that at a temperature of about 150° C. zinc became plastic and could be rolled into thin sheets. At once, it became a useful roofing material. The growing use of electricity disclosed the need for zinc plates in batteries. At the same time, the older uses

of zinc, in brass-making and in paints and pigments, expanded
and intensified the demand.

During this period of increased demand, the calamine
workings, which had been exploited for over two centuries,
were nearing exhaustion. Several were abandoned, and the domestic production of calamine had to be supplemented by imports. At this juncture the large deposits of the other zinc-
bearing mineral, blende, began to be mined. Blende is a
sulphide of zinc (ZnS). But the smelting of blende, like that
of calamine in the previous century, presented serious difficulties. It was not, like most sulphide ores, susceptible of
direct smelting in a furnace, because of the awkward physical
properties of the metal itself.[8] It was not until the 1840's that
a method was devised of extracting metallic zinc from blende.
The sulphide had first to be converted to an oxide ($ZnS + 30 = ZnO + SO_2$) which could then be reduced in the muffle furnace.

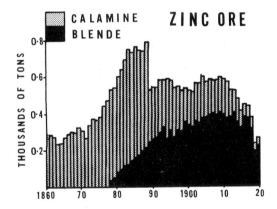

Figure 25: Production of calamine and zinc blende in
Upper Silesia, 1860-1920.

The oxidation process was less simple than the roasting of calamine. A higher temperature was necessary, and a more elaborate furnace, consuming vast quantities of coal, was used. The sulphur dioxide was at first allowed to escape into the atmosphere, with disastrous results on the vegetation of the area and the health of its inhabitants. The building of chimneys of exceptional height failed to draw off the sulphur fumes into the higher atmosphere, and it became necessary to remove the sulphur from the fumes before they were allowed to pass into the air.[9] At first limewater was used, but later the sulphur dioxide was used to make sulphuric acid.[10]

At first there was no difficulty in disposing of the sulphuric acid, which became a lucrative by-product of the smelting industry. But before long, the blende roasting furnaces were producing acid in quantities which greatly exceeded demand.[11] Nevertheless, the success that ultimately attended the efforts to smelt blende allowed it gradually to replace calamine, as the graph (fig. 25) shows.

The common pattern of the muffle furnace changed little during the century. Improvements were made in the design of the muffles and their heat-resistant qualities were improved. But the Upper Silesian furnace operators were conservative and showed little willingness to incorporate improvements in design that had been made in Belgium, the Rhineland and England. In particular they were far more extravagant of fuel than smelters could afford to be in areas where coal was more expensive.[13]

The Zinc Industry in the Nineteenth Century: Nor was there any significant change in the geographical distribution of zinc works during the century. The first zinc-smelter, the Lydognia works, lay close to the fiscal iron-works of Königshütte from whose furnaces it derived the Schwamm which it smelted. Thereafter furnaces were established close to the coal mines, rather than on the ore deposits (fig. 26). The volume of coal used was several times larger than that of calamine, and a site at the source of the fuel was very much more economical than one near the ore mines.

In those areas where the ore-bearing dolomite occurred, the surface of the ground was torn up by the workings. Large, open pits alternated with waste-heaps.[14] The deeper ores

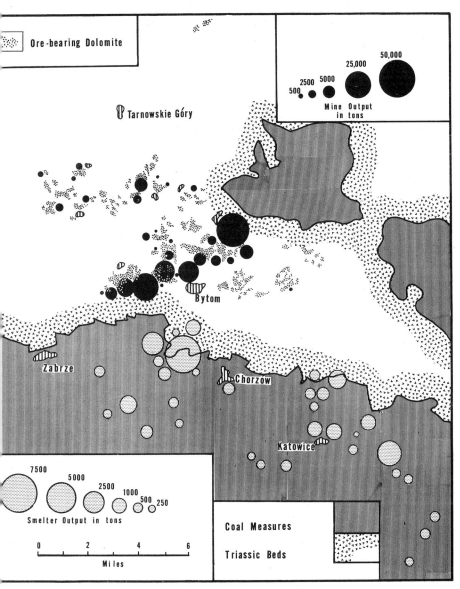

Ore-bearing Dolomite

Tarnowskie Góry

Mine Output
in tons

50,000
25,000
5000
2500
500

Bytom

Zabrze

Chorzow

Katowice

7500
5000
2500
1000
500
250

Smelter Output in tons

Coal Measures

Triassic Beds

0   2   4   6

Miles

Figure 26: The Mining and Smelting of Lead and Zinc, about 1860.

were reached by shafts and the galleries were kept dry by
steam pumps; the shallower workings could rely on natural
drainage. The scene resembled that in the Cornish tin-mining
region during the heyday of its prosperity.[15]

The ores were hand-sorted, before being despatched, usually by cart, to the roasting and smelting furnaces. In the
course of the century, the open-pits were abandoned and generally filled in, and mining came to be concentrated at a few
deep mines.

All aspects of zinc manufacture were to some degree unhealthy. The worst conditions were removed when the furnace chimneys ceased to pour sulphur dioxide into the air, but
it was impossible to keep all poisonous fumes under control.
In addition to sulphur gases, carbonic acid was passed into
the air at most stages in zinc smelting. Small quantities of
zinc fumes inevitably escaped, and were oxidized in the air.
These gases, with occasionally a trace of arsenic, could under
no circumstances maintain healthful conditions. The buildings
in which the smelting furnaces were erected were made as
tall as possible and everything possible was done to improve
ventilation. Nevertheless, the work of the zinc furnaceman
was one of the most unhealthy.[16] He was particularly subject
to bronchial and lung complaints, and the risks of poisoning
were considerable. And the improved ventilation, which
helped to remove sulphurous gases, exposed the workers to
cold and damp in winter, so that rheumatism also became an
occupational complaint of the zinc-workers.

Attempts were made at some of the smelters to improve
conditions in which workers lived and toiled, but the attitude
of some of the owners can only be described as apathetic.

Until the First World War, control of the mines and
smelters remained largely in the hands of the great landowners. Zinc-working required less capital—both in the mining and in the smelting—than the other branches of heavy industry that had been established in Upper Silesia. It was
easier for the landowners to retain control of zinc than of iron
and steel. Georg von Giesche's Erben, the oldest concern in
the zinc industry, continued throughout the period, though its
field of operations was drastically restricted after 1802 (see
page 34). A large part of the ore-field, which had in the 18th

century been worked by von Giesche's Erben, was developed
in the 19th century by Henckel von Donnersmarck.
We have already seen that there were two branches of
this wealthy and influential family, known for convenience
as the Beuthen and Tarnowitz lines.[17]   The Beuthen line possessed extensive deposits of zinc as well as of coal, which it
exploited quite early. The Tarnowitz line, which took up
heavy industry rather later, made up for its tardiness by the
intensity of its efforts. Count Guido Henckel of the Tarnowitz
line succeeded to his family's estates in 1848, at at once set
about developing their resources. In 1853 he founded the
Schlesische A. G. für Bergbau und Zinkhüttenbetrieb, which
grew within a few years to be one of the largest zinc producers in Upper Silesia.[18]

The Henckel interests became at this time by far the
largest in the zinc industry, and were followed in size by
those of Schaffgötsche, Tiele-Winkler, Hohenlohe and Ballestrem. In the 1860's half a dozen great families controlled
about 70 per cent of the industry. The only big producer outside their ranks was, of course, von Giesche's Erben, with at
this time about 12 per cent of the output. Von Giesche's share
of the total grew somewhat during the later years of the century, and appears on the eve of the First World War to have
outstripped the Henckel interests.[20]   Each of these holdings
was made up of concessions, mines, roasting or calcining furnaces, smelting furnaces and rolling mills.[21] Some had further
plant for the recovery of cadmium and lead.

The graph (fig. 24) shows the expansion of zinc production in Upper Silesia. It is a record of steady expansion, interrupted only by two short-lived recessions. The first of
these occurred about 1830, after a short period of very rapid
growth, and the second, also following a rapid expansion, in
the 1860's and 1870's. A third may have been imminent, also
following a period of sharp growth, in the 1880's, when Belgian and German producers agreed to limit their output.[22]
Quotas were allocated, and expansion thereafter pursued a
more steady course until the end of the century. The rate of
expansion was then increased, and a period of more rapid
growth lasted until the eve of the First World War.

"The statistics available on the world zinc industry, "

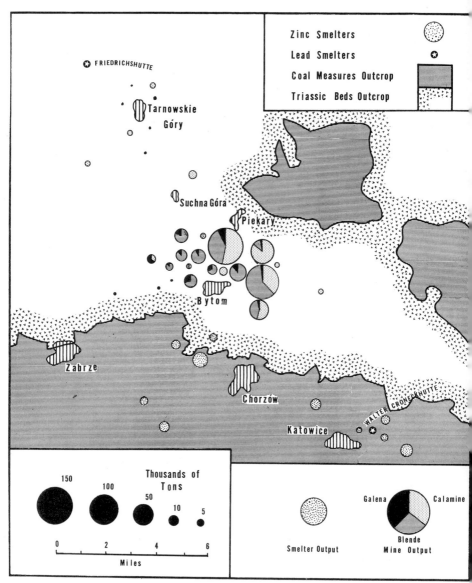

Figure 27: The Mining and Smelting of Lead and Zinc, about 1900.

wrote A. Skelton, "are outstanding among the base metals in their inadequacy."[23] Although reliable figures are available for production in Upper Silesia, it is not easy to relate these to production in the rest of the world. During the first half of the 19th century, Upper Silesia, with the Rhineland and the British Isles, had produced most of the world's zinc. Thereafter, although Upper Silesia succeeded in maintaining her relative position amongst European producers, her fraction of the world total declined. From about 25 per cent in 1880 it fell to about 22 per cent in 1900, and to about 17 when the World War began. These figures, of course, relate only to the German-held territory of Upper Silesia, and exclude the considerable production of Russian Poland and the small contribution of Galicia.[24] The ore-field as a whole remained at the end of this period a very significant producer, still producing nearly a quarter of the world's zinc.

Lead-working in Upper Silesia: The history of lead working is markedly different from that of zinc. Though occurring in the same geological deposits as zinc, lead ore was very much less abundant and its distribution was rather more localised. It occurred in only small quantities with the zinc deposits near Bytom, but was abundant between Tarnowskie Góry and Sucha Góra. At Miechowice, west of Bytom, it was in effect the only ore to be found. Thus the more important lead-workings were usually geographically distinct from the leading zinc mines, though there were mines—notably at Szarlej—which yielded the ores of both metals.

Secondly, lead was always a regalian mineral, and subject to the rigor of the regalian law. It was of importance in war and the small admixture of silver merely increased its value in the eyes of an eighteenth century prince. We have seen already (page 34) how von Reden revived the lead mines as a state undertaking and established the Friedrichshütte to smelt the lead ore obtained. He established the first steam engine in Upper Silesia to pump water from the Friedrichsgrube, and he and his successors cut adits to assist further in the drainage of the mines.[25]

The Prussian government reserved to itself the right to mine the lead deposits of Upper Silesia. In 1835 it defined its claims, limiting them to an area of 590 square miles which did,

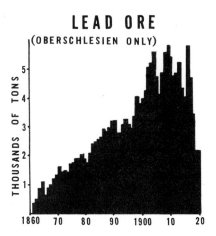

Figure 28: Production of lead ore in Upper Silesia, 1860-1922.

however, contain all significant deposits. But the Prussian claim was to lead only; zinc and iron ores were worked by concessionaires. These inevitably mined some quantity of lead ore, and the law prescribed that this should be sold to the Prussian State at a price equivalent to the cost of mining. In many instances the lead was recoverable from the zinc only after the latter had been smelted. The only lead-smelter in private hands was the Walther Cronek Hütte, built in 1863 by von Giesche's Erben to smelt the lead ores from the mixed deposits at the Biały Szarlej mine.[26] The lead which it produced had, of course, to be sold to the Prussian State. Although several other zinc companies produced small quantities of lead ore, the Hohenlohe holdings were the only other important source of lead.[27]

The royal lead mines and smelting works attracted much attention at the beginning of the 19th century,[28] and were regarded as technically amongst the most advanced in the world. The ore taken from the mines was hand sorted; some, in which the ore was intimately mixed with gangue minerals, was exposed to the air so that weathering might break it down.[29]

The method of smelting used was the "iron-reduction process." It took place in a high furnace, resembling a small blast-furnace. The ore was charged, together with over half its weight in iron and iron furnace slag, and with coke as fuel.[30] The iron combined with the sulphur in the ore, yielding metallic lead.[31]

Much of the lead was marketed in the form of the oxide, known as litharge, or red-lead. Lead oxidizes readily at a high temperature, and a good deal of lead oxide was produced in the ordinary smelting process. Commercial litharge was produced first by making the yellow, protoxide of lead (PbO) by heating the metal, and then by further oxidizing the yellow oxide to red or sesquioxide of lead (Pb_3O_4). Both processes were carried out in a simple furnace, heated by coal or coke.

Production of both metallic lead and also of litharge remained small from the time when von Reden revived the industry until the middle of the 19th century. Lead did not share in the expansion which characterized the zinc industry in the earliest part of the century. But after about 1860 production of both metallic lead and litharge increased sharply (fig. 28).

Conclusion: The non-ferrous metal industries of Upper Silesia were, except at the beginning of the century, less important than either the iron and steel or the coal mining, and their share in the total production of the region tended to decline during the century (see page 77). At the same time the world production of lead and zinc were rising steeply. From being the leading producer of zinc in the earlier years of the 19th century, Upper Silesia sank by the early years of the 20th to a relatively humble place.

Lead had been less important than zinc ever since the smelting of the latter had become established in Upper Silesia. The production of galena increased only very slowly and at the end of the period under consideration, it amounted to less than one tenth the volume of zinc ores produced. Lead became little more than a by-product of the zinc mines.

Notes

1. K. Seidl, "Die oberschlesische Zinkerzlagerstätte," Z.d.O.B.u.H.V., LXVI, 1927, 688-706; 762-776.

2. R. Michael, "Die Geologie des oberschlesischen Steinkohlenbezirkes," Abhandlungen der Königlich Preussischen Geologischen Landesanstalt, neue folge, LXXI, 1913, 270-380.

3. F. Krantz, Die Entwicklung der oberschlesischen Zinkindustrie, Kattowitz, 1911, 5-6.

4. Sabass, "Beitrag zur Grundungsgeschichte der Lydognia Zinkhütte zu Königshütte O-S," Z.d.O.B.u.H.V., IL, 1910, 534-549. A Rzehulka, "Zum hundertjährigen Bestehen der oberschlesischen Zinkindustrie," Z.f.d.B.H.u.S., LVII, 1909, 342-348.

5. Geschichte der Bergwerksgesellschaft Georg v. Giesche's Erben, Breslau, 1904, I, 147 ff; 213 ff; Bergwerksgesellschaft Georg von Giesche's Erben, Kattowitz, 1892.

6. L. Klemann, Die Zinkgewinnung in Oberschlesien, Breslau, 1860, 4 ff; W. R. Ingalls, The Metallurgy of Zinc and Cadmium, New York, 1906, 198 ff; J. S. G. Primrose, Lead and Zinc Smelting in Silesia, The Engineering and Mining Journal, LXXXVI, 1908, 265-269.

7. O. Pütz, "Die gegenwärtige Stand der Aufbereitung von Zink- und Bleierzen in Oberschlesien," Z.d.O.B.u.H.V., LII, 1913, 1-14.

8. H. Solger, Der Kreis Beuthen in Oberschlesien, Breslau, 1860, 97 ff.

9. F. Krantz, op.cit., 30-32; Bruno Knochenhauer, "Die Oberschlesische Montanindustrie," Die deutsche Wirtschaft und ihre Führer, IX, 1927, 18-20.

10. W. R. Ingalls, op.cit., 77 ff; 163-166; J. S. G. Primrose, op.cit.

11. Handbuch des Oberschlesischen Industriebezirks, Bd. 2, Kattowitz, 1913, 441-442.

12. J. S. G. Primrose, op.cit.; W. R. Ingalls, op.cit., 580-589.

Upper Silesia: 1800-1914: Lead and Zinc Industries   95

13. W. R. Ingalls, op.cit., 396.

14. F. Bernhardi, Geschichte der Bergwerksgesellschaft Georg v. Giesche's Erben, Breslau, 1904, 24 ff.

15. See lithographs (c.1855) in Georg von Giesches Erben. The areas of most intensive mining retain today this appearance of devastation.

16. Tracinski, "Die oberschlesische Zinkindustrie und ihre Einfluss auf die Gesundheit der Arbeiter," Deutsche Vierteljahrschrift für öffentliche Gesundheitspflege, XX, 1888, 59-86; Frey, "Die Zinkgewinnung im oberschlesischen Industriebezirk und ihre Hygiene....," Vierteljahrschrift für gerichtliche Medizin und öffentliches Sanitätswesen, Dritte Folge, XXXIII, 1907, 165-182; also Leopold von Wiese, Beiträge zur Geschichte der wirtschaftlichen Entwicklung der Rohzinkfabrikation, Jena, 1903, 79 ff; F. Krantz, op.cit., 59 ff.

17. B. Knochenhauer, op.cit., II, 57-62; H. Volz, Die Bergwerks- und Hüttenverwaltung des Oberschlesischen Industrie-Bezirks, Kattowitz, 1892, passim.

18. Z.d.O.B.u.H.V., V, 1866, 168.

19. P. Schmieder, "Die Fürstlich Hohenlohe'schen Hüttenwerke," B.u.H.J., XXXVII, 1889, 389-406.

20. F. Krantz, op.cit., 51-52.

21. These holdings are listed in B. Kosmann, op.cit., 41-43.

22. W. Y. Elliott, E. S. May, J. W. F. Rowe, A. Skelton, & D. H. Wallace, International Control in the Non-Ferrous Metals, New York, 1937, 698 ff; Leopold von Wiese, op.cit., 90 ff.

23. ibid., 688.

24. See figures of world production in E. A. Smith, The Zinc Industry, London, 1918, 10-18.

25. J. Partsch, op.cit., 55 ff.

26. F. Bernhardi, Geschichte der Bergweksgesellschaft Georg v. Giesche's Erben, 40-41.

96   The Upper Silesian Industrial Region

27. B. Knochenhauer, op.cit., 22.

28. Papers by Daubuisson, already cited; also, A. M. Héron de Villefosse, De la Richesse Minérale, III, Paris, 1819, 268-272.

29. Daubuisson in J.d.M., XVII, 1804, 325-344.

30. A. M. Héron de Villefosse, op.cit., 268-272.

31. John Percy, The Metallurgy of Lead, London, 1870, 357-368; Z.f.d.B.H.u.S., XIV, 139 ff; C. J. B. Karsten, System der Metallurgie, 1832, 157; The following equation is suggested (J. Percy, op.cit., 58): $3PbS+Fe^3=Pb^2+(PbS+Fe^2S+FeS)$.

32. J. Percy, op.cit., 508-521.

CHAPTER VI

UPPER SILESIA: 1800-1914 IRON AND STEEL

Von allen Provinzen ist Schlesien für das
Eisenhüttengewerbe die wichtigste, und be-
sonders ... Oberschlesien.

Berg- und Hüttenmännische Zeitung, 1842

The foundations of the iron and steel industry, established
by von Reden, were well and truly laid. At the beginning of
the 19th century the royal blast furnace and foundry were at
work at Gliwice, and although the pioneer works on the Małapanew reverted to the use of charcoal fuel, two new furnaces
of the largest size and most modern design were being planned at Königshütte. Von Reden may have been unduly optimis-
tic when he claimed that several land-owners were eager to
follow the example of the State, and set up coke-fired furnaces
of their own, but the lesson of Gliwice was not lost on them.
Political conditions at this time were not such as to encourage
enterprise, nor was the market for iron goods in Upper Silesia expanding sufficiently rapidly.

Scattered through the forests of Silesia and of neighboring parts of Poland and Austria, there were still numerous
charcoal-fired blast-furnaces. Along the rivers were Frischfeuer, or refineries, where iron from the blast-furnace was
converted into soft or malleable "bar-iron." Occasionally,
too, one found a Luppenfeuer or 'Bloomery,' where an ingot
of soft iron was produced directly from the ore on a small
hearth.

The Early Nineteenth Century: The example of the Prussian State was first followed by the princely families of Hohenlohe and Henckel von Donnersmarck. The Hohenlohehütte was
built in 1805, by the veteran Scottish iron-master, John Baildon.[1] At about the same time Hugo Henckel von Donnersmarck
established the Antonienhütte, but did not begin to use coke for
smelting until 1820.[2] At Königshütte a third blast-furnace

97

was blown in 1806 and a fourth in 1818. But the use of coke
spread only slowly. In 1831 John Baildon built his own blast-
furnace works, the Baildonhütte, at Katowice.[3] Seven years
later Count Hugo Henckel built the Laurahütte, thus laying the
foundations of what was to remain for many years the largest
private iron and steel works. Count Tiele-Winkler built a
blast-furnace, the Sophienhütte, on his lands at Mysłowice,
using John Baildon's works as a model, and a second furnace
was erected at Hugo Henckel's Antonienhütte.

Amongst the landowners who had been most impressed
by the success of the Małapanew furnace was Graf Colonna of
Strzelce Opolskie. Colonna built several charcoal furnaces
on his lands and operated them with success.[4] His holdings
passed to Graf Andreas Renard, an enthusiast for iron-works,
who not only maintained the Colonna undertakings but added
to their number. He built the Renard and Zawadzki works,
near the Małapanew river, and constructed a road to link
these and others of his works with the Odra River. Then, so
as to be able to smelt with coke, he bought and subsequently
rebuilt the Friedenshütte at Świętochłowice.

Throughout the first half of the century a large proportion of the iron smelted in Upper Silesia still came from the
small, charcoal-burning furnaces which lay scattered through
the forests. But about the middle of the century the scale began to tip in favor of the large, coke-fired works. The reasons for this were complex. Foremost amongst them was
the coming of the railway.[5] The first line into the industrial
area was built in 1845. It allowed goods to be sent quickly to
Wrocław and thence to Berlin and the northern ports.

This was followed by the establishment in Upper Silesia
of iron works by engineering and metal using firms in Berlin
or Wrocław. Foremost among these was the Borsigwerk,
founded by August Borsig to supply materials for his machine
shops in Berlin.

For many years the supply of charcoal to the older blast
furnaces had been growing more difficult. It was not that the
forests were exhausted: far from it, but the charcoal burners
were being obliged to move farther and farther into the forests, and the transport of charcoal to the furnaces was becom-
ing more difficult and costly. The same was true of the

iron-ore deposits which these furnaces used. The ores, many of them bog ores, were quickly exhausted, and the supply of ore from more distant sources stretched to the limits the labor supply and organizing powers of the iron-masters. On the other hand, the new, coke-fired furnaces were established close to the coal mines, which themselves yielded at this time a useful quantity or iron-ore. The iron deposits in the Shelly Limestone, furthermore, lay only a few miles to the north of the coal mines, and could supply all the ore that was needed for many years to come.

A further premium was placed on the use of coal by the introduction of puddling. Previously pig-iron, drawn from the blast-furnace, had been converted to soft or bar iron on a refining hearth. It required many refineries to handle the output of a sizeable blast furnace, and the fact that the only other use for pig-iron was in castings held back the growth of the iron-smelting industry.

Puddling consisted in boiling down the iron on a shallow, enclosed hearth, using the flames and hot gases from a coal fire to produce the heat. A long rabble, inserted through a hole in the side of the furnace, was used to stir the metal and expose it uniformly to the heat. This process allowed very much larger quantities of pig-iron to be refined, but also consumed greater quantities of fuel. It could, in fact, only be carried on close to coal mines.

The puddling process was brought to Upper Silesia in 1828. The older blast-furnace works added rows of puddling furnaces, and new works were founded, consisting only of puddling furnaces and their rolling mills, in which the "balls" of puddled iron were rolled into sheets and bars.

A puddling furnace had a very much greater capacity than a refinery, and did not depend on water-power, as was the practice in the refinery. It permitted the further expansion of the blast-furnace industry, because it removed the chief limitation on its usefulness—the slowness of the refining process. But the demand for puddled iron remained small until the railways created not only a demand for the iron but also the means whereby its own widespread market could be reached. Puddling works became numerous in the 1840's,[6] and their forests of chimneys and the clouds of smoke, made by their very generous

consumption of coal, began to give Upper Silesia the appearance, which it has never lost, of a "black country."
At about the same time the close supervision of the works, which the Prussian government had exercised, through the Bergamte, began to be replaced by a greater freedom. In 1865 the Direktionsprinzip was abandoned, and hence forward the iron concerns were free to choose their own staffs. In the opening years of the century iron technology in Upper Silesia had been amongst the most advanced in continental Europe. Then, in the 1820's and '30's, Upper Silesia fell behind Western Europe.[7] But at this moment L. Eck, manager of the Königshütte[8] and others, by their example and writings, again brought the Upper Silesian works to something near equality with those of Western Europe.[9] A handful of landowners, such as Graf Renard and the Henckel von Donnersmarck families[10] overcame the innate conservatism of many of their fellow countrymen, built larger furnaces, introduced new processes, and placed Upper Silesia again in the forefront of the German iron industry.

The Iron Industry in the Mid-19th Century: In the middle years of the 19th century industrial Upper Silesia held great promise. A writer in 1842 described its development as "the equal of England and foremost on the continent of Europe."[11] The Prussian government began to collect and publish statistics of mineral and metal production in 1823, and from that year until 1853 Upper Silesia produced over 40 per cent of the total Prussian output of pig-iron,[12] and a similar proportion of refined iron. Throughout this period Upper Silesia was undoubtedly the most important single industrial region in Germany. Its nearest rival was the Siegerland, lying to the east of the Rhine. The Ruhr area, later to become the most important centre of the iron and steel industries on the continent of Europe, was at this time of slight importance.

It is fortunately possible to reconstruct a very fair picture of the Upper Silesian industry about 1850, thanks to the writings of publicists in this field and the appearance at about this time of technical journals devoted to the iron and steel industry in general and to that of Upper Silesia in particular. The geographical pattern of the iron industry is shown in figure 29. The industry is clearly divisible into two parts: that

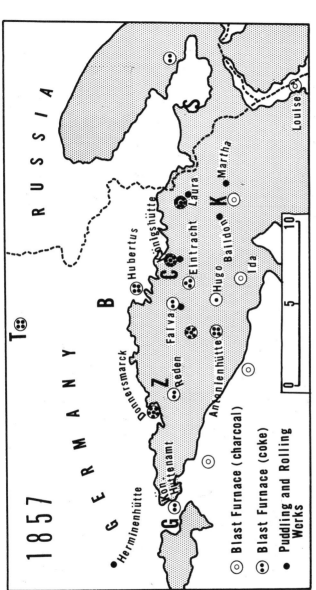

Figure 29: The iron industry of Upper Silesia in 1857. Letters indicate position of the chief cities: Bytom (B), Chorzów (C), Gliwice (G), Katowice (K), Sosnowiec (S), Tarnowskie Góry (T), Zabrze (Z).

based on charcoal and that on coke, and, in terms of output, the charcoal industry was still, in the middle of the 19th century, the larger.[13] In 1848 there were, in the whole of Upper Silesia, no less than 62 blast furnaces using charcoal as against only 19 using coke.[14] Nine years later there were 33 active coke furnaces, but there were still 61 charcoal furnaces. Most of the charcoal furnaces lay in the forested northern Kreise, particularly Lubliniec and Olesno, but they were not entirely absent even from the coalfield area itself. But many more coke furnaces were, in 1857, either planned or under construction, and coke-smelted iron soon began to exceed charcoal-smelted in quantity. There were also nine puddling works which used coal to refine pig-iron and rolled it into sheets, strips or rails.[15]

In Kreis Bytom, which contained almost all the works using coal and coke as fuel, scarcely more than a half of the pig-iron was refined to make bars, sheets or strips. The remainder went into castings. This high proportion of cast-iron was out of line with the general trend in Europe, where a larger and increasing proportion of the iron taken from the blast furnaces was being refined in the puddling furnace. The usefulness of puddled iron was much greater than that of cast iron, and, although foundry iron would continue to have many and important uses, the future was seen, even at this date, to lie with refined iron. In particular, refined iron, puddled and rolled, was used for railway lines. It was railway lines that dominated iron production in England, Belgium and Northwest Germany.[16] In Upper Silesia, the Laurahütte and Alvenslebenhütte, a fiscal works attached to the Konigshütte, specialized in rails, and rails made up, in 1857, over half the total output of refined iron goods. But demand in eastern Germany was smaller than in western, and was growing more slowly. With the cheapest coal in continental Europe, and with only very short hauls for both iron-ore and fuel, Upper Silesia had unique advantages in the production of puddled iron. But, by reason of its geographical location, it could not compete in the markets of western Europe with the products of hundreds of more suitably placed puddling furnaces.

In Western Europe there was a large, varied and at this time growing demand for soft iron for wire nails, chains and a multiplicity of small iron goods. These were made in countless factories and workshops, and with the growth of industries and cities, the demand for such goods inevitably grew. In Upper Silesia there was no such demand. The predominantly rural society, with generally a low standard of living, demanded few such goods. At best Upper Silesia could offer the rest of Germany a cheaper product, partly because the cost of some materials was lower, partly because labor was cheaper than elsewhere.

A FEUDAL INDUSTRY

In the middle years of the 19th century the iron industry was still firmly controlled by the Prussian state and the great landowners.

The Prussian State: The largest and most important undertakings were those of the government itself. The Gliwice works consisted of two blast-furnaces, one of them very up-to-date, and a foundry.[17] At the Königshütte were eight blast-furnaces, and, adjoining them the Alvensleben puddling and rolling works.[18] In addition the State operated the Małapanew works, still equipped with a charcoal furnace and an old-style refinery, and three similar works near Kluczbork.

Hugo Henckel von Donnersmarck: In 1835 Graf Hugo Henckel established the largest iron-works in private hands, the Laurahütte. Here, about 1850, there were eight blast-furnaces and a battery of 38 puddling furnaces. In addition, Graf Henckel owned the Antonienhütte, with four blast-furnaces, and the coal and iron-ore which supplied the materials.

Guido Henckel von Donnersmarck: His holdings consisted of the Donnersmarckhütte, with six blast-furnaces, and coal mines and iron-ore deposits.

Graf Hohenlohe von Ujest: In addition to his large holdings in coal and zinc, he possessed the Hohenlohehütte, with four blast-furnaces, and the Hugohütte, with a single furnace. He also owned several charcoal fired furnaces.

<u>Graf Renard</u>: He had inherited the ironworks that had been established by his father-in-law, Graf Colonna. They were mostly charcoal furnaces built on the Colonna estates, but Renard himself added a puddling works at Zawadzki and bought and rebuilt the Friedenshütte.

<u>Myłowice-Katowice</u> Holdings: Tiele-Winkler owned at this time several charcoal blast-furnaces and had recently built the Sophienhütte, a puddling works at which he refined much of the iron from his furnaces. It is interesting to note how, even in the second half of the 19th century, Hohenlohe, Renard and Tiele-Winkler clung to their old charcoal furnaces. The fact is that much of their lands were forested, and charcoal-burning was one of the few ways in which some profit could be derived from them.[19]

But, although the industry was dominated by the feudal interests of the great landowners, there were signs of the coming change. Small syndicates of merchants or manufacturers, located in Wrocław or Berlin, were seeking to establish their ironworks to supply their own needs for metal. As early as 1838 the Eintrachthütte was founded as a blast-furnace works by F. A. Egells of Berlin in order to supply iron to his foundry.[20] In 1854 August Borsig, also of Berlin, built the Borsigwerk at Biskupice for the same purpose.[21] A group of Wrocław merchants had built the original Friedenshütte, and another set up a puddling and rolling works, the Herminenhütte, at Łabędy.[22] Yet others founded wire-drawing, nail-making engineering establishments.

THE SECOND-HALF OF THE NINETEENTH CENTURY

About 1850 the iron industry of Upper Silesia was as important, relative to that of the rest of Germany, as at any time in its history. It still retained something of the momentum of its early years and the weakness of its competitive position had not fully shown itself.

Through the second half of the century the use of charcoal in the furnaces continued to decline. As we have seen, the balance was tipped in favor of coke during the 1850's, and during the following two decades of rapid expansion, the contribution made by the charcoal furnaces dwindled, until, by 1885, it

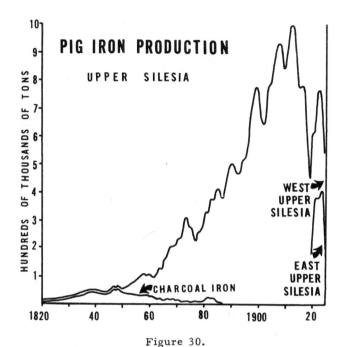

Figure 30.

had sunk to less than 1000 tons a year. Soon after this, the Prussian government ceased to publish separate figures for charcoal iron. But charcoal furnaces continued to work long after this date, and the last of them, the Wziesko works, did not close until the present century.

In terms of efficiency, however, the coke-smelting industry did not compare well with that in Western Europe. This was due in part to technical weaknesses at the works, in part to the poor quality of coke that was often used.[23] The coke-smelted iron was itself of no high quality, and was at first not thought suitable for steel-making.[24]

It is interesting that most of the landowners who possessed charcoal furnaces also built puddling furnaces on or very close to the coalfield to refine and roll their pig-iron.[25] Graf Renard established the Zawadzki works for this purpose;

Tiele-Winkler, the Sophienhütte; Guido Henckel, the Falva-
hütte, and Graf Henckel, the Hugohütte.

The supply of pig-iron from the charcoal furnaces was
irregular; its quality was often poor, and it was not long before the puddling works were drawing their iron from nearby
coke-fired furnaces rather than from the remote charcoal furnaces.

Capital Investment and Company Formation: Although
most of the iron industry in the middle of the century was the
private possession of the great landowners, a few undertakings
were in the hands of merchants and industrialists, and some
of the small ironworks were leased by syndicates of Jewish
merchants.[26] A Wrocław syndicate had established the original Friedenshütte; another, the Herminenhütte, and the Berlin engineering firm of August Borsig founded the Borsigwerk.
Before 1850 only a few iron consuming industries had been
established in Upper Silesia. But their number was increasing: the Gliwice wire works of Hegenscheidt, the Fitzner
boiler works at Siemianowice, the iron foundries of Jakob-
shütte; Ganz und Cie at Racibórz, and the Heinrichswerk at
Friedrichshütte, were only the more enduring of these works
founded about this time with outside capital.

Most of the older works had been operated as appendages
of the feudal estates. They suffered from a lack of investment
capital. The new firms were more adequately capitalized,
chiefly, as in West Germany, by the banks.[27] The new firms
were in many instances directed by able and farsighted entrepreneurs, who, following the pattern set by those in western
Germany, tried to bring under their own control the raw materials on which their industry depended.[28] This they could
only do by taking over the feudal undertakings. In the course
of some forty years the ironworks of the feudal aristocracy
either closed or passed one by one into the possession of joint-
stock companies.

The pattern of this process was set when in 1853 the extensive coal and zinc holdings of Graf Guido Henckel passed
to the Schlesische A. G. fur Bergbau und Zinkhüttenbetrieb.[29]
Two years later the considerable though scattered holdings of
Graf Renard became the nucleus of the A. G. Schlesische Hüt-
ten-Först-und Bergbaugesellschaft Minerva. This company

merged a few years later with a Wrocław group headed by Friedlander and Löwenfeld, and created the Oberschlesische Eisenbahnbedarf A. G.

In 1891, the Prussian State, withdrawing, in the spirit of the time, from its large and direct participation in industry, sold its Königshütte works.[30] These, along with the neighboring Laurahütte, belonging to Hugo Henckel von Donnersmarck, were taken over by the newly constituted Vereinigte Königs und Laura A. G.[31]

The Oberschlesische Eisenindustrie A. G. was formed in 1889 by the fusion of several smaller units among them the holdings of Hegenscheidt and Caro, the Herminenhütte and the Vulkan (Julienhütte) blast furnaces. The Bismarkhütte A. G. was founded in 1872 as a steel works by an outside group of merchants, but later took over the Falva blast furnaces from Henckel.

The iron works of Guido Henckel were in 1872 formed into the Donnersmarckhutte A. G.,[32] and the Tiele-Winkler holdings in 1889 were absorbed into the Kattowitzer A. G. Other combinations and transfers took place, so that by the end of the century the feudal interests had been entirely displaced by a dozen Allgemeinegesellschaften, whose share capital was still owned in some small degree by the old, landowing families, but was mainly in the hands of German banks and financiers. The change was undoubtedly to the advantage of Upper Silesian industry. Most of the Upper Silesian industry had passed into the hands of companies, but it remained short of capital.

The lack of investment in the Upper Silesian iron industry was basically due to a lack of confidence in it. Its local market was very small. Its costs of production were less than those in Central and West Germany, but not sufficiently so for its products to compete effectively in those markets. Indeed, the greater economies of scale and organization, achieved in the Ruhr made it possible for the latter to produce certain grades of iron more cheaply than Upper Silesia before the end of the century.[33]

Technological Change: The second half of the 19th century was a period of rapid and fundamental changes in the processes of iron and steel-making. During the middle years of

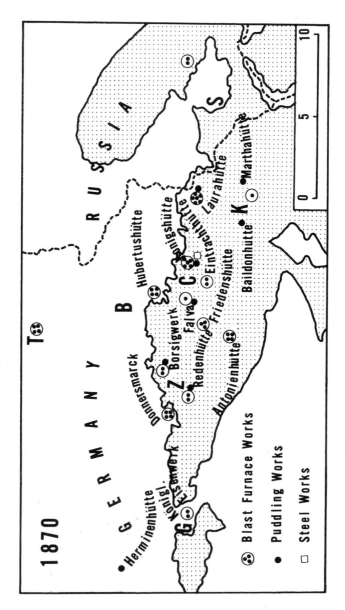

Figure 31: The iron industry of Upper Silesia about 1870.
For symbols, see figure 29.

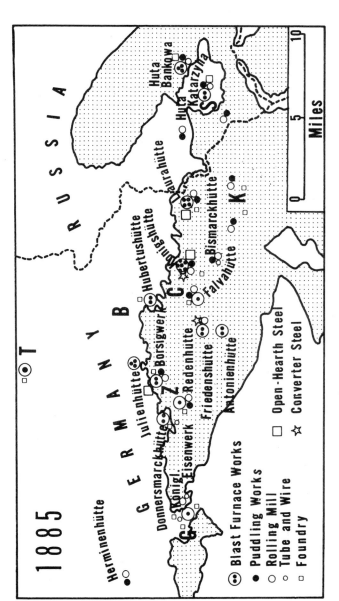

Figure 32: The iron and steel industry of Upper Silesia and adjoining areas, 1885 (based on B. Kosman). For symbols, see figure 29.

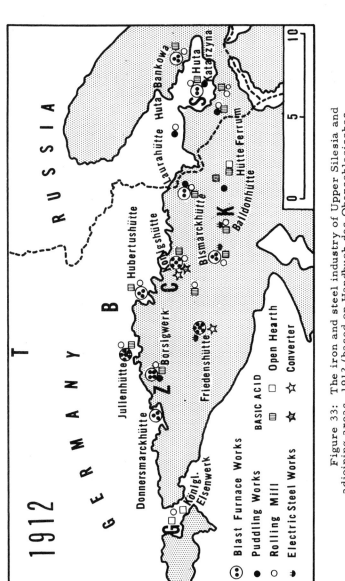

Figure 33: The iron and steel industry of Upper Silesia and adjoining areas, 1912 (based on Handbuch des Oberschlesisches Industriebezirks and technical journals). For symbols, see figure 29.

the century the puddling furnace used sometimes to " puddle"
steel instead of soft iron, represented the highest development
in iron-refining. Steel was made in only very small quantities
and generally by the clumsy and costly process of first removing the carbon in a puddling furnace or refinery and then
putting back just enough to impart to the metal the qualities of
steel. During the 1850's Sir Henry Bessemer's experiments
led to the perfecting of the process which bears his name.
Hot air was blown through liquid iron, tapped from the blast-
furnace. Excess carbon was burned out of the metal. The
heat generated by this process raised yet higher the temperature of the iron, keeping it in a molten state, so that other im-
purities were oxidised or combined with the slag and removed.

At once a means was found by which the speed and scale
of refining could be brought into line with that of smelting.
Furthermore, the decarbonizing of the iron could be stopped
at any appropriate stage or, if carried to completion, the
metal could be recarburized to any desired degree. This
meant of course that in the Bessemer "converter" steel production was as easy as the making of soft iron, and no one
doubted the immense superiority for most purposes of steel
over iron.

The Bessemer process was so quick that a fine control
over it was impossible to achieve. In the 1860's the French-
man, Pierre Martin, combined with William Siemens to introduce the open-hearth. Here the pig-iron, together with scrap
metal, was melted down on the shallow pan of a furnace by
burning pre-heated gases. By careful control of the metal,
the slag and the materials of which the hearth was made, a
similar decarbonization of the iron could be achieved. Furthermore, the slower speed of the process allowed a finer control
to be exercised over it, and the quality of metal produced was
better than that of the Bessemer steel.

Both processes, it was soon discovered, could be used only
with iron that was free, or nearly so, of phosphorus. Phosphorus was not removed during either process and, left in the
steel, made it brittle and almost useless. It was not until
1879 that Gilchrist and Thomas, lined the converter with a
"basic" refractory brick, thus permitting the phosphorus to

be removed in a basic slag. A few years later a basic lining
was used in the open-hearth.

These new processes were quckly adopted in Western
Europe, but the slowness of the response of Upper Silesia con-
trasted with the receptiveness of its industries in the days of
von Reden. This was not however due entirely to lack of enterprise. The raw materials with which the Upper Silesian industrialists had to work were much less suited to the new processes than those available to Western Europe.

Bessemer's converter process was tried at Königshütte
in 1856-7, very soon after it had been patented in England.[34]
It met with only indifferent success because, unknown to those
who introduced it, pig-iron smelted from the local ores contained just enough phosphorus to make the converter process
inapplicable. A few years later the same works made steel
quite successfully by the Bessemer process by using a non-
phosphoric pig-iron which was imported from England. The
failure of the Bessemer process was due to extensive phosphorus in the iron, but this did not mean that the Thomas, or
basic, process was particularly suited to Upper Silesian pig-
iron. It was adopted at the Königshütte in 1883 and shortly af-
terwards at the Friedenshütte, but the Thomas process demanded an iron fairly rich in phosphorus. No external heat
was used in the Thomas process because the chemical changes
which took place themselves generated sufficient heat for the
process to continue until its completion. In effect, if iron contained phosphorus, it was best to have it in abundance. Where
the Thomas process was used successfully in Upper Silesia,
the phosphorus content of the metal was enriched by the addition of a highly phosphoric slag from the refineries and puddling furnaces.[35]

The open-hearth process suffered from none of these dis-
advantages. It could be used either with or without a basic
lining, and as heat was supplied by burning gases, the amount
of phosphorus was not of great significance. But the open-
hearth process was operated best when large quantities of iron
and steel scrap were added to the charge. In Western Europe,
where the supply of process-scrap from the engineering machine shops and of old scrap from disused plant and equipment
was large, the open-hearth offered considerable economies.[36]

But in Upper Silesia machine shops were few and plant and equipment had mostly not been in use long enough to have become obsolescent. The first open-hearth was built at the Borsigwerk in 1872, and the first basic open-hearth in 1898. But at the end of the century puddling still remained the dominant means of refining iron. Over half the pig-iron smelted was destined for the puddling furnace, and there were no less than 277 active puddling furnaces in the area, as against only some ten open-hearths. But the first decade of the present century saw a sharp change: an increase in the number of basic open-hearths and in the production of open-hearth steel, and a sudden decline in the number of puddling furnaces, from nearly 300 in 1900 to less than a hundred in 1913. This change in the relative importance of wrought iron and open-hearth steel reflected the greater usefulness of the latter. It also resulted, in part, from the greater availability in more recent years of steel scrap, the use of which added greatly to the economies of the open-hearth.

The geographical distribution of the iron industry of Upper Silesia in the middle years of the 19th century is shown in figure 29. The trends just described are reflected in the maps of the industry about 1885, and about 1912, based respectively on the writings of Kosmann[37] and Voltz.[38]

The Supply of Iron Ore: For almost a century the ore deposits of Upper Silesia, though poor in quality and widely scattered, sufficed for the needs of the local industry. Broadly speaking, the ores belonged to three distinct geological horizons. Lowest in the geological scale were those ores which occurred in the coal-measures. At best these ores contained from 30 to 40 per cent iron.[39] Next came the brown ore deposits of the Triassic limestone, the most abundant though by no means the best ores in Upper Silesia.[40] Lastly there were small and scattered deposits of bog ores and of other similar superficial deposits, which fed the industry in its earliest stages, but were soon exhausted.

During the early years of the 19th century the smelting industry was based on the easily mined ores of the Trias, but during the middle years these were supplemented by the richer coal measures ores. Until the '60's the region was on balance self-sufficing in the supply of iron ore. Although the

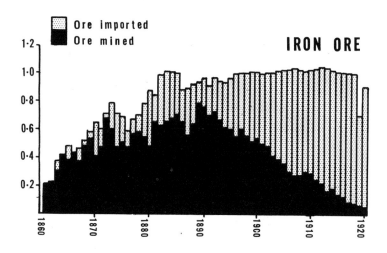

Figure 34: Source of iron-ore smelted in Upper Silesia, 1860-1920.

local production continued to increase until about 1890, it failed to keep pace with the expansion of the iron industry.[41] Even if the slow rate of growth of iron-mining in Upper Silesia had not necessitated an increasing volume of import, some ores from without would have been needed both to blend with the local ores and to smelt particular qualities of metal, such as Bessemer and Thomas iron. The graph (figure 34) shows the relative proportions of Upper Silesian, other German and foreign ores used during the twenty years preceding the first World War.

Comparatively little ore was obtained from other parts of Germany. A little came from Lower Silesia and Poznan province, but all large German deposits lay at too great a distance. On the other hand, good ores, some of them low in phosphorus and rich in manganese, were to be had in the

mountains of northern Hungary—the present Slovakia. The
high-grade ores of Styria and Carinthia lay at no great distance. There were good ores in Poland, and those of Sweden
and Ukraine, though distant, were not beyond the reach of
Upper Silesian industry at this time. The ore reserves of Austria and Hungary were limited in volume, and the imports of
ore from Sweden and the Ukraine were in fact increasing
steadily during the pre-war years.[42]
The imported ores were in general of a much higher
quality than those obtained locally, but their price at the works
was also relatively high. There was no reason, however, why,
with the improvement of water transport on the Odra and Kłodnicki Canal, Swedish ore should not be delivered as cheaply
to Upper Silesia as to the Ruhr. And Russian ore was actually
delivered to Upper Silesia at a price per ton of iron content
slightly lower than that of Swedish ore.[43]

Volume of Production: Figure 30 shows the expansion of
pig-iron production during the century that elapsed between
the close of the Napoleonic Wars and the beginning of the First
World War. In contrast with the earlier and sharper rise in
the production of lead and zinc, it was not until about 1850 that
any considerable activity was manifested in the iron industry.
Thereafter, with only short-lived recessions in the 1870's,
about 1885-87, 1891-94, and 1908-10, the iron-smelting grew
at an accelerating pace until the outbreak of the First World
War.

Steel production had been of only trifling importance before the introduction of the Bessemer process, and it did not
expand rapidly until the open-hearth had been adopted. Some
part of the blast-furnace production went to iron foundaries;
a steadily diminishing amount went to the puddling furnaces,
and the remainder, supplemented by iron and steel scrap and
imported pig-iron, went to the steel works.

Notes

1. L. Beck, IV, 181.

2. L. Beck, op.cit., IV, 181.

3. W. Paley Baildon, Baildon and the Baildons, n.d., II, 492.

4. J. Partsch, op.cit., II, 133 ff; B. Knochenhauer, "Die oberschlesische Montanindustrie," Die deutsche Wirtschaft und ihre Führer, IX, 1927, 26-9.

5. M. Frank, "Przyczynek do badania wydobycia węgla w Polsce na tle rozwoju sieci kolejowej w Śląsko-dąbrowsko-Krakowskim Zagłębiu Węglowym do pierwszej wojny światowej," Zeszyty Naukowe Wyższej Szkoły Ekonomicznej w Katowicach, I, 1957, 8.

6. Some of these works were very progressive in their technology; see L. Eck in B.u.H.Z., II, 1843, 611-16.

7. Fritz Redlich, History of American Business Leaders, I, Ann Arbor, 1940, 44-46.

8. B. Knochenhauer, "Die Oberschlesische Montanindustrie," Die deutsche Wirtschaft und ihre Führer, IX, 1927.

9. L. Wachler, Betrachtungen über die jetzige Lage des Hohofenbetriebes in Oberschlesien, Oppeln, 1857, 27-33.

10. F. Redlich, op.cit.

11. B.u.H.Z., I, 1842, 58. See also A. M. Héron de Villefosse, De la Richese Minérale, I, 383, III, 427-434.

12. L. Beck, IV, 358 ff.

13. B.u.H.Z., VIII, 1849, 121-124.

14. L. Wachler, Betrachtungen über die jetzige Lage des Hohofenbetriebes, Oppeln, 1857, 25-26; 38; "Bemerkungen über einige in der Nähe von Gleiwitz liegende Privat—Eisenhütten und andere gewerbliche Etablissements," B.u.H.Z., X, 1851, 838-40; also, B.u.H.Z., X, 1851, 337-40; 753-56; 833-38; B.u.H.Z., XII, 1853, 184-88; O.Z.f.B.u.H., II, 1854, 333-34; J.d.S.V.f.B.u.H., I, 1859, 67 ff; Z.f.d.B.H.u.S., V, 1858, 101-13.

15. "Lage der Eisenindustrie," J.d.S.V.f.B.u.H., I, 1859,
67-9; L. Wachler, op.cit., B.u.H.M., VIII, 121-24; "Ueber
Stabeisen-Erzeugung in Oberschlesien, " J.d.S.V.f.B.u.H., II,
1860, 54-6.

16. N. J. G. Pounds and W. N. Parker, Coal and Steel in
Western Europe, London, 1957, passim.

17. Brand, "Die Königliche Eisengiesserei bei Gleiwitz
in Oberschlesien," B.u.H.Z., X, 1851, 337-40; S. Golachowski,
"Gliwice u progu industrializacji, " Studia Śląskie, Przegląd
Zachodni, (zeszyt dodatkowy), VIII, 1952, 266-309.

18. "Betrieb-Vorrichtungen auf den Königl. Eisenhütten-
werken in Oberschlesien, " B.u.H.Z., X, 1851, 833-38.

19. H. G. Heymann, "Die gemischten Werke in deutschen
Grosseisengewerbe, " Münchener Volkswirtschaftliche Studien,
LXV, 1904.

20. H. Volz, Die Bergwerks- und Hüttenverwaltung des
Oberschlesischen Industrie-Bezirks, Kattowitz, 1892, 35-37.

21. ibid., 9-25.

22. Cornelius Netter, "Die Geschichtliche Entwicklung
der Herminenhütte in Laband ....," S.u.E., LI, ii, 1931, 1189-
1192; 1306-1313.

23. B. Osann, "Der hohe Koksverbrauch in den oberschlesischen Hochöfen, " Z.d.O.B.u.H.V., XXVII, 1888, 382-87. Sabass, "Das Hochofenwerk Wziesko in Oberschlesien,"
Z.d.O.B.u.H.V., LIII, 1914, 141-6.

24. L'Industrie du Fer en 1867, Paris 1869, III, 496.

25. "Ueber Stabeisen-Erzeugung in Oberschlesien, "
J.d.S.V.f.B.u.H., II, 1860, 54-56; L. Wachler, Betrachtungen
über die jetzige Lage der Stabeisen-Erzeugung in Oberschlesien, Oppeln, 1858, 7-19.

26. See Z.f.d.B.H.u.S., II, 1855, 138-39 for a list of these.

27. The sources of investment capital are reviewed in:
Franciszek Ryszka, "Kapital monopolistyczny na Górym Śląsku
i formy jego polityki, " Studia Śląskie, 203-65, Przegląd Zachodni, VIII, 1952.

28. "Zur geschichtlichen Entwicklung der oberschlesischen Walzwerkserzeugung, " S.u.E., LVIII, 1938, 900-01; Kazimierz Popiołek, "Koncentracja i centralizacja produkcji w górniczo-hurniczym przemyśle Górnego Śląska w II poł. XIX stulecia, " Kwartalnik Historyczny, LXIII, 1956, nr. 4-5, 255-267.

29. H. Volz, Die Bergweks- und Hüttenverwaltung des Oberschlesischen Industriebezirks, Kattowitz, 1892, 37-42, H. G. Heymann, op.cit., 186; B. Knochenhauer, op.cit., 111-16.

30. H. Voltz, op.cit., 163-80.

31. Oskar Stillich, "Eisen- und Stahlindustrie, " Nationalökonomische Forschungen auf dem Gebiete der grossindustriellen Unternehmung, I, Berlin, 1904, 181-238.

32. Donnersmarckhütte 1872-1922, Berlin, 1923.

33. "Preise für Eisen, Eisen-Artikel und Maschinen, " Z.d.O.B.u.H.V., XXXII, 1893, 216.

34. Handbuch des Oberschlesischen Industriebezirks, Band 2, Kattowitz, 1913, 697.

35. K. G. Heymann, op.cit., 189.

36. K. G. Heymann, op.cit., 193.

37. B. Kosmann, Oberschlesien sein Land und seine Industrie, Gleiwitz, 1888.

38. Handbuch des Oberschlesischen Industriebezirks, Band 2, ed. H. Voltz, Kattowitz, 1913.

39. G. Einecke & W. Köhler, "Die Eisenerzvorräte des Deutschen Reiches, " Archiv für Lagerstättenforschung, I, 1910.

40. F. Raefler, "Die Brauneisenerzlagerstätten Oberschlesiens, " Z.d.O.B.u.H.V., LIV, 1915, 47-71.

41. R. Rassmann, "Das Auswanderungsproblem der oberschlesischen Schwerindustrie, " Veröffentlichungen des Schlesischen Gesellschaft für Erdkunde, II, Breslau, 1922; F. Jüngst, "Ueber den Einfluss des Bezuges auslandischer Eisenerze auf die Roheisenerzeugung in Oberschlesien, " Z.f.d.B.H.u.S., XLVIII, 1900, 519-36; B.u.H.R., I, 1904-5,

109-11; G. Bresson, "Note sur l'industrie du fer et de l'acier dans le bassin de la Haute Silésie," R.d.M.M., I, 1904, 141-54.

42. S.u.E., XVII, 1897, i, 40, 65.

43. Fritz Jüngt, "Ueber den Einfluss des Bezuges auslandischer Eisenerze auf die Roheisenerzeugung in Oberschlesien," Z.f.B.H.u.S., XLVIII, 1900, 519-36.

CHAPTER VII

POLAND, GALICIA AND MORAVIA

"Not till about 1870 did the peasants begin to
build proper brick chimneys, when the iron
cooking stoves came in, which are now used
everywhere in the kitchens."
Jan Słomka, From Serfdom to Self-Government.

We have already seen how the Upper Silesian coalfield and industrial area came to be divided between Prussia,
Russia and Austria. The largest and by far the most valuable
share of this territory fell by the accident of partition to Prussia, and we have seen in the last five chapters what use the
Germans made of the lands they thus acquired.

Russian and Austrian Silesia: The Russian share of this
territory was acquired when, in 1815, the Napoleonic Grand
Duchy of Warsaw was annexed by the Tsars, and became the
so-called "Congress" Kingdom of Poland. It included a small
area, sometimes known as Russian Silesia, which had belonged to Prussia from the Third Partition of Poland in 1795
until the creation of the Grand Duchy of Warsaw, and thus had
for a short time known the energy of Prussian administration.
After the suppression of the Polish rising of 1830, "Congress"
Poland, was absorbed administratively into the Russian Empire.

Austria held her share of the mining and industrial area
by a variety of titles. The South-western corner of the coalfield lay in the Duchy of Moravia, which had belonged to the
Hapsburgs from the 16th century. The county of Cieszyn had
been a part of the ancient Duchy of Silesia, but had been allowed to remain in Hapsburg possession when Frederick II
conquered the rest of the duchy. Galicia, which included the
most easterly extension of the coalfield, fell to Austria as
her share of Polish Territory in the First and Third Partitions.

Both Russian and Austrian held parts of the region contained an area of exposed coalfield, which was opened up in

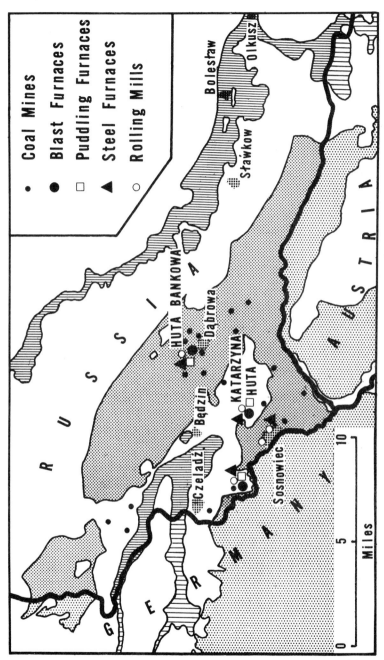

Figure 35: The Dabrowa Industrial District, about 1900.

the course of the century. Both contained also deposits of
the ores of lead, zinc, and iron. In effect, each held in minia-
ture the resources and potentialities which the Germans enjoyed in fuller measure in Upper Silesia. And in each a minia-
ture industrial region, similar in nature to that of Upper Silesia, but smaller in resources and output, was evolved during
the century.

Within the Russian and Austrian-held lands there grew up
three centers of industrial growth, dependent upon outcrops
of the coal measure: the Dąbrowa region of Russian Poland;
Western Galicia, between Kraków and the German border, and
northern Moravia and adjoining Cieszyn, where the most vigorous growth outside Germany took place. It is upon these
three geographical divisions that this chapter is based.

RUSSIAN DĄBROWA

The Russian share of the coalfield was by far the smallest, some 77 square miles, or 3.7 per cent of the whole. But
over a large part of this area the coal-measures were exposed, and mining was easier than in most other parts of the
coal basin.[1] Although the coal seams diminish toward the east
both in number and in total thickness, the disappearance of
some of the intervening beds results in seams of quite exceptional thickness.

Coal Mining: The existence of coal was probably recognized earlier here than in any other part of Upper Silesia. A
coal mining company was established by one of the last kings
of Poland, but it does not appear that mines were regularly
operated before 1796. In that year von Reden opened a mine
in the small area of Poland which Prussia had acquired in the
previous year. Several other mines were also developed, and
the names of ten are preserved. In 1807 this region passed
out of Prussian control, and in 1815 came under the rule of
the Tsars.

One of the first acts of the new rulers was to establish a
mines administration, with its headquarters in Kielce, and for
a few years, under the direction of Staszic and Lubecki, there
was a vigorous policy of mining development. But this ended
in 1830.[2] In the 1840's the Russian state opened coal mines,

but these were not successful either in themselves or as examples to the local landowners, and in time they passed from the control of the State to that of small companies which operated with German or French capital. The volume of output increased very slowly, and it was not until 1860 that it reached a quarter of a million tons in a year. Thereafter expansion was very much more rapid. It reached a million tons in 1879; two million within less than ten years, and three million by 1893. This more rapid increase, which characterized the last quarter of the 19th century, resulted from the increasingly important role of foreign capital in this area and followed the clarification of the old Polish mining law.[3] After the abortive Polish rising of 1863, estates confiscated from certain of the landowners who had participated, passed to industrialists and investors. The increased output of the following years owed much to these German entrepreneurs. Towards the end of the century, in keeping with the changed direction of Russian political alliances, the German capital tended to be replaced by French.[4] On the eve of the First World War the French controlled about 60 per cent of the Dąbrowa coal-mining industry, including the Sosnowiec Company, which produced nearly a quarter of all the coal mined.[5]

Coal mined in the Dąbrowa field was mostly a lean coal, good for most industrial purposes, though not for metallurgical coke. Coking-coal was imported into this area for use in the blast-furnaces, but an import duty effectively protected the Russian market in other respects from coal from German Upper Silesia.

The mines were shallow, and few exceeded 600 feet in depth.[6] There had formerly been a great number of quarry-like workings, which could be opened with very little capital wherever the coal outcropped. But in the 19th century these gradually gave place to deep mines. In 1907 there were 55 shafts; in 1912, 130, which at this time belonged to 39 separate mines. Most of the coal was used in "Congress" Poland, nearly half of it in Warsaw itself. Very little was sent to Russia proper.

The Iron Industry: The fortunes of iron-working in Dąbrowa resembled those of coal-mining. Iron ores had been

mined and smelted in Poland long before the Partitions, but
no works had been established in or near Dąbrowa until the
Panki furnace was established in the 18th century. This, of
course, passed eventually to Russia.[7] The plans of Staszic
and Lubecki for the development of an iron industry failed to
materialize for many years. After 1830, however, the success,
achieved in German Silesia, of smelting iron with coke inspired similar attempts in Dąbrowa. During the thirties the
Bank of Poland was active in promoting and financing iron-
works. In particular it established the Huta Bankowa, a coke-
using iron-works, close to the Dąbrowa coal mines.[8]

But in 1843 the Russian State intervened, belatedly and
unsuccessfully, in the operation of the diminutive iron-indus-
try. It took over the assets of the Polish Bank, but under its
control the output of iron dwindled.[9] In 1870, the furnaces
were closed, and six years later the derelict premises sold
to a private group which reopened them as the A. G. Huta
Bankowa.

During the years when the Huta Bankowa had first been
active, its market was protected by the relatively high import
duty of 15 kopeks per pud of crude iron. In 1868, two years
before the works closed, this was reduced to 5 kopeks.[10]   At
the same time, however, the earlier duty was maintained on
all fabricated iron goods. Crude iron, smelted in German Upper Silesia, could be exported easily across the River
Przemsza to Russian Poland; the market for iron goods in
Russia was expanding, and German companies in Upper Silesia were thus encouraged to establish branches beyond the
Russian border. In this way the Ver. Königs- und Laurahütte,
formed in Upper Silesia only a few years before, established
the Katharinahütte at Sielce in 1881.[11] Its purpose was to refine pig-iron, imported from the company's furnaces near
Katowice, and to roll and fabricate it for sale in Russia. In
the next year the Oberschlesischer Eisenbahnbedarfs A. G.
founded the Alexanderhütte at Milowice with similar objectives
and, at the same time, Henckel von Donnersmarck built the
Puschkin works. Other works established within the Russian
borders by German interests included two tube mills at Sosnowiec, a bridge-building, boiler-making and engineering
works at Sielce, and a foundry and engineering works at Poręba.

In 1884 the import duty on crude iron was raised to 9 kopeks per pud, and then by successive stages to 35 kopeks in
1891. The earlier duties had been high enough to exclude
from Russian territory most iron goods made in Germany;
the new tariffs had the effect of excluding also pig-iron and
imposed upon the newly established works the obligation to
smelt their own iron. Thus, in 1890 a blast-furnace was
added to the Katharinahütte, and another five years later, the
owners of the Alexanderhütte leased and then enlarged an old
Polish blast-furnace works.

Reference had been made only to those ironworks that
were established actually on the Dąbrowa section of the Silesian-Moravian coalfield. There was a contemporary expan-
tion of the iron industry in other parts of Poland, particularly near Częstochowa, to the north of the coalfield, and near
Radom.[12] German participation in these works was very
much smaller than in those of the Dąbrowa region, and Russian, French and Belgian capital was proportionately more
important. In the ironworks located on the coalfield the participation of German capital diminished as the political relations between Russia and Germany deteriorated, and control
of several works passed to the French.

The Triassic beds which occurred in the vicinity of the
coalfield yielded small quantities of iron-ore, as in German
Silesia, and, in the early days of the industry this was supplemented by the output of coal-measures ore.[13] But these ores
were inferior both in quality and quantity to the iron-ore obtained in German Upper Silesia, and were soon for practical
purposes exhausted. Ore from the bedded deposits near Częstochowa was used, but had to be supplemented by ores from,
first, other parts of Congress Poland and then from Russia
itself.[14] The Russian contribution grew steadily. From about
100,000 tons in 1895,[15] the Polish consumption of Russian ore
rose to over half a million tons in 1912.[16] By this time iron-
ore had virtually ceased to be mined in the vicinity of the Dąbrowa furnaces, which relied mainly on ores brought by rail
from Krivoi Rog in the Ukraine.[17]

An industry which had thus come to depend on iron ore
brought 700 miles from the Ukraine, and upon coking coal
from Germany, was hardly in a strong economic position. In

all there were only four combined iron-smelting and steel-making firms and two further works made steel and rolled goods.

It is difficult to trace the expansion of iron production in Dąbrowa because the statistics for this region were normally included in those for "Congress" Poland as a whole. It may, however, be assumed from what is known about the size of the works, that Dąbrowa contributed less than half the Polish total. This would suggest that output in Dąbrowa can rarely have amounted to much more than 10 or 15,000 tons of pig-iron a year from the time when the Huta Bankowa was established in the 1830's until the expansion of the 1880's.[18] The production of pig-iron in Poland rose from about 50,000 tons a year in 1885 to about 200,000 tons in 1900 and 400,000 on the eve of the First World War. Considerably less than half of this came from the coalfield area of Dąbrowa; the rest was mainly from furnaces near Częstochowa, Kielce and Radom. It is improbable that the production in Dąbrowa amounted to over 20,000 tons in 1885; 80,000 in 1900, and 150,000 in 1910.[19]

The puddling and later the steel-making industries were relatively strongly developed in Dąbrowa. Indeed, the modern iron industry in this area consisted first in the refining of pig-iron imported from German Silesia.[20] The puddling furnaces and later the open-hearth furnaces indeed consumed a much greater volume of pig-iron than was actually smelted by the local blast furnaces. Steel production in Poland rose to considerably more than half a million tons a year. The Huta Bankowa was the largest single steel producer, and the Dąbrowa area produced between a third and a half of the Polish total.

Lead and Zinc Mining: The similarities between Dąbrowa and German Upper Silesia extended also to the extensive deposits of lead and zinc ores in the former. These occurred in the Triassic dolomite, which extended (see figure 35) from the German-held area of Upper Silesia south-eastwards into Russian territory.[21] The ore-deposits constituted two narrow belts; one continued the Tarnowskie Góry-Bytom deposits of Germany as far as Będzin; the other, a narrow belt of much less highly mineralized dolomite, stretched northwest from Olkusz towards Częstochowa (fig. 9).[22]

These deposits were worked intermittently in the 18th century, and with greater vigor during the short period when this area was in Prussian hands, but mining declined in importance soon after the territory had been transferred to Russia.[23] The chief difficulty appears to have been the excessive water in the mines, and when this had been overcome by cutting adits and the installation of a steam-engine, the industry revived. A number of mines was opened near Będzin and Olkusz, but mining dwindled towards the end of the century, and came to be concentrated in two mines—the "Ullyses" and "Bolesław"—near Olkusz.[24]

Several zinc-smelters were established during the course of the century, most of them close to Będzin, where coal was readily available. Some of these were short-lived, and by the end of the century only three were still active.[25]

Though developed primarily for zinc ores, the mines in the Dąbrowa region produced also small quantities of lead. There was no lead smelter in the area, and ores seem as a general rule to have been exported to be smelted in German Silesia. The production of zinc remained relatively small. Until the middle of the 19th century output of metallic zinc scarcely exceeded 3000 tons a year. Thereafter output increased steadily and in 1904 exceeded 10,000 tons for the first time.

WESTERN GALICIA

South of the Biała Przemsza river lay the Austrian province of Western Galicia, acquired in the First Partition of Poland. It included a sector of the coalfield, somewhat larger and more richly endowed than the Russian, and also an extensive area of the ore-bearing dolomite.[26] Like the German and the Russian sectors, the Galician also possessed reserves of iron-ore, both in the Triassic beds and in the foothills of the Beskid Mountains further to the south.

The coal measures come to the surface in four areas in Western Galicia. The largest of these and the earliest to be worked was the so-called Jaworzno region, lying within the bend formed by the Przemsza and its tributary, the Biała Przemsza. An outcrop of Triassic beds, which included the

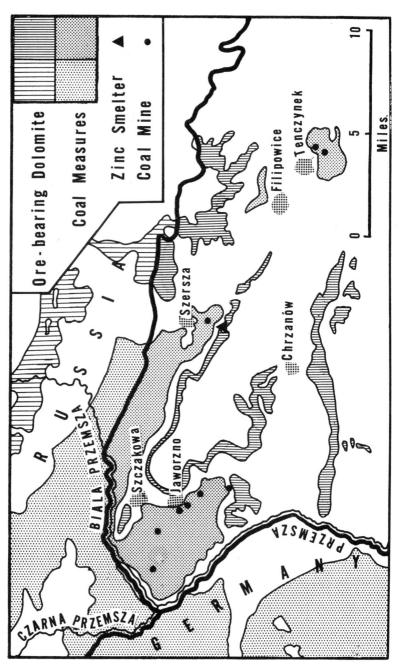

Figure 36: Industry in West Galicia, about 1900.

deposits of lead and zinc ores, separated this from the Szcza-
kowa-Siersza area. The remaining areas of the exposed coalfield were quite small and lay farther to the east, near the villages of Tenczynek and Filopowice.[27] All the coal mines were
opened on the exposed coalfield, and no attempt was made to
tap the vast resources of the hidden field.[28]

The Jaworzno mines, opened in the 18th century, were
the oldest, but those of Siersza and Tenczynek were in production early in the 19th century.[29] The coal from the West Galician field was mostly lean and unsuitable for making coke, and
output remained very small until the second half of the century.
In the '70's production began to increase more rapidly, as demand grew for coal and newly built railways permitted it to
be distributed more widely. Output exceeded a quarter of a
million tons in 1872, half a million in 1886, and a million in
1900.

The lead and zinc deposits of Galicia[30] occur in the dolomite formation which extends south-westward from the Bytom
and Będzin area. The production of lead and zinc ores rose
slowly during the century, but was smaller than that in Russian Dąbrowa and only a fraction of that from German territory.[31]

Iron-ore was also worked, but the output, never large, declined during the century, and ceased before its end. The iron-
working industry of Galicia was only of trifling importance.[32]
It used charcoal rather than coke, and was practiced in several
small and widely scattered works. Earlier in the century iron
was refined, but later the diminishing production went wholly
into castings.

MORAVIA AND AUSTRIAN SILESIA

The resources and industries of Moravia and Austrian
Silesia were of much greater significance than those of West
Galicia. This sector of the coalfield was second in importance
only to the German. But it differed in two important respects
from the three sectors already discussed. The area of exposed coalfield, in the first place, was very small. It consisted
only of a few square miles of outcrop near Moravska Ostrava
and Karvinna. Over the rest of this very extensive area the

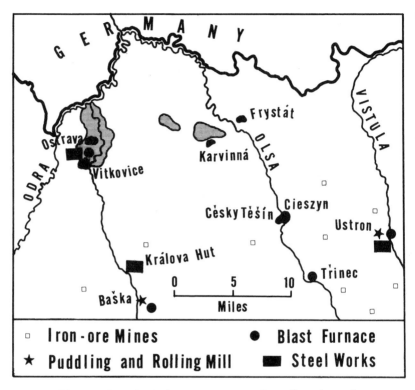

Figure 37: The industrial region of Těšín and northern Moravia, about 1900.

coal measures were so deeply buried under later deposits as to be beyond the range of profitable mining. Indeed, along its southern margin the extent of the coal-basin was far from clearly known.[33]

In the second place, the territory of Moravia and Austrian Silesia was entirely lacking in those Triassic beds which in the remaining sectors were the source of the ores of lead, zinc and iron. Both Moravia and Austrian Silesia produced iron-ore, but it came from other beds than the ore-bearing dolomite.

The Ostrava-Karvinná Coalfield: Towards the south of
the coal-basin the coal seams, in general level and but little
disturbed, become very much more folded.[34] They are still
very numerous—no less than 300 are enumerated—but their
total thickness is less than in Upper Silesia. The upper coal-
measures yield only a poor quality coke, but some of the
seams of the lower, or Margin Group, contain the best coking
coal in the whole coal-basin.

The outcrops were mined in a desultory fashion in the
18th and early 19th century, but serious mining did not begin
until the middle of the 19th century.[35] During the 1840's there
was active prospecting, and the extent of the coal reserves
that were revealed aroused great interest. By about 1850,
some eight mines were producing some 140,000 tons.[36] A
large part of this came from von Rothschild's mine at Polska
Ostrava, and the other mines were very small.[37] But production was expanded steadily in the second half of the century.[38]
Statistics were generally published separately for Moravia
and Austrian Silesia. The former, which contained the mines
of Moravska Ostrava, was producing 739,000 tons yearly by
1870; 1,479,000 by 1900 and 2,500,000 by 1913. Austrian Silesia, which contained the mines of Karvinná and Polska Ostrava,
was always more important than Moravia. Its output rose to
1,556,000 tons in 1840, 4,697,000 in 1900, and 7,595,000 in
1913.

A rising proportion of the coal obtained was converted
into metallurgical coke for use here and in other parts of the
Austro-Hungarian Empire. By 1913 this amounted to about a
quarter of the total.[39] There was a considerable export of
coke to the iron-works in Russian Dąbrowa, and coal was supplied to the Austrian railways as well as to industrial centers
elsewhere in Hungary.

The Iron and Steel Industry: In Moravia and Austrian
Silesia, as well as in the neighboring mountains of Slovakia,
there were small works in which from early times iron had
been made with charcoal.[40] Here, in 1826, the Archduke
Rudolph, Archbishop of Olomouc, established a puddling works
which used coal from the Ostrava-Karvinná section of the coalfield and iron from the charcoal-furnaces of the region. This
was the Vítkovice works, the earliest puddling works to be

established within the Austro-Hungarian Empire.[41] In 1839, they were sold to von Rothschild. At once new blast furnaces were built to use coke made from the good coking coal found there. Rothschild had already got possession of a coal mine and had built a battery of coking ovens. Vítkovice had become, like the Königshütte in Upper Silesia, the model iron-works from which neighboring ironmasters were to learn the new methods of smelting and refining iron.[42]

The following years were a period of considerable activity.[43] Blast furnaces were built at Třinec, Obschar, and Węgierska Górka and a puddling works at Karlova Huta. The attraction of this region lay rather in the facilities which it offered for the new puddling process than as a source of coke for the blast furnace. For many years the Vítkovice works were alone in smelting with coke. About 1850, mixed coke and charcoal were used in the furnace at Stefanau, but elsewhere only charcoal. The charcoal-using works were not, as a general rule, converted to the use of coke.[44] They and the many Frischfeuer went gradually out of use, and production came to be concentrated in a few large, modern works.

Foremost amongst these were, of course, Vítkovice in northern Moravia, and also Třinec, in Austrian Silesia. The former was notable in Central Europe for its experiments with new metallurgical processes. It was the first works in the Hapsburg Empire to smelt with coke[45]; the earliest experiments with the Bessemer process were made here in 1866, and the first use of the Thomas process here in 1879 was one of the earliest in continental Europe. It is claimed further that the duplex method of steel making was invented here.

Gradually the older furnaces and refineries were closed, but at the end of the century small charcoal blast furnaces were still active at Frydek, Stefanau and Blansko, but they were producing only iron castings.

The Vítkovice iron and steel works, together with rolling mills, foundry, engineering construction works, coal mines and coke ovens, passed to the Vítkovice Mining and Steel Company,[46] in which the Rothschild family continued to have a strong interest. The Rothschild Bank of Vienna acquired a controlling interest in the Koskulls iron-ore field in northern

Sweden, from which ore was sent via the river Oder to supply
the furnaces in Vítkowice.[47]
The Třinec works, established to the south of Cieszyn
by the Austrian Archduke Charles, were transferred in 1906
to the Czech Mining and Smelting Company.[48] This company
also controlled several small iron-works in Moravia, Austrian Silesia and neighboring parts of Galicia, but their activities and, in certain instances also their plant, were gradually transferred to Třinec.[49]
The iron ores mined in Moravia and Silesia had formerly
sufficed for the needs of the industry.[50] But output declined
during the later years of the century, and in Austrian Silesia
mining ceased in 1895. Long before this, however, the blast
furnaces had come to rely on ores from the mountains of
northern Hungary and central Bohemia and on rich, mangani-
ferous ores from Styria. This placed an unaccustomed strain
on the industry. The Ostrava-Karvinná coal was the most
suitable in Central Europe for the metallurgical processes,
and an attempt was made to reduce transport costs by taking
coke to the ore. Fuel was sent to blast furnaces in Styria,
Carinthia and Hungary, and a blast furnace was even built at
Schwechat, near Vienna, midway between the Moravian coal
and the Styrian iron-ore. But only near the coalfield did the
iron smelting attain the proportions of a major industry. Its
growth was slow until about 1880, after which there was a
much more rapid expansion, which coincided with the introduction of the converter and open hearth processes.
It has been necessary to describe the industrial development of the whole Silesian-Moravian coalfield in four separate
sectors, two of them Austrian and the others German and Russian. The Austrian, German and Russian sectors were separated from one another throughout most of the period by high
tariff walls. The movement of raw materials and of part and
fully finished goods between them was on only a very small
scale. The temporary break in the Russian tariff barrier in
the 1870's and '80's sufficed to show the kind of co-operation
and integration that might have developed under a more liberal
tariff regime. There emerged, however, three separate industrial regions, each located just within the borders of one of
the great imperial powers which shared the coal-basin. At

least one of them was kept in being only high tariffs. Each of
the three drew raw materials as far as possible from its own
national hinterland. Indeed, the only commodity to cross the
national boundaries in significant quantities—apart from German exports of pig-iron to Russia during the short period of
the latter's more liberal tariff policy—was coking-coal.
There was, in addition, a very small movement of lead ore
from West Galicia into Germany because the Austrian territory had no smelter.

The geographical pattern of industrial development in the
Silesian-Moravian region accorded rather with the alignment
of political boundaries than with the location of industrial resources. Each was geographically marginal to the country to
which it belonged. The market of each lay, by and large, in
one geographical direction. Each was denied the facility not
only to locate its industries on the best sites within the coalfield area, but also to export its products to the whole of the
surrounding area. It follows that the industrial practice was
more extravagant and wasteful than it might have been under
a more beneficent political regime.

Notes

1. A. Schwarz, "Das Steinkohlenrevier von Dombrowa,"
M.R., IX, 1917, 187-89.

2. N. Gąsiorowska, Gornictwo i Hutnictwo w Królestwie
Polskim, 1815-1830, Warsaw, 1922: "Die Montanindustrie im
Königreich Polen," Z.d.O.B.U.H., LV, 1916, 9-29: Jan Pazdur,
"Gornictwo i hutnictwo zagłębia staropolskiego w połowie XIX
w (1846-1864)," Kwartalnik Historyczny, LXIII, 1956, nr. 4-5
200-220.

3. Goroll, "Überlick über die Geschichte und Grundzuge
des polnischen Bergrechts," Z.d.O.B.u.H.V., LX, 1921, 7-11;
"Die Kohlen-Versorgung Russisch-Polens," Z.d.O.B.u.H.V.,
XXXVII, 1898, 264-65.

4. "Die Kohlen-Versorgung Russisch-Polens,"
Z.d.O.B.u.H.V., XXXVII, 1898, 264-265.

5. Kurt Flegel, Die wirtschaftliche Bedeutung der

Montanindustrie Russlands und Polens, Osteuropa Institut,
Breslau, 1920, 16.

6. A. Gerke, "Bergbau, Hüttenindustrie und Industrie
der Steine und Erden im Kunftigen Polen," Z.d.O.B.u.H.V.,
LVIII, 1919, 1-25.

7. Wacław Oziębłowski, "Erzbergbau im Polen: II,
Geschichtlicher Ueberblick uber den Erzbergbau im Polen,"
Z.d.O.B.u.H.V., LXVIII, 1929, 518-27, 570-80, 626-36; O.
Vogel, "Zur Geschichte der Montanindustrie Polens,"
Z.d.O.B.u.H.V., LXVI,1927, 308-11, 382-84, 443-46: N.Gasiorowska,
op.cit., Mieczysław Radwan, "O prawdziwy obraz dziejow hutnictwa
żelaznego w Polsce," H., XIV, 1947, 363-65; F. Popiołek,
Dzieje Hutnictwa żelaznego na ziemiach polskich, Katowice,
1947.

8. "Jetziger Zustand des Eisenhüttengewerbes im Koni-
greich Polen," B.u.H.Z., I, 1842, 333-38.

9. "Verkauf der Fabriken und Bergwerke im Königreich
Polen," O.Z.f.B.u.H., XII, 1864, 271-72.

10. J. Kuczynski and G. Wittkowski, Die Deutsch-Russi-
schen Handelsbeziehugen in den letzten 150 Zahren, Berlin,
1947, 21-30; Valentin Wittschewsky, Russlands Handels- Zoll
und Industriepolitik, Berlin, 1905, 118-25; Z.d.O.B.u.H.V.,
XXXIII, 1894, 31-35; Irena Pietrzak-Pawłowska, "Z dziejów
monopolizacji górnictwa i hutnictwa w Krókstwie Polskim,"
Kwartalnik Historyczny, LXIII, 1956, nr. 4-5, 341-367.

11. Handbuch von Polen, ed. E. Wunderlich, Berlin, 1918,
431-32; Paul Thrasenster, "L'Industrie siderurgique russe,"
R.U.d.M., 3e serie, XLVII, 1899, 43-54.

12. Jan Rutkowski, Historia Gospodarcza Polski, (do
1864 r), Warsaw, 1953, 351-61; F. Popiołek, op.cit., 32-41.

13. B.u.H.Z., I, 1842, 333-38.

14. Handbuch von Polen, ed. W. Wunderlich, Berlin, 1918,
424-29; G. Behagel, "Die Eisen- und Manganerze Osteuropas,"
Osteuropa Institut, Quellen und Studien, 3 Abt., Heft 5, 1922,
95-101; S. Kontkiewicz, "Złoża rudy żelaznej w południowej
części ziemi wieluńskiej," H., XVII, 1950, 175-82.

15. R.U.d.M., XLVII, 1899, 46.

16. Z.d.O.B.u.H.V., LV, 1916, 25.

17. A. Gerke, op.cit., 13-14; Report on the Industrial, Commercial and Economic Situation in Poland, D.O.T., London, 1921, 14.

18. B.u.H.Z., I, 1842, 333-38.

19. Revue Économique Internationale, II, 1911, 561.

20. Revue Économique Internationale, II, 1911, 561; Handbuch von Polen, ed. E. Wunderlich, Berlin, 1918, 432.

21. Kurt Flegel, Die wirtschaftliche Bedeutung der Montanindustrie Russlands und Polens, Osteuropa Institut, Breslau, 1920, 61-64; W. Oziębłowski, op.cit., 524-25.

22. Handbuch von Polen, 423.

23. "Der Bleierz- und Galmei-Bergbau zu Olkusz im Königreich Polen," B.u.H.Z., I, 1842, 317-320.

24. Paul Martell, "Mitteilung über die Zinkindustrie in Russisch-Polen," Z.d.O.B.u.H.V., XLVII, 1908, 193-5; Przewodnik po Zagłębiu Dąbrowskim, Sosnowiec, 1939, 133-4.

25. K. Flegel, op.cit., 62.

26. B.u.H.R., IX, 1912-13, 13-20; 25-34.

27. Franz Schwackhöfer, Die Kohlen Österreich-Ungarns und Preuss.-Schlesiens, Vienna, 1901, 57-58.

28. Austrian Poland, Foreign Office (Peace) Handbook No. 46, London, 1920, 58.

29. Hermann, "Ueber den Bergbau im Kreise Chrzanow in Galizien," Z.d.O.B.u.H.V., XXXVI, 1897, 16-23; Franz Bartonec, "Die Steinkohlenablagerung Westgaliziens und deren volkswirtschaftliche Bedeutung," O.Z.f.B.u.H., XLIX, 1901, 321-5; 336-40; "Das galizische Kohlenrevier," M.R., X, 1918, 639 ff.

30. W. Oziębłowski, op.cit., 525-27.

31. "Der Bergwerksbetrieb im Kaiserthum Österreich im Jahre 1855," Vienna, 1857, 135.

32. Die Verwaltungs-Berichte der k.k. Berghauptmann-schaften, 1858, Vienna, 1859, 285; Der Bergwerksbetrieb im Kaiserthum Österreich im Jahre 1855; Vienna, 1857, 133-35; Henryk Jost, "Górnictwo i Hutnictwo w Tatrach polskich," Studia i Materiały z Dziejów Nauki Polskiej, IV, 33-61, War-saw, 1956.

33. W. Petrascheck, "Die Kohlenreviere von Ostrau-Kar-win-Krakau," Z.d.O.B.u.H.V., LXVII, 1928, 272-81, and in five sebsequent installments of this volume.

34. E. Gruner & G. Bosquet, Atlas Général des Houillères, Paris, 1911, 179-82; F. Schwackhöfer, op.cit., 42-48; W. Pe-trascheck, op.cit., 404-15 and later installments: E. Mládek, "Der Zusammenhang der westlichen mit der östlichen Flöz-gruppe des Ostrau-Karwiner Steinkohlenreviers und die Or-lauer Störung im Lichte der neueren Aufschlüsse," B.u.H.R., VII, 1910-11, 201-08, 211-21; Geisenheimer, "Das Steinkoh-lengebirge an der Grenze von Oberschlesien und Mahren," B.u.H.R., III, 1906-07, 1-8; 15-20.

35. Das Ostrauer Kohlenrevier, S.u.E., X, i, 1890, 574-75; R. Drapala, "Wie die Steinkohle zu Schlesischen- (Pol-nisch) Ostrau wirklich entdeckt wurde," M.R., XIX, 1927, 235-38, 259-65.

36. "Die früher k.k. Kohlenwerke bei Mährisch-Ostrau," O.Z.f.B.u.H., V, 1857, 27-29; 35-37; B.u.H.J., XXI, 1873, 118-66.

37. "Auszug aus dem Jahresbericht der schlesischen Handels und Gewerbekammer für 1851 und 1852," O.Z.f.B.u.H., I, 1853, 235.

38. F. Pospíšil, "Über das Ostrau-Karwiner Steinkohlen-revier," M.R., XIII, 1921, 313-18; 333-37; 353-57.

39. E. Fanta, "Fünfzig Jahre tschechoslowakischer Stein-kohlenbergbau," M.R., XVIII, 1926, 38-42.

40. The Iron and Steel Industry of Czechoslovakia, Prague, 1930, 105-06; Otakar Quadrat, "La Situation de l'industrie sidérurgique en Tschécoslovaquie," Revue de Métallurgie, Mémoires, XXXII, 1935, 469-81.

41. "Das Eisenwerk Witkowitz," O.Z.f.B.u.H., II, 1854, 315-17; 340-42; L. Beck, op.cit., IV, 368; R. Doderer, Ge-schichte und Entfaltung der tschechoslowakischen Eisenindus-trie," M.R., XVIII, 1926, 44-47.

42. L. Beck, op.cit., IV, 1899, 743.

43. F. M. Friese, "Die Eisenwerke Sr. kaiserl. Hoheit
des Erzherzogs Albrecht in Schlesien," O.Z.f.B.u.H., V, 1857,
257-61 and later installments.

44. "Koaksroheisen in Mähren," O.Z.f.B.u.H., I, 1853,
343-34; "Die Entwicklung der Roheisenindustrie Oesterreichs
in neurer Zeit," Z.d.O.B.u.H.V., XXXV, 1896, 352-26; "Die
Entwicklung der Eisenindustrie im XIX Jahrhundert und die
Betheiligung Oesterreichs an derselben," S.u.E., XX, 1900, i,
666-68; "Zur mährischen Berwerksstatistik," O.Z.f.B.u.H., I,
1853, 127; "Auszug aus dem Jahresbericht der schlesischen
Handels und Gewerbekammer für 1851 und 1852," O.Z.f.B.u.H.,
I, 1853, 235 ff; C. A. M. Balling, "Die Eisenindustrie in Mähren und in österr. Schlesien," B.u.H.J., XVIII, 1869, 173-229;
Der Bergwerksbetrieb im Kaiserthum Österreich, Vienna,
1857, 118-32; Die Verwaltungs-Berichte der k.k. Berghaupt-
mannschaften, 1858, Vienna 1859. Alojzy Waszek, "O hutnictwie w Ustroniu," W.H., X, 1954, 51 ff. L'Industrie du Fer en
1867, Tome III, Paris 1869, 560-62; O. Quadrat, op.cit., 469 ff;
L. Beck, op.cit., IV, 743-44.

45. O.Z.f.B.u.H., XVI, 1868, 316-17.

46. Vitkovické horní a hutni rézírtvo.

47. "Schwedische Eisenerze für Witkowitz," S.u.E., XIX,
i, 1899, 51.

48. Báňská a hutní společnost (Prague).

49. O. Quadrat, op.cit., 474-76.

50. "Die Eisenerze Oesterreichs und ihre Verhüttung,"
O.Z.f.B.u.H., XXVI, 1878, 356-58; C. A. M. Balling, op.cit.,
175-7.

CHAPTER VIII

NEW BOUNDARIES IN SILESIA-MORAVIA

O wojnę powszechną za wolność ludów,
Prosimy Cię, Panie.
O broń i orły narodowe,
Prosimy Cię, Panie.
Adam Mickiewicz.

The First World War was brought to a close by the defeat of the German and Russian Empires and the disintegration of the Austro-Hungarian. But before it ended the American President had proposed a number of principles on which a lasting peace should be based. Though they had no binding force on those who gathered at Paris to draw up the treaties of peace, it was assumed that the settlement would be not inconsistent with these principles.

Amongst the proposals made by President Wilson were the recreation of an independent State of Poland and the granting of political freedom to the national groups of the Austro-Hungarian Empire. There was no doubt that these would be implemented. The creation of new political units, satisfying the political aspirations of Poles, Czechs, Slovaks and other minority peoples was made relatively easy by the military defeat of the older imperial powers of Central Europe. The most urgent problem was the delineation of the new boundaries in a way that would satisfy the aspirations of the peoples without disrupting the economic life of the boundary areas.

We are concerned here only with the new boundaries as they were drawn in and near the Upper Silesian industrial area. The problems here reduce themselves, in effect, to two questions: if it be assumed that the new Poland would take Dąbrowa and Galicia, how much of German Upper Silesia should she also take. Secondly, would Czechoslovakia, heir to the Hapsburg lands of Bohemia, Moravia and Slovakia, possess also those nominally Silesian territories which had remained under Hapsburg rule. The latter question was the less important

139

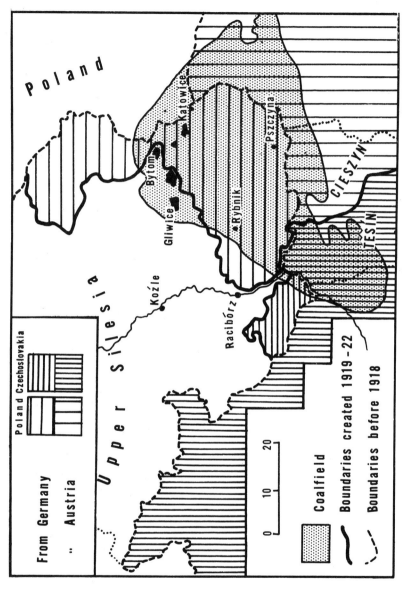

Figure 38: New boundaries in Silesia and Cieszyn (Těšín), 1919-1922.

although it caused bitter feelings between Poland and Czechoslovakia.

The Question of Austrian Silesia: The claims of Czechoslovakia seem to have been based upon the assumption that a
need for coal would justify the annexation of territory that on
linguistic and cultural grounds should go to Germany or Poland.[1] The territory of Hlucin or, as it is sometimes called,
Opava, had been a part of the ancient Duchy of Silesia, from
which it was separated in the 15th century.[2] It was left in
Austrian hands when the rest of Silesia was conquered by
Frederick II, and Czechoslovakia, which inherited much of the
northern boundary of the Austro-Hungarian Empire, also took
the small territory. Though formerly it had possessed some
importance as a source of iron-ore and had contained a few
small iron-works, its industrial importance was now limited
to a couple of coal mines.[3]

The territory of Cieszyn was economically more important, and the struggle for its control between Poland and
Czechoslovakia endangered good relations between these two
countries throughout the inter-war years.[4] The claim of
Czechoslovakia to Cieszyn was based on the historic association of Silesia with the Bohemian crown, the reliance which
Czechoslovakia placed both upon the coal mined in the territory and the railway which ran through it, and the alleged
Czechoslovak and Protestant character of the population.[5]

The Czechoslovak claim that "Karvinná and Ostrava
form a geological and economic whole" was based entirely on
the fact that, as the Czech memorandum to the Peace Conference pointed out, the Vítkovice works in northern Moravia
were dependent in large measure on coking coal from the Karvinná mines in the territory of Cieszyn.[6] These mines, very
much more productive, as statistics given in the previous
chapter have shown, than those of Moravska Ostrava, made
this area a prize of very considerable value.

The territory of Cieszyn was first occupied by Polish
troops, under protest by Czechoslovakia.[7] The question was
then referred to the League of Nations and a plebiscite ar-
ranged. Before, however, this could be held, the Council of
ministers decided to partition the area between Poland and
Czechoslovakia. The boundary, which followed roughly the

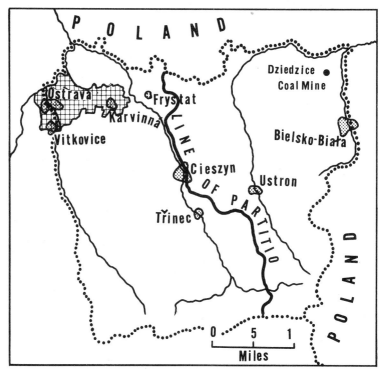

Figure 39: The partition of the territory of Cieszyn (Těšín), 1920.

river Olza, divided the city of Cieszyn, but gave to Czechoslovakia almost all the developed area of the Karvinná coalfield. In fact, the part that went to Poland, Śląsk Cieszyński,
contained only one unimportant mine. The portion of the
Cieszyn territory that remained in Czechoslovak possession[9]
continued to be an important source of coal for Czechoslovakia
and the Danubian Basin. But statistics of its coal production
are henceforward included with those of Moravia, and the Ostrava–Karvinná coalfield is henceforward treated as a unit
(see pages 181 to 184).

THE PARTITION OF UPPER SILESIA

The wartime declarations of President Wilson, confirmed by the actions of the allied leaders at the Paris Conference, had emphasized the right of national groups to determine their political future. The industrial region of Upper Silesia was in part Polish in language and culture, and inevitably the newly formed Polish government claimed the whole region. As soon as the fighting ceased, there broke forth from Germans and Poles a flood of claims and counter-claims. German and pro-German writers emphasized and exaggerated the German character of the region, and Polish apologists pointed out that it had been indisputably Polish until the German authorities under Bismarck eradicated Polish language and customs from the area. Germans claimed that the coal and metal production of Upper Silesia was essential for the well-being of Germany, and Polish writers declared that without it the new Poland could not live. Both sides supported their theses with studies based on the production statistics of the region, and exaggerated both their needs and their claims. The only matter on which both sides agreed was that the developments in Upper Silesia during the previous century had made it a functional unit which it would be disastrous to partition.[10] Upper Silesia, they claimed, must go intact to either Germany or Poland.

German writers stressed the dependence of Upper Silesian industries on iron-ore and steel scrap from Germany and emphasized that the Upper Silesian coal industry was heavily dependent on markets in the rest of Germany.[11] The steel industry of Upper Silesia had come to use large quantities of scrap in its open-hearth furnaces, and it could be assumed that the new Poland had little to offer. It was forgotten on the other hand that without Lorraine, Germany, was ill-equipped to supply the industrial area with ore, and might even experience a shortage of scrap.

Before the war the territory of the new Poland had relied heavily on imported coal.[12] In 1913, only about 43 per cent of the coal consumed within this area was actually mined within its borders. Almost as great a quantity had been obtained

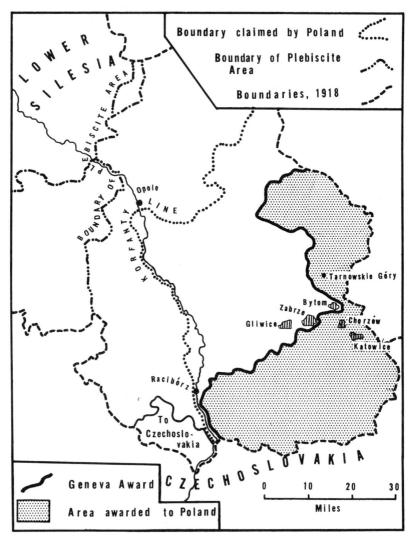

Figure 40: The partition of Upper Silesia, 1919-1922.

from Germany.[13] In fact, much of the market for Upper Silesian coal lay within the new Poland.

The Plebiscite: But it was not such economic considerations that decided the issue, but rather the feelings of the people who lived in Upper Silesia. The draft treaty of May, 1919 gave most of Upper Silesia to Poland. As might have been expected, news of this aroused such deep resentment in Germany that Lloyd George proposed a plebiscite and succeeded in converting the Supreme Council of the Allies to his view.[14] A commission was appointed to supervise the plebiscite and the area within which the plebiscite was to be held was defined in the Treaty of Versailles.[15]

This area embraced the whole of the Regierungsbezirk Opole, except certain Kreise to the west of the river Odra, and also Kreis Namysłow (Namslau), which was part of Middle Silesia. The plebiscite was to be held in all territories in which there was a significant non-German minority. In reaching this decision, the Allies relied heavily on the German census of 1910, much less partisan in its findings than German statements had since become.

In Upper Silesia itself, neither Poles nor Germans placed great trust in the forthcoming plebiscite. There was an armed rising of the Poles. After this had been suppressed and an Allied military force established, the territory was deluged with propaganda from both sides. The odds were heavily in favor of the Germans. They controlled most of the wealth in the area and they lived in the cities, where they could organize their efforts more effectively. The Poles, who predominated in most rural area, were frequently organized in German-controlled labour unions or were tenants of German-owned estates, and were thus subjected to severe German pressure. Furthermore, the Germans claim that the economic well-being of Upper Silesia was bound up with that of Germany herself, and that a prosperous Germany was a condition of world prosperity, was one likely to appeal to neutral opinion in Great Britain and America.[16]

Feelings were so inflamed in Upper Silesia, that quite small incidents provoked rioting and armed risings. The negotiations which preceded the plebiscite caused much bitterness. The question whether the right to vote extended to all who had

been born in the plebiscite area, irrespective of their present
domicile, or only to those living there at the time, was decided in favor of the former. This decision clearly favored
the Germans, among whom were many children of former local officials and industrial employees who had settled elsewhere in Germany. Similarly the organization of voting on
the great estates was probably calculated to favor the German
cause.

The plebiscite took place on March 20, 1921, and a very
high proportion of the eligible population voted. The report,
published on May 7, was as confusing as the events leading up
to the plebiscite. The north and west of the plebiscite area
had voted heavily in favor of Germany. Elsewhere the com-
plexity of the voting picture made any equitable line of division
quite impracticable, and nowhere was the picture more con-
fused than in the industrial area itself. The larger cities,
notably Gliwice, Bytom, Chorzów and Katowice, showed a con-
vincing German majority. The medium-sized cities were
evenly divided, and the small cities and rural communities,
with very few exceptions, showed a large Polish majority.[17]

The only conclusion that emerged was that an equitable
line of partition, acceptable to both parties, could not possibly
be achieved. Apart from the extreme claims of Poles and Germans (fig. 40), several compromises were suggested by mem-
bers of the Plebiscite Commissions which would have had the
effect of giving Germany almost the whole of the industrial
area. It was the duty of the Commission to make recommenda-
tions for the division of the area, and when news of these proposals ultimately leaked out, many Poles prepared to seize by
force what they had been unable to obtain by the use of the bal-
lot. At the beginning of May, a Polish force, organized and
led by Korfanty, entered Upper Silesia.[18] Within a few days
the Poles were in control of all Upper Silesia east of the river
Oder. At the same time German bands, armed from secret
stores of weapons, entered the area from the West. The Allied troops in the area succeeded in keeping German and Polish
forces apart, but it was not until July that their authority was
restored, and the rising was over.

In the meanwhile the Interallied Commission had failed
to agree on a line of partition, and in August referred the matter

to the League of Nations. In September the League Council
set up a small committee charged with settling the problem.
The Council of the League decided that a partition of the actual industrial area was practicable and that the wishes of
the people, rather than economic and technical considerations,
should guide their decisions. On October 12, 1921, the League
Council published its report and proposed the line of demarca-
tion which was accepted by the Council of Ambassadors (the
continuing organization of the Allied Powers) and ultimately,
though under protest, by both Germany and Poland.

The International Regime of Upper Silesia: The boundary
defined by the League's committee[19] left within Germany the
cities of Bytom, Zabrze, and Gliwice, together with their im-
mediate surroundings, but gave to Poland the cities of Katowice and Królewska Huta, renamed Chorzów, together with
the very considerable number of small industrial cities which,
together made up the greater part of the industrial area. The
economic unity of the area had been sacrificed in order to permit as full a degree as possible of self-determination.

In order, however, to counter the ill-effects of the partition on the economy of the region, the League recommended
that the area should, for a period of fifteen years, continue to
be organized and run as an economic unit under the supervision of a Mixed Commission. An Arbitral Tribunal was also
to be set up to determine private cases arising from the inter-
pretation of the international agreement. Both Germany and
Poland nominated representatives on the Mixed Commission
and the Arbitral Tribunal, and also sent plenipotentiaries to
Geneva to draw up the Convention prescribed by the League
Council.

The purpose of the Convention had been defined as "To
preserve, for a certain time, for the industries of the territory separated from Germany their former markets, and to
ensure the supplies of raw material and manufactured products
which are indispensable to these industries...to prevent the
working of the railways serving Upper Silesia from being af-
fected by the shifting of the political frontier; to regulate the
supplies of water and electricity; to maintain freedom of movement for individuals across the new frontier."[20] These objectives,

together with the rights and privileges of the local people,
were ensured by the Geneva Convention.

THE SOCIAL GEOGRAPHY OF UPPER SILESIA

Both parties to the Convention had previously protested
that Upper Silesia formed a whole which it would be folly to
partition. The detailed manner in which the agreement was
drawn is a measure of the gravity of this surgical operation.
Yet the patient did not die, as had been so confidently pre-
dicted. The Convention and the Mixed Commission together
smoothed over the many difficulties that inevitably arose with
extraordinary ability and success.

In the course of the preceding century a vast and complex
industrial area had grown up in Upper Silesia. The increase
of the population of the industrial Kreise from about 12,300 in
1781 to 835,000 in 1910 in itself created problems in transport
and housing and in food and water-supply.[21] It is a mistake
to assume that Upper Silesia became a focus of migration
during the period of industrial growth. There was a movement
towards this area early in the 19th century, but this was not
large, and appears to have become insignificant by 1845. After about 1860 there was a steady migration from Upper Silesia, made necessary by the extraordinarily high birthrate
in the area. This was much greater than was necessary to
supply even the needs of a rapidly expanding industry, and of
a slowly growing agriculture.

The Kreise of Toszek-Gliwice (Tost-Gleiwitz), Bytom,
Katowice, Zabrze and Królewska Huta, in each of which industrial growth was prominent, showed a very rapid rate of
growth.[23] A number of neighboring Kreise, which mined coal
and iron, lead and zinc ores, or took the industrial overflow
of the more developed Kreise, showed a less rapid growth.
Tarnowskie, Góry, Pszczyna and Rybnik belonged to this group.
Lastly, the predominantly agricultural Kreise, which made up
the rest of Upper Silesia, maintained a slow but steady growth
until near the end of the century and then remained static or
even declined slightly in population.

The three cities of Gliwice, Bytom and Katowice marked
the corners of an "industrial triangle" within which, through

the 19th century, the farms and villages were gradually turning themselves into sprawling industrial towns. Two of these three cities retained something of their old, urban character. The walls of Bytom and Gliwice were pulled down, but the Ring, or Market place, dominated by the brick-built towers of the older churches, gave these cities some distinction and character.[24] But around them spread the works, railways and spoil-heaps, interlaced with ribbons of brick-built tenement houses and cottages. Several of these mushroom cities, such as Katowice, Zabrze, Królewska Huta, Swiętochłowice and Zaborze, grew rapidly and without plan. Like the contemporary cities in the Ruhr, they lacked that order which market place, church and walls had imposed on older cities.

Thus the cities grew into one another, reaching out with the long tentacles of their roads and railways, each lined with factories and dwellings, to embrace and engulf farms and forests. In the vicinity of mines and industrial works "colonies" were established by the owners. At best, these were small but neat cottages, well-built, each with a small garden.[25] But there were also large, gloomy tenement blocks of four or five stories. Supplementing these "family" dwellings were the "Schlafhauser" for unmarried men.[26] These were barracks, sometimes of the most primitive order, built and maintained by the management of several of the works. In 1890 these provided accommodation for about 3000 workers. By 1913 there were 220 of these Schlafhauser, equipped with no fewer than 28,586 beds. Seventy per cent of these were at the coal mines. Thus about 15 per cent of the total employed in Montanindustrie[27] and nearly 20 per cent of coal miners were housed under such conditions.

The majority of the unskilled and semi-skilled workers who lived in the "colonies" and "sleeping houses" were Poles, though their Wasserpolnisch dialect was distinct from orthodox Polish. German political writers frequently claimed that the "Water Poles" had no right to be considered Poles and that their cultural affinities were rather with Germany. It was difficult, however, to substantiate this case, and the actions of these people in the troubled times before and just after the plebiscite left no doubt that their loyalties were to the new Polish state.

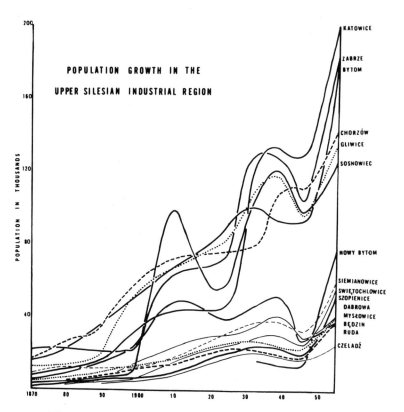

Figure 41: Growth of population in the industrial area of Upper Silesia.

The Polish population was in general Catholic, but is is wrong to assume that the German population was by contrast Protestant. About a quarter of the latter were also Catholic. Nevertheless the antithesis between Catholic Pole and Protestant German was widely assumed to hold goods.

Poles formed a majority in the smaller industrial cities, in which mining and metal-working formed the dominant occupation. But in the few larger cities — Gliwice, Bytom, Królewska

Huta—they were outvoted by a sizeable middle class, made
up of German officials, merchants, shop-keepers and the like.
The supply of agricultural produce to the industrial region created difficulties chiefly because much of the surrounding countryside was naturally unproductive.[28] Within the
framework of the great estates much of the cultivable land
was divided among holdings of minute size. In the Kreise of
the industrial region considerably over half the total holdings
were each of less than a hectare (2.47 acres). Most of these
undoubtedly represented the part time agricultural employment of families engaged mainly in mining or factory work.
But even in the mainly agricultural Kreise, where industry
did not offer part time employment, almost half the holdings
were of less than five acres.[29]

It is evident that the agriculture practiced in Upper Silesia was mainly subsistence farming. Until recent years a
three-field system, with periodic fallow, had been practiced,
but the use of artificial fertilizers had made the latter unnec-
essary.[30] In 1914 the cultivated area amounted to little more
than half the total area; 70 per cent of it was under grain crops,
and almost half of this rye. Potatoes and sugar beet occupied
about a quarter of the cultivated land, and it is interesting to
note a small area under the grape vine.[31]

The diet of the miner and industrial worker consisted
mainly of potatoes, cabbage and rye bread.[32] Meat and dairy
produce were eaten in only small quantities, but spirits were
drunk more copiously than was generally desirable.[33]

Upper Silesia was very far from supplying the food needed
by its industrial population. Most of the meat consumed was
brought into the area in the form of hogs, and there was a considerable import of bread crops and of potatoes. In the years
preceding the war the annual import of foodstuffs amounted
to over a quarter of a million tons.[34] Nearly 80 per cent of
this came from Germany, and 60 per cent from the territory
which remained German after 1922. This fact was used too
by German propaganda to demonstrate the inter-dependence
of Upper Silesia and the rest of Germany. It is true that imports into Upper Silesia from Russian-held territory were relatively small and were made up mainly of potatoes, but this
was probably due more to the high protective duties which

separated Upper Silesia from her non-German neighbors, than to any inability on the part of the latter to supply the food needs of the industrial area.

Clearly then the supply of foodstuffs could be adjusted without great difficulty to the political pattern created by the partition of Upper Silesia. The supply of water was less elastic. The industrial area spans the watershed between the rivers Odra and Vistula. Surface drainage is limited to a few small streams, and local water supply came at first mainly from wells. As demand arose towards the end of the century, the municipalities turned to the growing number of abandoned mines. These were an abundant source, but much of it was so acid or so salt that it was unfit for human consumption.[35]

This objection, however, did not in general apply to mines that had been opened in the Triassic limestone in search of lead and zinc ores, and these rocks furthermore, were an abundant source of water owing to their highly porous nature.[36] The abandoned mines capable of being used for water-supply lay at a considerable distance from the larger cities. Pumps had to be erected, filter beds laid down and a complex system of pipe-lines constructed. This did not, however, prevent serious shortages and also an acute typhus epidemic in the 1890's.[37]

The map, figure 42, shows the network of pipelines that had grown up on the eve of the war, connecting the more important mines with the chief industrial cities. Gliwice depended on shafts at Zabrze, and Łabędy; the Donnersmarckgrube supplied Zabrze and Bytom, Królewska Huta and Katowice by a more intricate system of pipes drew water from the Szyb Staszic (Adolf-Schacht), Rosaliegrube and Zawada mine.[38] The boundary established by the Geneva decision truncated this system of water supply. In spite of the complexity of the system, there were parts of the industrial area still dependent at the end of the war on shallow wells, the purity of whose water was far from certain.

Part V of the German-Polish Convention of May, 1922, consisting of clauses 336 to 369,[39] regulated the movement of water through the network of pipes. Certain pipes in German territory were reserved exclusively for Polish use, and vice versa. For a period of fifteen years the water from such

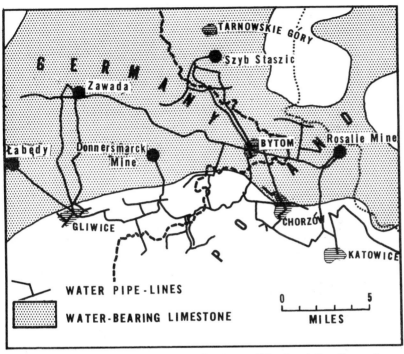

Figure 42: Water supply in Upper Silesia at the time of the Partition (after R. Michael).

important sources as Zawada and Szyb Staszic had to be shared equitably. Both countries agreed to allow specified quantities of water to pass to named communities across the boundary, and Germany was guaranteed a share in hitherto un-developed sources of water in the Triassic beds in Polish terri-tory. Kaeckenbeeck makes it clear that, in spite of the com-plexity of the "international experiment" in Upper Silesia—or, perhaps, because of it—the terms of the convention were obeyed both in spirit and letter.

The supply of electric power raised similar though more tractable problems. The main sources of power were two large thermal stations at Chorzów and Zaborze. The effect of

the partition was to give the former to Poland and to retain
the latter in Germany. But both lay close to the boundary,
and both had obtained fuel from and supplied current to locali-
ties on the other side. As in the case of water, the supply of
electric power was guaranteed[40] to consumers through the
facilities in existence before the partition. This arrangement
was to last for three years, at the end of which it was assumed
that the supply of electricity would have been adapted to the
new political situation.

It was assumed, also, that, as soon as it had been demar-
cated, the new political boundary would become also a customs
boundary. The Convention merely excepted from normal customs regulations certain commodities for a limited period of
time, in order to avoid hardship and distress. Most important
of the exceptions was the provision that "the natural products
which originate in and come from one of the two zones of the
plebiscite area, and are destined for consumption or use in
the other zone, shall cross the frontier free of duty."[41] This
exception was made for fifteen years. Although there was an
acrimonious discussion of the extent to which agricultural
products were covered by this clause, there was never any
doubt that it covered the movement of coal and the ores of
metals.

Part-finished factory goods raised a more difficult question, because they constituted a commodity against the import
of which most countries protected themselves. It was agreed,
however, to permit unrestricted movement of unfinished goods
for a period of six months after the coming into effect of the
Convention and then, for a period of fifteen years, to allow the
movement of such goods across the boundary, provided that
after further processing they returned to their country of origin. This clause was intended to regulate, for example, the
movement of pig-iron to steel works on the other side of the
boundary, or of steel ingots to rolling mills or forges.

The assumption, which we have already noted, that eastern
Germany was heavily dependent upon the mineral products of
Upper Silesia was the basis of a further exception. For a period of fifteen years Poland was required to permit the export
to Germany of coal, coal products and mineral ores. Germany
for her part had to allow the import of such goods without duty

for a term of three years. The action of Germany when, in
the summer of 1925, this latter obligation no longer rested on
her, will be discussed in the next chapter.

It was no less important that the inhabitants of the plebiscite area should be free to move about in both parts of the
area as their business and private affairs required. The Convention guaranteed to the permanent residents of the area for
a period of fifteen years the right to have a "circulation permit" which allowed them to cross the international boundary
within the plebiscite area at will.

During the years between the two World Wars the bitter
feelings between Poland and Germany, engendered by the
Treaty of Versailles and the Geneva decisions, showed no
signs of healing. For many of these years there was in fact
a tariff war between the two countries. It is easy to see how
the two parts of Upper Silesia would have suffered if the pas-
sions and policies of the two countries had been given full rein.
"If the disaster was not greater," wrote George Kaeckenbeeck,
who was through these years President of the Arbitral Tribunal of Upper Silesia, "it was ..to a large extent due to that
settlement which, within the area most likely to suffer, imposed a minimum of obligations, of restraint, of intercourse,
of co-operation, of discussion."[42]

DĄBROWA

The contrast between the physical appearance of the lands
on each bank of the Przemsa river was a common-place of
German writers. The rude villages, the unpaved roads and the
lack of sanitation and water-supply to the east of the river
merely confirmed, in their view, the superiority of German
culture to the polnische Wirtschaft to be found beyond its borders. Hartshorne has commented on the predominantly "brick
or stone houses west of this line" and "the frame and rough-
hewn log huts, commonly with thatched roofs that predominate
east of this cultural divide...The total impression of all these
differences is such that anyone travelling ten miles across
this cultural landscape boundary between Silesia and Poland,
feels that he has travelled farther than from Chicago to Silesia."[43]

The contrast is, in reality, not between Silesia and Poland, but between Germany and Russia. In Dąbrowa modern
industry had been superimposed, as in Upper Silesia, upon a
proverty-stricken peasant society. But in Silesia the industry was, judged by the standards of the 19th century, efficient
and orderly. Indeed, a pretension to a planned development
was achieved by the pervasive Prussian bureaucracy. Above
all, some small part of the wealth that stemmed from the Silesian mines and factories was ploughed back in improved
roads, sanitation and water-supply, in workers' colonies and
the whole appratus of Prussian welfare institutions. But no
such thing occurred in Dąbrowa. There, inefficient and bully-
ing Russian officials attempted little and achieved less.[44] The
local Polish nobility, who at least had some stake in the land
and stood for a more effective and humanitarian development
of its resources, had in part been expropriated after the Rising of 1863, and their places taken by Russians.

There were no ancient cities in Dąbrowa. When the Russians left the country during the First World War there remained behind them a region half urban, half rural, half industrial, half agricultural. The two parts and the two functions
were intermixed, and the result was an ugly sprawl of ram-
shackle cottages and rundown factory buildings. Upper Silesia
was very far indeed from being a place of physical beauty and
mental and moral enlightenment, but it was incomparably better
than the squalor that lay beyond the dark valleys of the Brynica
and Przemsza.

West Galicia: The easy-going rule of Austria had done
better in Western Galicia than had the Russians in Old Poland.
More by luck than judgment they had avoided a forced and hur-
ried development of their mineral and industrial resources.
Although these could have supported a much more intensive
growth, the mining of coal, zinc and iron ore had remained
small-scale and scattered. The result was that Western Galicia was still, as it had always been, predominantly rural. The
rural population was unbelievably dense; squalor was no less
real than in Dąbrowa, but in a country setting it was less conspicuous.

Notes

1. Hermann Janosch, Das Hultschiner Ländchen, Ratibor, 1930; La Documentation Internationale: La Paix de Versailles-Questions Territoriales, Paris, 1939, Mem. 8, 110-13.

2. L. Eisenmann, "Les Silésies dans l'histoire," La Silésie Polonaise, Paris, 1932, II, 1-14.

3. Charlotte Thilo, "Die Bevolkerungs-, Siedlungs- und Wirtschaftsverhältnisse im Hultschiner Ländschen," in Beiträge zur Schlesischen Landeskunde, ed. M. Friedrichsen, Breslau, 1925, 77-114.

4. K. Witt, Die Teschener Frage, Berlin, 1935.

5. H. W. V. Temperley, A History of the Peace Conference of Paris, IV, 1921, 348-56; La Documentation Internationale: La Paix de Versailles - Questions Territoriales, Paris, 1939, Mem. 4, 59-75.

6. La Documentation Internationale: La Paix de Versailles, - Questions Territoriales, I, Paris, 1939, 65-75.

7. H. W. V. Temperley, History of the Peace Conference of Paris, IV, London, 1921, 348-63.

8. Victor H. Winston, The Polish Bituminous Coal-Mining Industry, American Slavic and East European Review, XV, 1956, 38-70.

9. Called by the Poles "Śląsk Zaolziański."

10. See especially: Denkschrift des oberschlesischen Berg- und Hüttenmannischen Vereins und der Handelskammer, Kattowitz n.d., but published before the plebiscite of 1921; "Beiträge zur oberschlesischen Frage," Osteuropa Institut, Vorträge und Aufsätze, III, ii, Berlin, 1921.

11. ibid., 14-23; also Sidney Osborne, The Problem of Upper Silesia, London, 1921.

12. The Economic Value of Upper Silesia for Poland and Germany respectively, London, 1921.

13. G. Kramsztyk, La Pologne, l'Allemagne et l'Industrie de la Haute Silésie, Nicolai, n.d.

158   The Upper Silesian Industrial Region

14. Sarah Wambaugh, Plebiscites since the World War, Carnegie Endowment for International Peace, Washington, 1933, I, 206-70, contains a good, balanced account of these events; see also, H. W. V. Temperley, History of the Peace Conference of Paris, London 1920, II, 207-15; J. Ancel, "Géographie politique de la Haute Silésie," La Silésie Polonaise, Paris, 1932, 37-62.

15. Treaty of Versailles, Section VIII, Art. 88.

16. J. M. Keynes, The Economic Consequences of the Peace, London, 1919, 77-79; Sydney Osborne, The Problem of Upper Silesia, London, 1921, especially 49-142; see also, J. Weinstein, Upper Silesia: a Country of Contrasts, Paris, 1931 The Polish case is best expressed by A. Benisz, Górny Śląsk w walce o polskość, Katowice, 1930.

17. This is expressed cartographically in S. Wambaugh, op.cit., I, 259.

18. Novel by Arnold Bronne, S. O. S., London 1930 (A translation of O. S., 1929) gives an interesting though partisan account of the rising.

19. League of Nations Official Journal, Dec., 1921, 1220-1232.

20. Quoted in G. Kaechenbeeck, The International Experiment of Upper Silesia, Oxford, 1942.

21. The Kreise are Beuthen, Kattowitz, Hindenburg, Konigshütte and Tarnowitz. Estimates are given by W. Volz, "Oberschlesien und die oberschlesische Frage," Veröffentlichungen der Schlesischen Gesellschaft fur Erdkunde, I, 1922, 50.

22. Wilhelm Volz, Die wirtschafts-geographischen Grundlagen der oberschlesischen Frage, Berlin, 1921, 45-81; Handbuch des Oberschlesischen Industriebezirks, Bd. 2, Kattowitz, 1913, 216; also see Z.d.O.B.u.H.V., XLIII, 1904, 369-76; W. Volz, "Oberschlesien und die oberschlesische Frage," Veröffentlichungen der Schlesischen Gesellschaft für Erdkunde, Heft I, 1922.

23. G. E. Graf, "Die geographische Lage des oberschlesischen Industriereviers," Geographische Zeitschrift, XXV, 1919, 195-210.

24. Franz Gabrysch, "Die räumliche Entwicklung der Städte Beuthen, Hindenburg und Gleiwitz," Zur Wirtschaftsgeographie des deutschen Ostens, Bd. 14, Berlin 1937; also "Beuthen O/S.," Monographien deutscher Städte, Bd. XV, Berlin, 1925, and "Gleiwitz, eine oberschlesische Stadt," ibid., Bd. XII, Berlin, 1925.

25. Frief, Die wirtschaftliche Lage der Fabrikenbeiter in Schlesien, Breslau, 1876, for a very full discussion of housing conditions at this date; also, Sattig, "Ueber die Arbeiterwohungsverhältnisse im oberschlsischen Industriebezirk," Z.d.O.B.u.H.V., XXXI, 1892, 1-50.

26. F. Raefler, "Das Schlafhauswesen im oberschlesischen Industriegebiet," B.u.H.R., XIV, 1917-18, 1-6; 9-14; 17-21; 25-29; 33-37.

27. The useful German term which covers iron & steel as well as coal industries.

28. Bruno Dietrich, Oberschlesien, Breslau, 1920, 15-16.

29. J. Partsch, Schlesien, vol. II, Breslau, 1911, 19-20; W. Volz, "Die Ostdeutsche Wirtschaft," Veröffentlichungen des Geographischen Seminars der Universität Leipzig, I, Langensalza, 1930; Hermann Freymark, "Schlesiens Wirtschaft - eine deutsche Lebensfrage," Schriften der Industrie- und Handelskammer, Breslau, X, 1927.

30. Seweryn Wysłouch, "Kapitalistyczna przebudowa rolnictwa Śląskiego i jej skutki w latach 1850-1880," in Studia Śląskie, 1-119, Przegląd Zachodni, VIII, 1952, (Zeszyt dodatkowy). Upper Silesia, Foreign Office (Peace) Handbooks, no. 40, London, 1920, 26-27.

31. John Quincy Adams had noted extensive viticulture in Lower Silesia, Letters on Silesia, London, 1804, 19.

32. J. Partsch, op.cit., II, 20; also Z.d.O.B.u.H.V., XLIII, 1904, 369-76.

33. Bonikowsky, "Die wirtschaftliche Verhältnisse der oberschlesischen Montanindustrie," in Handbuch des Oberschlesischen Industriebezirks, Bd. II, 239-59; Kuhna, Die Ernahrungsverhältnisse der industriellen Arbeiterbevölkerung in Oberschlesien, Leipzig, 1894.

34. Wilhelm Volz, Die wirtschaftsgeographischen Grundlagen der oberschlesischen Frage, Berlin, 1921, 39.

35. Geisenheimer, "Die Wasserversorgung des Stadtkreises Kattowitz," Z.d.O.B.u.H.V., IL, 1910, 243-49.

36. Geisenheimer, "Die geologischen Verhältnisse der oberschlesischen Wasserversorgungsanlagen," Z.d.O.B.u.H.V., LII, 1913, 313-20.

37. "Die Entwicklung der staatlichen Wasserversorgungsanlage im oberschlesischen Industriebezirk," Z.f.d.B.H.u.S., LVII, 1909, 379-404; Geisenheimer, "Die Wasserversorgung des Stadtkreises Beuthen, O-S.," Z.d.O.B.u.H.V., IL, 1910, 470-82; G. Behagel and K. Knoedl, "Der Wasserverbrauch und Wasserbedarf im Polnischoberschlesischen Industriebezirk," Z.d.O.B.u.H.V., LXIII, 1924, 238-53.

38. "Das Wasserwerk Rosaliegrube," Z.d.O.B.u.H.V., LXII, 1923, 121-40.

39. The French texts of the Convention is given in full in G. Kaeckenbeeck, op.cit., 567-822.

40. Clauses 370 to 380, in Kaeckenbeeck, op.cit., 719-24.

41. Kaeckenbeeck, op.cit., 460.

42. G. Kaeckenbeeck, op.cit., 466.

43. R. Hartshorne, "Geographic and Political Boundaries in Upper Silesia," Annals of the Association of American Geographers, XXIII, 1933, 195-228.

44. See J. Słomka, From Serfdom to Self-Government, London, 1941, for observations on Russian rule.

CHAPTER IX

SILESIA DIVIDED

"Dieser gewaltige Wirtschafts-Organismus."
Wilhelm Volz.

The Partition of Upper Silesia, despite the precautions taken to preserve some functional unity, was a cruel blow to its industries. But the wounds had begun to heal long before the period of fifteen years, prescribed for the Upper Silesian "common market," had elapsed. The alleged wrongs of the Partition, however, continued to rankle, and their political significance grew as their real economic importance began to fade.

PROBLEMS OF PARTITION

The line of partition had taken no account of the intricate arrangements of individual works, of the movements of fuel and ore, of pig-iron, steel scrap, ingots, rolled goods—forgings and castings. In terms of crude statistics, Germany retained about 600 square kilometers of the coalfield area out of the 2800 which she possessed before the Partition, and her estimated reserves of coal were reduced from about 57.8 to about 8.7 milliard tons. Her losses in coking coal were yet more severe.[1]

Of twenty-two major mining and metallurgical concerns which had operated before the war in the plebiscite area, only five remained wholly within the new German boundaries. They were:

> Borsigwerk A. G.
> Donnersmarckhütte A. G.
> Oberschlesische Kokswerke und Chemische
> Fabriken A. G. (Oberkoks)

and two of the enterprises of the Prussian State:

> Staatliche Hüttenamt in Gleiwitz
> Staatliche Hüttenamt in Malapane

161

Six major concerns found themselves, as a result of the
Partition wholly in Poland:

> Fürst von Pless'sche Generaldirektion
> Rybniker Steinkohlengewerkschaft
> Bismarckhütte A. G.
> Ver. Konigs- und Laurahütte A. G.
> Fürst von Donnersmarck'sche Bergwerks und
>   Hüttendirektion
> Oberschlesische Zinkhütten A. G.

Eleven firms, just half the total, but representing a great deal
more than half the Upper Silesian productive capacity, found
themselves divided: mines from coke ovens and furnaces,
rolling and finishing mills from steelworks and steelworks
from blast furnaces.
The divided works were:

> Staatliche Bergwerksdirektion
> Gräfl. Schaffgotsch'sche Werke
> Gräfl. von Ballestrem'sche Verwaltung
> Oberschlesische Eisenbahnbedarfs, A. G.
>   (Oberbedarf)
> Oberschlesische Eisenindustrie A. G. für Bera-
>   bau und Hüttenbetrieb (Obereisen)
> Kattowitzer A. G. für Bergbau und Eisenhütten-
>   betrieb
> Bergwerksgesellschaft Georg von Giesche's
>   Erben
> Schlesische A. G. für Bergbau und Zinkhütten-
>   betrieb
> Hohenlohewerke A. G.
> Graf Henckel von Donnersmarck-Beuthen
> Staatlichle Hüttenamt Friedrichsgrube

Extreme cases of division, almost paralyzing the work
of the companies, were the partitions of the Oberbedarfs and
Obereisen concerns. The former was left with its chief smelting works, the Friedenshütte, and its coal mines in Poland,
and a good deal of its refining and finishing works, chiefly in
Gliwice and Zawadzki, on the other side of the boundary. The
latter was divided by the new boundary into two more comparable

units, with the Julienhütte blast furnace and steelworks and
the finishing works at Łabędy and Gliwice in Germany and the
Baildon smelting and steelworks in Poland.
   This dismemberment of industrial units, which had been
pieced together during the previous half century and had grown
slowly into functional units, appeared to be a greater tragedy
than in fact it was. It nevertheless afforded material in abundance for German irredentist propaganda. The Oberschlesien-
Atlas,[2] a elegant but tendentious regional atlas of Upper Silesia, showed in a series of maps the ways in which the former
German-owned companies were broken up. But, in fact, the
severed fragments of industrial firms in time merged into
new and to outward appearance no less effective units.
   The following table illustrates how, on the basis of 1920
figures of production and output, the industrial resources of
Upper Silesia were divided between the two countries:

	West (German) Upper Silesia			East (Polish) Upper Silesia		
	Number of mines or works	Output(tons)	Per-cen-tage	Number of mines or works	Output(tons)	Per-cen-tage
Coal	14	7,859,074	24.8	53	23,861,794	75.2
Coke ovens	9	1,281,637	51.5	9	1,206,015	48.5
Coal briket-ting plants	1	124,603	42.9	3	165,415	57.1
Iron smelting works	3	191,923	33.4	5	383,879	66.6
Steelworks	3	404,977	33.4	7	808,247	66.6
Rolling mills	4	134,112	16.4	8	683,511	83.6
Iron and steel foundries	12	30,133	33.1	13	60,790	66.9
Other iron and steel finish-ing works	26	119,892	50.3	27	118,456	49.7
Zinc ore	5	44,708	15.5	10	243,651	84.5

   In addition to its industrial plant, Poland acquired all the iron
and lead mines in the area, and all of the lead and zinc smelting capacity.
   The partitioned companies faced the problems — technical
and commercial — in a variety of ways. The Henckel von Donnersmarck company, concerned primarily in zinc mining and

smelting, was registered as an English company, "The Henckel von Donnersmarck Estates, Ltd., London," and continued to operate its holdings in both countries. The Georg von Gliesche's Erben, a larger and more complex company, maintained its chief office in Germany, but established the Giesche Społka Akzyjna as a Polish subsidiary. In other instances, also, the smaller portion of the concern became a subsidiary of the larger on the other side of the boundary.[3]

But on each side of the new boundary new combinations were gradually built up between the truncated fragments. In Polish Upper Silesia a cluster of firms, which had emerged from the disruption of Obereisen and Oberbedarf, merged with the Kattowitzer A. G. to form the Neue Kattowitzer A. G. On the German side of the boundary, the remnants of the same two companies fused to make the Vereinigte Oberschlesische Huttenwerke A. G.

More serious, in the long run, was the cutting off of Polish Silesia from German sources of investment capital. We have seen already how heavily dependent these firms had been on German banks. The new Poland was quite unable to fulfill this role,[4] and the Polish companies and even, to some extent, the German became dependent on foreign capital.

French capital was the most important. It not only played an important role in the reorganization of Upper Silesian industry, but was used to finance the railways that were necessary to link the industrial area with the rest of the Polish state and with its new Baltic port of Gdynia. There was a considerable foreign investment also in various municipal undertakings, including the construction of tramways.[5] The Polish portion of the Prussian state-owned coal mines became the Skarboferm, with a heavy French capital investment.

Second in importance to French capital was American. The Silesian American Corporation was created in 1926 by the banker W. W. Harriman as a holding company. Its major investments were in von Gliesche's Erben, but it had considerable investments also in iron and steel both in Germany and in Poland.

A number of industrial firms in Polish Upper Silesia remained under direct German ownership and control. The Poles accused the Germans—and not without reason—of favoring the

plants remaining on German soils both in orders and investment.[6]

The Genéva Convention had provided for the unrestricted
movement of raw and part-finished materials across the boundary for a number of years. It was intended however that this
period should be used in each country to prepare for the full
rigors of national competition. There was a degree of rationalization in individual works. Some units were closed, and
fresh mines were dug and smelters built to round off the possessions of a company. Thus far the problems faced by the
two parts of Upper Silesia were similar, and were faced in
broadly similar ways. But each had also its peculiar problems
which could be faced only in the context of its own national setting.

GERMAN UPPER SILESIA

The division of Upper Silesia undoubtedly dealt more
harshly with that part which remained in Germany than with
what passed to Poland. Firms which were left entirely on the
German side of the boundary were relatively small, and Ober-
koks, one of the strongest of them, was dependent on coal
from the other side.

Coal Mining: Germany retained only fourteen coal' mines,
with less than 25 per cent of the former productive capacity of
the region. The Radzionków mines was actually intersected
by the boundary, and a fresh mine, the Beuthen Mine, was developed from a shaft which had been left in German territory.[7]
Only 8 per cent of the German share of the coal reserves was
of coking quality, and it seemed likely that German Upper Silesia would remain dependent on Polish for a large part of its
metallurgical coke. A single coal bricketting plant, at Zaborze,
was left in Germany, but in 1924 another was built at the Ho-
henzollern (Szombierki) mine.

It had been assumed that Germany, and West Upper Silesia in particular, would be obliged to import coal in considerable quantity from East, or Polish Upper Silesia. Provision
had been made for this in the Geneva Convention, and, indeed,
Poland's commercial policy was based upon the assumption
that there would be a continuing demand in eastern Germany

for Polish coal. But such expectations proved ill-founded.
Coal production was so stimulated in West Upper Silesian that
Germany terminated her coal imports from Poland at the earliest date permitted by the Geneva Convention.
The area of the coalfield that remained in Germany produced in 1920 less than eight million tons of coal. In 1923,
the first complete year after the partition, output was about
8.75 million tons. Thereafter a policy of rationalization and
modernization achieved an unusually rapid expansion of output.
In 1925 output was over 14 million tons and in 1929, it reached
almost 22 million. The recession in West Upper Silesia was
less marked than in the Polish and Czechoslovak sections of
the coalfield, and by 1938, production had recovered, and
reached over 28 million tons.

This quite remarkable achievement in West Upper Silesia resulted mainly from a greatly increased output by each
miner, and this in turn was made possible by the introduction
on a large scale of mechanical picks, coal cutters and coal
conveyors.[8] The seams were of course, suited to mechanical
mining; they were thick, level and little disturbed. Very few
of these seams however were of coking quality. In fact coal
from the Lower Silesian mines was generally used in the Upper Silesian coke-ovens.[9] Upper Silesian coal, on the other
hand, yielded a high percentage of fine coal. Bricketting was
relatively important, and the capacity of bricketting plants was
greatly increased.

Upper Silesian coal made a good domestic and boiler fuel.
It also served well as a gas coal. It served most of the fuel
needs of eastern Germany, and its area of distribution was
similar to that of the pre-war years, except of course, that
West Upper Silesia no longer supplied the areas that had
passed to Poland.

The Iron and Steel Industry: Germany retained a rather
larger proportion of the iron-smelting and steel-making industries than of coal mining, and although she was left somewhat
short of rolling mill capacity, she had a similar proportion of
finishing works. But taken by and large they were an ill-as-
sorted bunch of small units. Three blast furnace works with
together 15 furnaces that could not turn out more than 200,000

tons of pig-iron in a year were certainly neither modern nor efficient. West Upper Silesia was in fact ill-placed to continue production of iron and steel. None of the few, small iron mines of Upper Silesia was left in Germany; local supplies of coking coal were inadequate, and the chief advantages which the region possessed lay in its body of skilled labor and technicians. Much of the plant was obsolescent. West Upper Silesia was thus a high-cost producer, and the price of its steel goods, category for category, was a little above that of the products of the Ruhr. Its market was restricted to eastern Germany, where it was insulated to some extent by distance, and to Central Europe. Even in Silesia it was fighting a losing battle against the competition of the Ruhr and Rhineland.[10]

The iron-smelting industry was indeed expanded in the first years after the partition, but output failed to increase significantly during the boom years of the 1920's. It sank to negligible proportions during the depression and, even under the stimulus of Nazi rearmament did not regain the level of its peak years in the early 1920's. Just after the First World War, Upper Silesian industry had attracted investment from West German industrialists. But developments after about 1924 seem to reflect a certain disillusion. The older smelting works, such as the Borsigwerk and the Gliwice and Donnersmarck works were first closed and then dismantled. Indeed, the Julienhütte at Bobrek alone remained significant.

Steel-making and the manufacture of rolled and foundry goods did not altogether share the decline which characterized smelting. There was no spectacular expansion, but the position was at least maintained and in favorable years improved. The shortage of steel rolling capacity in West Upper Silesia was to some degree remedied when the Zawadzki works were re-equipped in 1922-3. Plans to establish yet another rolling works resulted in the complete rebuilding of the Herminenhütte at Łabędy,[11] and the replacement of the Julienhütte by a new, integrated works was anticipated by the outbreak of the Second World War.

The unevenly matched development of iron-smelting and steel-making is explained by the great importance assumed by

the open-hearth. West Upper Silesia retained a single puddling
works, which was closed soon after the partition, and the manufacture of converter steel (either Bessemer or Thomas) was
given up in favor of open-hearth. The open-hearth process
had the unique advantage that it permitted the use of scrap metal in almost unlimited quantities. In fact, in West Upper Silesia, pig-iron was little more than a supplement to scrap metal
in the steelworks. It was this fact, that an average no more
than a third of the steel processed actually represented pig-
iron derived directly from the blast furnace, that prevented
the diseconomies of site from being prohibitive in the iron and
steel industry.

The supply of steel scrap was of greater significance than
that of iron ore. But a country, such as Germany, with a long
established industry and a high rate of replacement of equipment, was not generally short of scrap metal. But the industrial area of Upper Silesia, unlike the Ruhr, was able to supply only a very small part of its requirements of scrap; the
rest came from the interior of the country, though at a fairly
high cost in freight.[12]

Certain changes were necessarily effected in the supply
of iron ore. None came now from the diminished resources
of the Triassic beds of Upper Silesia, and the scanty reserves
of coal-measures ore lay almost wholly on the Polish side of
the boundary.[13] In general, about a third of the ore used was
from Sweden, imported through the Baltic port of Szczecin
and brought, either by rail or by river and canal barge to the
industrial area. Domestic German ore played only a small
part. It came from mines in Lower Saxony and Bavaria, and
two of the West Upper Silesian iron works (the Donnersmarck
and Julien works) actually bought iron deposits in these areas.

The problem of transport costs was, however, dominant.
The German railways permitted iron ore to be carried at preferential rates, but this did not suffice to offset the immense
advantage conferred on the Ruhr, Silesia's chief rival, by the
facility of cheap, water transport. The river Odra had indeed
been made navigable, under normal weather conditions, for
medium-sized barges, but the Kłodnicki Canal, which joined
the industrial area with the Odra river-port of Koźle remained
as it had been left after the improvements made in the 1880's.

In the 1920's the traffic on the canal was only a minute fraction
of that carried on the Odra itself. Clearly the advantages of
water-transport could be achieved only if barges could be
brought right into Gliwice itself. The completion of the Adolf
Hitler Canal, now the Gliwicki Canal, in 1939 along the route of
the old Kłodnicki Canal was designed to achieve this end. Indeed, the Germans envisaged a veritable network of canals
linking the Odra with the Vistula, Danube and Upper Elbe.[14]
The completion of such a project would certainly have lowered
the costs and widened the market for the industries of Upper
Silesia. The Second World War came before the consequences
had become fully apparent of the opening of the new canal, but
there were indications before 1939 that industries might be re-
located and revived along the banks of the new waterway.[15]

POLISH UPPER SILESIA

The Polish sector of the industrial area was made up of
three separate and distinctive areas, which never during the
years between the two wars, entirely merged their individuality.
The Dąbrowa area (see pages 122) was from the historical
point of view the nucleus of this group of territories because it
alone had been part of the "Congress" Kingdom of Poland. To
the southeast of it lay the territories, West Galicia and Cieszyn,
taken from the former Austro-Hungarian Empire. To the west
lay Upper Silesia proper, that part of former German Silesia
which was allotted to Poland at the Partition.

The former Austrian territories were the least developed
and were the more easily integrated into the new State. The
differences between East, or Polish Upper Silesia and Dąbrowa
were more serious. The boundary separating them had formerly been one of the least easily surmounted in Europe. On
one side of it lay the larger and more efficient part of the Upper Silesian industry. On the other had grown up the iron industry of Russian Poland, small-scale, relatively inefficient and
heavily dependent on imported materials. Such an industrial
area would inevitably face severe competition as soon as its
protective tariff barrier was broken down.

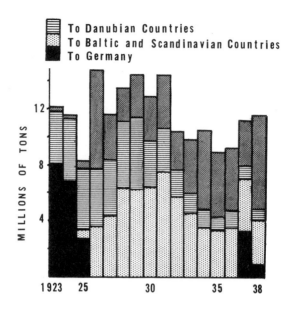

Figure 43: The export of coal from Poland, 1923-1939.

In the field of coal-mining rivalry between the several sectors was yet more intense, because throughout the inter-war years the productive capacity of Polish mines greatly exceeded effective demand. Of the major industries of the region, only the mining and smelting of lead and zinc raised no insuperable problems, chiefly because the industry was small and demand remained consistently high.

The Coal Industry: To her extensive reserves in Dąbrowa and Galicia[16] Poland added about three-quarters of the productive capacity of Upper Silesia. She now had mines and equipment capable of producing some 33 million tons of coal a year; her problem was to dispose of this quantity of fuel. The Geneva Convention guaranteed a market in Germany for half a million tons monthly for three years. The rest of Poland's export

was to the Danubian countries. Figure 48, which illustrates
the direction and volume of this trade, shows how important
to Poland was this guaranteed market. But it held for only
three years, after which Germany was at liberty to exclude
Polish coal.[17] This, in June 1925, Germany did not hesitate
to do. The blow was a serious one for Poland, and might have
been disastrous for her economy but for the British General
Strike of the following year. British competition in North
European markets had been very severe,[18] and the sudden
disappearance of British coal gave Poland a large and ready-
made market.

The Scandinavian and Baltic countries had been important
purchasers of British coal.[19] Henceforward they became the
chief foreign market for Polish coal, and the market which
Great Britain lost she never wholly regained. By 1930, the
Scandinavian and Baltic countries were taking almost a half
of Poland's export of coal, and this proportion was maintained
until 1937, when Germany again took a significant fraction of
Poland's export.

This new orientation in Poland's coal trade necessitated
the building of fresh means of transport. In the past some Upper Silesian coal had moved down the river Odra to the port
of Szczecin. This was now clearly impossible, and the river
Vistula offered no satisfactory alternative. The coal therefore had to be taken to the Polish Baltic Sea ports by rail.

The pre-war railway connections between German and
Russian territory had been scanty in the extreme, and now that
the line of this boundary lay entirely within Poland, it constituted a serious barrier to movement. Additions were made
to the former German and Russian railway systems in order
to permit a more intensive movement between East Upper Silesia and the rest of Poland. A new railway line was laid down,
from Katowice, through Bydgoszcz to the Baltic coast, but
was not opened for through traffic until 1931.[20]

The port of Gdańsk (Danzig) was quite inadequate for the
Polish coal trade, and the newly built port of Gdynia, equipped
for such bulky cargoes, handled almost the whole of Polish
coal exports to northern Europe.

The development of this export trade was costly to Poland
in more ways than one. The railway and docks developments,

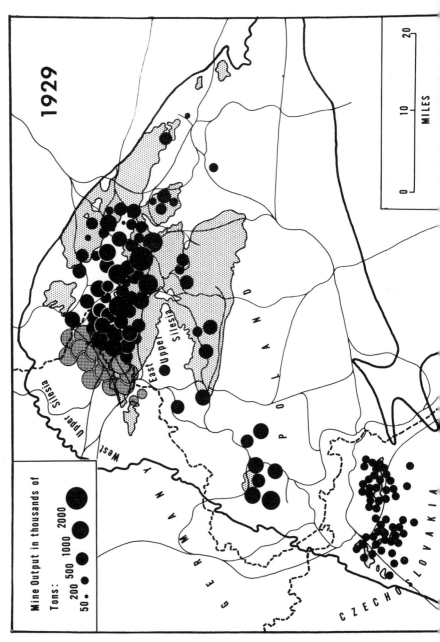

Figure 44: Coal mines and coal output from the Upper
Silesian-Moravian coal basin, in 1929.

though financed in part with French capital, represented nevertheless a substantial drain on the Polish national income. The
coal export was also heavily subsidized by highly preferential
freight rates on the State Railways, and miners' wages were
lowered to enable Poland to undersell her rivals.[21] It was no
doubt highly irritating to fuel consumers in Warsaw to pay
more for their coal than Swedes in Stockholm were paying for
coke from the same mines. But the alternative was unem-
ployment in the mining areas and a dangerous loss of foreign
exchange. The subsidized coal export therefore continued
throughout the years between the two wars.[22]

Foreign sales absorbed in favorable years up to half the
total production. North European and Danubian countries absorbed most of this, with these two major regions taking generally approximately equal quantities. Sales from the Czechoslovak sector of the coalfield were much smaller, but these
contained—as Polish sales did not—a considerable proportion
of coking coal. The total quantity of coal exported from the
Moravian mines was very much smaller than that from the Polish and, furthermore, was incapable of any considerable expansion.

In 1930, a commercial agreement with Germany allowed
Poland to regain something of her German market, particularly
desirable in view of the sharp decline in sales to northern Europe.

In the face of overproduction throughout the interwar
years, the rivalry between the Dąbrowa and East Upper Silesia
sectors of the coalfield threatened to become acute. Dąbrowa
had long supplied coal to Congress Poland, protected in its
market by the Russian import duty on fuel. But after 1922,
Dąbrowa coal, obtained from relatively small and inefficient
mines, was faced with the powerful competition of coal won
from larger and more economic pits on the other side of the
Przemsza river. The identity of the two groups of mines and
mining companies had each been cemented by sales organiza-
tions, and these two groups were prepared in 1922 to fight for
mastery in the Polish market with whatever resources were
available. Fortunately such competition was avoided by an
agreement, reached in 1925, to share the market, both national

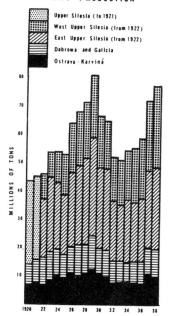

Figure 45: Coal production the Upper
Silesian-Moravian coal basin, 1920-1938.

and foreign, in the proportions of approximately three for East Upper Silesia and one for Dąbrowa and Galicia.[23]

The rationalization and modernization of coal mining was more necessary in the Polish sector of the coalfield, so greatly at the mercy of the world price of coal, than in any other. A number—about a dozen—of the less effective mines was closed.[24] There was a sharp drop in the number of miners employed, but a great increase in the output of coal per miner. Mechanical picks and coal cutters were widely adopted, together with mechanized underground transport of coal by rail, cable and conveyor-belt.[25]

In the very thick seams of Upper Silesia a "pillar-and-stall" method of mining had been widely adopted. Pillars of coal were left to support the roof of the working as mining advanced. Such pillars could not be allowed to remain when mechanical methods of underground haulage were introduced, and a "longwall" method of mining was adopted.[26] As the extraction of coal advanced through the seam the roof was allowed to collapse behind the workings. In seams of only moderate thickness enough waste was obtained in the course of coal-cutting to stow away behind the working face, and thus diminish the extent of roof collapse. But in the thickest Silesian seams it was not necessary to cut away anything but coal. There was thus nothing to cushion the collapse of the roof just when the extent of that collapse was greatest. In Upper Silesia mines were relatively shallow, and extensive collapsing of the roof was disastrous for occupations carried on the land surface above the mines. A partial solution was found in passing down into the mines, usually in water and through iron pipes, large quantities of sand and gravel.

There was some geographical extension of coal-mining during the years between the wars. Mines had already been opened in the so-called "Central Region" of Rybnik and Pszczyna.[27] This area had vast reserves of coal; seams were level and thick, but lay deeper beneath the surface than in the older established mining area. Production from this area was greatly increased.[28] But the recruitment of mine labor was made difficult by the sparse settlement of the region as a whole, and the building of miners' "colonies" was more important here than elsewhere.[29]

One of the obstacles to the growth of the iron and steel industry in Polish Silesia was the shortage of coal of coking quality. Its use necessitated a low blast furnace, so that furnace output was smaller in Upper Silesia than in almost every other European industrial center.[30] Attempts were being made throughout the interwar years to improve the quality of Polish coke, but the region remained heavily dependent on coke and coking coal imported from Czechoslovakia and Germany.[31]

Whereas in West Upper Silesia there was a steady increase in coal production, output in Poland was very much more erratic. Being more dependent on exports, it suffered more severely than the German during the Depression. Its advances during the 1930's were only temporary, and production at the end of the inter-war period was in fact less than at the beginning.

The Dąbrowa and Galician regions shared in the fortunes of East Upper Silesia. Indeed, any expansion of output from one at the expense of another was precluded by the All-Polish Coal Convention.[32] Mines in these divisions of the coalfield were somewhat smaller than those in Upper Silesia proper, and there was a greater number of very small, shallow mines, worked by addit or open pit.

The <u>Iron</u> and <u>Steel</u> <u>Industry</u>: The iron and steel industry suffered from the same kinds of problem as those which afflicted West Upper Silesia. In Poland, however, they were eased to some extent by the rather larger scale of the industry and by the fact that it was protected by the government and had a near monopoly in the domestic market.

After the partition of Upper Silesia Poland found herself in possession of several small and rather old works in the Dąbrowa district and of firms or parts of firms in East Upper Silesia. The Dąbrowa industries had been damaged severely during the war; factories had been brought almost to a standstill by lack of materials, and their revival was slow.[34] Coke, iron-ore and steel scrap had all to a greater or lesser degree to be imported. The Huta Bankowa, oldest of the Dąbrowa ironworks, was brought back into production, together with a number of small steelworks, tube-mills, foundries and enamel works in Sosnowiec, Sielce and Milowice.[35]

By 1918, iron-working had ceased in West Galicia and also

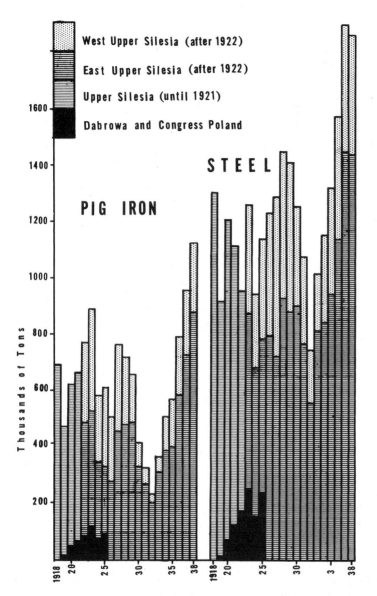

Figure 46: Production of pig-iron and steel in the Upper Silesia-Dąbrowa industrial region. Figures for Dąbrowa are included with those of East Upper Silesia after 1925.

in that part of Cieszyn which went to Poland. It was not until September 1938, when Poland annexed the rest of the Cieszyn territory, that she got possession of the Třinec (Trzyniec) works. For most of the interwar years these works lay in Czechoslovakia and are discussed below.

In East Upper Silesia itself an extensive re-organization was necessary of the splintered firms to which Poland had succeeded. Four out of the seventeen major concerns, which emerged from the partition, were joined to make the Kattowitzer A. G. fur Bergbau und Eisenhüttenbetrieb.[36] This became a large, integrated concern. It controlled about a sixth of the coal mining capacity of East Upper Silesia and between a half and two-thirds of the smelting and steel-making capacity, together with coke-ovens adequate to supply its own needs. There was extensive re-organization within the newly constituted company; several coal mines were closed and the blast-furnaces of the old Hubertushütte were dismantled.[37]

The Friedenshütte A. G., which derived from the former Oberbedarf, merged with Baildonhütte A. G., a splinter from the old Obereisen, to form the second largest iron and steel concern, the Friedenshütte A. G. The only other works of importance was the A. G. Ferrum, formerly a part of Obereisen. It was a steel-making and finishing works, and after a somewhat precarious existence for a number of years, it formed a close association with an engineering and construction works in Kraków.

This reconstruction of the iron and steel companies in East Upper Silesia was accompanied by a considerable investment of outside capital. Shortly after the end of the war Friedrich Flick, the West German iron and steel magnate, invested heavily in the Bismarckhütte A. G. and the Kattowitzer A. G. When, in 1922, the assets of these two companies passed under Polish control, he sold his holdings. These were henceforward held by a Dutch company, but, on his own evidence, Flick maintained, though indirectly, his interest in the Polish companies.[38] Not without reason, contemporary Polish writers represent Upper Silesian industry at this time as controlled by Flick and Harriman.[39]

Shortly after the partition of Upper Silesia, Harriman formed corporations which invested in Upper Silesian industry.

It has been claimed that American interests were really quite
small, and that they served rather as a camouflage for the
Germans, who really owned the stock.[40] This is probably so
with regard to coal, iron and steel, though American holdings
in the Silesian zinc industry (see page 185) were not inconsiderable. French capital, so conspicuous in transport and municipal developments, was relatively unimportant in iron and
steel in East Upper Silesia.[41] In the Dąbrowa region, on the
other hand, where French investment had been considerable
before the war, it continued to be important.

We have already seen what problems confronted the iron
and steel industries of West Upper Silesia. The industry of
East Upper Silesia was no better placed in these respects.[42]
Coking coal was in short supply at first and had to be supplemented by imports from Czechoslovakia. Methods of coking
were, however, improved, and the local production of coke
came to be adequate for local needs. On the other hand,
local production of iron-ore had long been insufficient, and
during the 1920's, the Upper Silesian deposits were for practical purposes, exhausted.[43] Although Poland at large was by
no means rich in iron-ores, there were substantial deposits
in the Jurassic beds near Częstochowa and in the Kielce district.[44] Import duties were imposed on low-grade foreign ores
in an attempt to increase the use in Upper Silesia of domestic
ores.[45] But most Polish ores had a high phosphorus content,
and this greatly limited their usefulness.[46] The duties, imposed after 1926 on imported ores of less than 50 per cent
metal, focussed attention on sources of high-grade ore, such
as the Ukraine and Sweden. It also emphasized the need to
make the most of such domestic sources of iron as slag, scale
and pyrites. In 1926, the blast furnace charge in East Upper
Silesia consisted of[47]:

Polish ore	115,485 tons	23%
Imported ore	192,810 "	37
Imported manganiferous ore	39,939 "	7
Pyrites, scale, slag	171,386 "	33
	516,620 tons	100%

Such remained very approximately the relative importance of
the different sources of iron-ore until 1939.[48]

As in West Upper Silesia, the production of steel greatly
exceeded that of pig-iron, and the difference roughly represented the consumption of iron and steel scrap. Germany,
with a long established manufacturing industry, was able to
produce most of the iron and steel scrap needed by her steel
industries. In Poland, on the other hand, both the rate and
the volume of obsolescence of iron and steel plant were slower.
In the more prosperous years, about three-quarters of the
scrap used in the open-hearth furnaces was imported. In
1928, over half a million tons of scrap was imported, and the
traffic was benefitted by a preferential freight rate from the
Baltic ports to the industrial area.[49]

The obligation to use as much local ore as possible,
coupled with the shortage of scrap, imposed a particular pattern on the steel industry. The open-hearth furnace was relatively less important than in West Upper Silesia, and the
basic, or Thomas, converter, more so. The result was that
Polish steel was, on balance, of a somewhat lower quality
than the German, and served a more restricted range of uses.

From 1924 the Polish iron and steel industry was united
into a single cartel,[50] which fixed prices and determined production quotas. This cartel extended to the industries of the
Dąbrowa district as well as to those of other parts of Poland.

The production of both pig-iron and of crude steel were
expanded during the later 1920's, as works were amalgamated
and re-equipped with the aid of foreign capital. Steel production reached a peak in 1928. The drop in production during
the following years was proportionately less than in West Upper Silesia. Recovery from the depression was also more
rapid and by 1937 the output of steel was again over 900,000.

The considerable political importance which the iron and
steel region of Upper Silesia has attained must not lead us to
suppose that its economic significance was equally great. The
whole of Silesia was really only a minor producer. The loss
of East Upper Silesia in 1922 made a difference of only about
7 per cent to the German steel-producing capacity, and its importance was small compared with that of the formerly German area of Lorraine, or even of the Saar. There had been

no effective expansion in the industry as a whole since the beginning of the century, and if the total output of pig-iron and
steel on the eve of the Second World War approached that of
about 1900, it was only because a small expansion of the industry in East Upper Silesia had compensated for a contraction
in West. As a proportion of the total German production of
iron and steel, the Upper Silesian output had been in continuous
decline since the middle years of the 19th century. And this
trend was continued in West Upper Silesia after the Partition.
It was checked in East Upper Silesia only by the policy of the
Polish government. Considerations which have already been
examined: high cost of coke and high freight charges on iron-
ore, made Upper Silesia a comparatively expensive producer.
Yet its abundance of fuel, other than coking coal, gave it certain advantages. It might have been thought that its destiny
was to become a center for fabricating iron and steel goods
and for the construction of tools and machines needed in the
Central European market. Crude iron and steel, meanwhile,
would be produced in the Ruhr or on the ore-field of Lower
Saxony, where costs of production were lower. Indeed this
trend was apparent in West Upper Silesia during the period
between the wars. There was a contraction in the smelting
industry, but an expansion of the steel-making and finishing
branches. New capital in West Upper Silesia went into the
finishing branches; in East Upper Silesia a more even balance
was maintained between the smelting, steel-making and finishing branches of the industry.

NORTHERN MORAVIA

The Coal Industry: After the division of the Cieszyn territory, the Czechoslovak republic found itself in possession of
about 18 per cent of the area of the whole coalfield and of some
5 per cent of its reserves.[51] Most of the Czechoslovak sector
of the coalfield was hidden by varying thicknesses of Secondary
and Tertiary beds, and the coal beds outcropped only over very
small areas near Moravska Ostrava, Karvinná and Hlucin.
Mining is carried on only in the vicinity of these outcrops.
Over three hundred coal seams have been enumerated,

but they nowhere attain the great thicknesses found near the northern edge of the coal-basin.[52] Mining was to some extent mechanized, but was somewhat more expensive than in the Polish sector. The mines furthermore contained gas, and this in turn imposed restrictions that were unknown in the north of the coal-basin. On the other hand, the coking coals from this corner of the coal basin were superior and also more abundant than those of any other part. Whereas Ostrava–Karvinná coal in general lost ground in the Central European market before the powerful Polish drive of the 1920's, its coking coal gained, and was in demand even in Polish Silesia.

There were between 35 and 40 mines in northern Moravia and in that part of Cieszyn which went to Czechoslovakia. They were grouped in three small areas: to the west of Ostrava, between Ostrava and Karvinná, and south of Karvinná. With the exception of a single state-owned undertaking, they were owned and operated by eight companies. Two of these— the Báňská a Hutní Společnost and the Vítkovické Horni a Hutní Řěžířtvo—were also producers or iron and steel. They were also the largest coal mining concerns, with 16 pits, over half the total coal production and two thirds of the coke.

Coal production was restricted in the years following the war by lack of labor and equipment.[53] It then expanded to a level of between ten and eleven million tons a year, which was maintained until the Depression. Output fell to less than eight million tons, and did not recover until 1937.

Ostrava-Karvinná accounted for about three-quarters of the total production of Czechoslovakia, and for almost all its output of coking coal. During the period between the wars, the coke ovens at Ostrava and Karvinná supplied blast-furnaces in Bohemia with fuel. There was an export to Austria, which could produce none from her domestic coal reserves, and small quantities were sent to Hungary, and Poland. But the export market was sluggish. Demand did not increase appreciably, and competition from the subsidized Polish exports was severe in the Danubian countries. Czechoslovakia improved her export position somewhat as a result of the French occupation of the Ruhr in 1923 and the resulting diminution of German coal exports, but her market continued to be mainly that provided by her own homes and industries.

Iron and Steel Industry: We saw in chapter seven that
during the 19th century there were many small iron-works in
northern Moravia and in the Austrian held parts of the ancient
Silesian duchy. But gradually the smaller and more remotely
placed works were closed or converted into workshops for
fabricating iron goods. When the boundaries of Czechoslovakia and Poland were finally drawn, only four iron and steel
works remained in this area. Two of these—at Vítkovice and
Třinec—were large, modern undertakings. At Bohumin was
a small blast-furnace works, closed a few years later, and
the fourth was a small smelting and refining works at Węgierska Górka.[54]
     Largest of the iron and steel works were those of Vítko-
vice.[55] At the end of the war the works consisted of two blast-
furnaces with up-to-date steel and rolling mills. The company, the Vítkovické Horni a Hutni Řěžířtvo, owned eight coal
mines; it had coke-ovens both at the mines and at the iron-
works, and also possessed iron-ore deposits at Koskullkulla,
in northern Sweden, as well as in Slovakia and Hungary.[56]
The works continued to be, not only by far the largest, but also one of the most efficient in Central Europe. Its output, at
least of pig-iron, was generally higher than that of all the
works in East Upper Silesia.
     The second largest works both in Czechoslovakia and in
Central Europe was the Třinec plant of the Báňská a Hutni
Společnost of Prague, a company formed in 1906 from assets
previously owned by the Archduke Frederick of Hapsburg.[57]
The Třinec works lay close to the river Olza, in the Cieszyn
territory. Their growth resulted from the concentration here
of the operations of several scattered furnaces and refineries.[58]
The Třinec company, like that of Vítkowice, controlled a number of coal-mines; possessed iron-ore mines in Slovakia, and
coke-ovens both at the mines and at Třinec. In addition to its
blast-furnaces and steel works, the company possessed a rolling mill and steel construction works in Karlova Huta, a wire-
drawing mill at Bohumin and a chain works at Mala Moravka,
all of which were supplied with crude metal from the Třinec
works. The capacity of the Třinec works was expanded from
about 140,000 tons of pig-iron in 1922 to 475,000 in 1929.
     It is difficult to isolate the statistics of iron and steel

production for the Moravian and Silesian districts of Czecho-slovakia.[59] In general it formed about two-thirds of the Czecho-slovak pig-iron production and a somewhat lower proportion of the steel. In 1929, a peak year, it amounted to about 1,195,000 tons of pig-iron and 1,300,000 tons of crude steel. Steel-making and steel-using firms in other parts of Czecho-slovakia were regularly supplied with pig-iron and ingot steel from the works in this area. Steel production, both here and elsewhere in Czechoslovakia, was overwhelmingly by means of the open-hearth, although the supply of scrap from domestic sources was altogether inadequate. Like Poland, Czechoslo-vakia was obliged to rely heavily on imported materials.

Although iron-ore mines were practically exhausted in northern Moravia, Czechoslovakia as a whole was better en-dowed than Poland. There were still deposits of importance in Bohemia as well as in Slovakia. The Bohemian ores, how-ever, were used in the furnaces near Plzen and Kladno, and the Ostrava-Karvinná area had to rely mainly on Slovakian and imported ores. The latter were mainly from Sweden and South Russia. The Swedish ores were commonly brought by barge up the river Odra to the frontier port of Bohumin, but freight charges on ore were, as in Upper Silesia, very high. The Czechoslovak sector of the coalfield possessed, however, adequate reserves of coking coal, an advantage denied to both West and East Upper Silesia.

LEAD AND ZINC INDUSTRIES OF UPPER SILESIA

The line of partition in Upper Silesia did greater violence to the lead and zinc industries than to any other. While it left ten mines in East Upper Silesia and five in West, a not inequit-able division, it gave to Poland all the zinc roasting and smelt-ing furnaces, both the lead smelters and the single lead roll-ing mill. All that West Upper Silesia retained to help it to handle the ore from its five mines was three zinc rolling-mills.[60] We saw in the previous chapter that the Geneva Con-vention provided for the movement of German ore to smelters on Polish territory, and for the return of the metal to Ger-many. Such a solution, however, did not for long recommend itself to the Germans, who set about building the smelters they needed.

Of the six companies which mined, smelted and refined zinc in the pre-war area of Upper Silesia, two went intact to Poland. The remainder, which included the two largest—von Giesche's Erben and the Generaldirektion der Grafen Henckel von Donnersmarck—were divided by the new boundary. Most of these zinc-producing firms had owned also the coal-mines which supplied the fuel needed by the smelters in such generous quantities. In certain cases the smelters were cut off from the source of their coal supply.

Clearly, a reorganization of the zinc industry was no less necessary than that of the iron and steel. On the Polish side of the boundary this was marked by the closing of certain pits, the merging of some of the operating units, and an extensive re-equipment of the industry with foreign capital.

The zinc undertakings in the former Russian Poland represented by and large French capital.[62] After the partition, French and Belgian capital became important also in the companies of East Upper Silesia. It controlled the former Schlesische A. G. für Bergbau und Zinkhüttenbetrieb and was invested in Hohenlohe works as well as in the lead works.[63] At the same time the American company, W. W. Harriman Inc., which already dominated American zinc production, was negotiating for the control of the von Giesche company, largest in the Upper Silesian field.[64] The German government was reluctant to allow it to take over the section of von Giesche then operating in West Upper Silesia, but Harriman virtually bought out the holdings in East Upper Silesia and undertook, in partnership with the German government, to erect a furnace works in Germany, capable of smelting the German ores.

The Silesian Company[65] and von Giesche then commenced a program of modernizing and re-equipping their works. The flotation process was introduced and both companies erected plant for the electrolytic refining of zinc in East Upper Silesia, and the West Upper Silesian branch of von Giesche built a large electrolytic smelter at Magdeburg in Central Germany.[66] In East Upper Silesia, new roasting furnaces were built for the sulphide ores, a modern galvanizing plant

was erected, and several of the old furnaces were closed and
smelting restricted to four large, modern works.[67]

During the previous century, the zinc resources of Upper Silesia had been heavily worked. We have already seen
that reserves of calamine ore had been reduced to small proportions, and that the mines had been obliged to rely more
and more on blende. At the same time the average grade of
the ore obtained was declining.[68] The use of the flotation process made it possible to use ores of lower grade, but at the
same time attention began to be diverted from the long established ore-fields of Bytom and Tarnowskie Góry to those
of the former Russian Poland and of West Galicia, where
mining had been less intensive.[69] The production of zinc ores
from these areas increased steadily in relation to the total
Polish production, and most of the ore was calamine, evidence
of the relative youthfulness of mining here.[70]

Demand for zinc, which had greatly increased during the
war, remained high for several years following. In West Upper Silesia the production of zinc ore remained low on account
of the uncertain political situation. But as the movement of
crude ore to Polish smelters, in accordance with the Geneva
Convention, came to be organized, the output of the mines expanded.[71] By 1930 it had reached a level of more than four
times as high as in 1923. On the Polish side of the boundary
expansion was less rapid, but here too pre-war levels were
soon exceeded, and in 1930 the zinc-mining area produced
more than 50 per cent more ore than in the best pre-war year.

This rapid expansion of output was made possible by the
rationalization of the mines and the increase of smelter capacity. By 1928 the danger became apparent of an overproduction of zinc. In that year the European Zinc Cartel was
formed,[72] embracing all significant European producers. In
1929 it was agreed to curtail production, but the allocation of
quotas aroused discontent, and their enforcement proved to be
almost impossible. In Poland, the sulphuric acid that came
as a by-product of the roasting of zinc ore was in demand,
and helped to balance the low price of the metal itself. In
both countries the working of the silver-lead deposits was intensified owing to the high price of silver, bringing with it an
increased production of zinc ore from the same workings.

The acute overproduction of zinc led to a sharp reduction
of output in the early 1930's. In Poland, ore production fell
to less than a sixth of its 1930 level and in West Upper Silesia it was reduced to little more than a half. Output of refined zinc fell to a smaller extent. The smelting industry of
East Upper Silesia used large quantities of imported ores.
Much of these came from West Upper Silesia, but an increasing proportion were from the New World. The very high fuel
comsumption of the traditional zinc smelter made Upper Silesia a suitable location for the industry. It was clearly more
necessary to run the smelters at capacity during the Depression than to operate the mines to the full. The opportunity was
accordingly taken to run the smelters to an increasing extent
on cheap imported ores.

One of the clearest indications of progress in mining and
smelting technology is the ability of one generation to process
again and with profit the slag-heaps of a previous age. The
waste heaps of the zinc mines and smelters contained a small
percentage of metal. The flotation process, however, allowed
some of them to be re-used, thus restricting the mining
branch of the industry.

The Polish zinc mining and smelting industries recovered
slowly from the Depression, but by 1939 had regained their position of 1930. In West Upper Silesia, mine output recovered
more quickly, and the bringing into production of the new
smelter at Magdeburg greatly increased Germany's capacity.[73]
At the same time it deprived Polish smelters of one of their
chief sources of ore, and brought about the closing of the Hohenlohe smelter.

Before the war only one mine had been developed primarily for lead, the extensive, State-owned Friedrichsgrube.
This was divided by the line of partition. The part remaining
in Germany became a company; that acquired by Poland continued under governmental ownership and control.

A little lead ore was produced inevitably from the zinc
mines, but the metal had previously to be offered for sale to
the State. Von Giesche and Hohenlohe both maintained small
lead-smelters, which, together with the large State-owned
smelter at Szopienice, went to Poland in 1922. Much of the

ore mined in West Upper Silesia was sent to be smelted in
Poland, and the metal was then returned to Germany.

Upper Silesia as a whole constituted only a minor producer of lead ore. Production both of ore and metal declined
in the depression of the early '30's, but the decline in output
was restricted to some extent by the association of lead with
silver, the price of which remained high.[74]

One must beware of exaggerating the scale of both the
zinc and the lead industries. During much of the 19th century Upper Silesia had been the most important single producing area in the world, but during the present century its percentage of the world's zinc output fill from over 30 to less
than 14 per cent. Poland, nevertheless, remained the most
important source of zinc ore in Europe, and, after Belgium,
the biggest producer of the refined metal.

Upper Silesia's contribution to the world's lead supply
had always been much smaller. It declined during the 19th
and early 20th centuries and after the First World War was
rarely more than 2 per cent of the world's total.

Notes

1. Gerhard Wende, "Die Auswirkungen der Grenzziehung
auf die Oberschlesische Montanindustrie," Schriften des Deutschen Ausland-Instituts Stüttgart, Reihe E, Bd. 7, 1932, 3; W.
Volz, and H. Schwelm, Die Deutsche Ostgrenze, Langensalza,
1929; L. de Launay, "Après le Partage," Revue des Deux Mon-
des, XCII, 1922, 416-40.

2. Walter Geisler, Oberschlesien-Atlas, Breslau, 1938.

3. Paul Deutsch, Die oberschlesische Montanindustrie
vor und nach der Teilung des Industriebezirks, Bonn, 1926,
49 et seq.

4. Leopold Wellisz, Foreign Capital in Poland, London,
1938, 42-47.

5. L. Wellisz, op.cit., 59, 64 ff.

6. W. J. Rose, The Drama of Upper Silesia, London, 1936.

7. Hans Otto von Borcke, Die Entwicklung der wirtschaftlichen

und sozialen Verhältnisse in Westoberschlesien nach der Teilung, Berlin, 1937, 55-56.

8. J. Blitek, "Die Entwicklung der Leistungskurve im polnisch Oberschlesien," Z.d.O.B.u.H.V., LXVII, 1928, 154-64.

9. Handbuch der Kohlenwirtschaft, ed. K. Borchardt & K. Bonikowsky, Berlin, 1926, 211-31; Maurice Baumont, La Grosse Industrie Allemande et le Charbon, Paris, 1928, 58-70.

10. Most illuminating figures are quoted by I. Borejdo, "Hutnictwo na Ziemiach Odzyskanych," Ż.G., III, 1948 (Lipiec-Sierpień), 43-47. See also P. H. Seraphim, Deutschlands verlorene Montanwirtschaft, Verwaltung und Wirtschaft, XIV, Stuttgart, 1955, 57-65; "Zur geschichtlichen Entwicklung der oberschlesischen Walzwerkserzeugung," S.u.E., LVIII, 1938, 900-901.

11. C. Netter, "Die geschichtliche Entwicklung der Herminenhütte in Laband," S.u.E., LI, 1931, 1189-1192; 1306-1313.

12. Walter Langner, "Die Verkehrs- und Frachtlage der deutsch-oberschlesischen Eisenindustrie," Archiv für Eisenbahnwesen, LIII, ii, 1930, 1215-1236; 1567-1598; LIV, 1931, 73-118.

13. R. Kreide, "Entwicklung des Hochofenbetriebes in Oberschlesien seit dem Jahre 1913," S.u.E., LII, 1932, 365-67.

14. Hans F. Zeck, Die Deutsche Wirtschaft und Südosteuropa, Leipzig, 1939, 81.

15. "Oberschlesien als Standort einer Eisenschaffenden Industrie," Vierjahresplan V, 1941, 472-76.

16. "Das Galizische Kohlenrevier," M.R., X, 1918, 639.

17. N. Dobis, "Die polnisch-oberschlesische Montanindustrie," Z.d.O.B.u.H.V., LXV, 1926, 30-37; D.O.T., 1925, 7; Józef Popkiewicz and Franciszek Ryszka, "Górnośląski przemysł ciężki w latach 1922-1929," Kwartalnik Historyczny, LXIII, 1956, nr. 4-5, 417-439.

18. Bruno Mynett, "Der Steinkohlenverkehr in Polen," Petermanns Geographische Mitteilungen, LXXXIII, 1937, 171-75; P.G.-H., XVI, 1924, 3232, quoting Przemysł i Handel, 1924, no. 1; D.O.T., 1927, 22.

19. A. Szczepański, "The Export Trade of Upper Silesia," Baltic and Scandinavian Countries, III, 1937, 263-69; D.O.T., 1928, 25.

20. C. Smogorzewski, Poland's Access to the Sea, London, 1934, 385-88; see also H. Bagiński, Poland and the Baltic, London, 1946; François Michel, "Le Charbon silésien et ses débouchés," La Silésie Polonaise, Paris, 1932, 161-74.

21. P.G.-H., XVI, 1924, 391. D.O.T., 1927, 22; 1928, 25.

22. See D.O.T., Reports, passim, published in most years.

23. P.G.-H., XXIII, 1931, 173-75; K. Rasch, Die Teilung Oberschlesiens und ihre Bedeutung für die Kohlen-, Eisen- und Zinkindustrie, Diss., Fried.- Wilhelms Universität, Berlin, 1926, 50-51.

24. "Die Produktionsergebnisse der oberschlesischen Montanindustrie im Jahre 1925," Z.d.O.B.u.H.V., LXV, 1926, 623-26; D.O.T., 1929, 26-27; 1935, 14.

25. J. Blitek, "Die Entwicklung der Leistungskurve im polnisch-oberschlesien," Z.d.O.B.u.H.V., LXVII, 1928, 154-65.

26. W. Budryk, "Le développement de la science et de la technique des minières polonaises au cour des dix années écoulées, R.d.L.M., XIII, 1933, 309-16; 329-36.

27. R. Wachsmann, "Der Steinkohlenbergbau im Rybniker Revier," Z.d.O.B.u.H.V., LXII, 1924, 233-38.

28. P.G.-H., XVI, 1924, 324, quoting Przemysł i Handel, 1924, no. 7.

29. Gerke, "Ueber den Plesser Bergbau und die Boerschachte," Z.d.O.B.u.H.V., LXVIII, 1929, 124-29.

30. W. Meyn, "Die Verbesserung des oberschlesischen Kokses," Z.d.O.B.u.H.V., LXIV, 1925, 472-75.

31. M. Durnerin, "La question du coke en Silésie et en Sarre-Lorraine," R.d. l'I.M., II, 1922, 415-34; 446-60.

32. Ogólno-Polska Konwencja Węglowa.

33. These were regularly listed in P.G.-H.

34. "Die Eisenwerke Polens im Jahr 1917," S.u.E.,
XXXVIII, 1918, 205-6; "Der Wiederaufbau der polnischen
Eisenindustrie," S.u.E., XL, 1920, 562.

35. Pologne 1919-1939, Neuchatel, vol. II, Vie économique, 303 ff; Handbuch von Polen, Berlin, 1918, 430-32; R. Huet,
"L'industrie du fer en Pologne," La Silésie Polonaise, Paris,
1932, 175-95; W. Petrascheck, "Die Grundlagen der Montanindustrie im Königreich Polen," M.R., IX, 1917, 401-4; 425-7;
451-4; 476-8; 506-9.

36. "Die Wirtschaftslage der polnisch-oberschlesischen
Montanindustrie in dem Monaten April, Mai und Juni, 1929,"
Z.d.O.B.u.H.V., LXVIII, 1929, 492-95.

37. G. Behagel, "Der Aufbau der Industrie Oberschlesiens im Wechsel der Zeiten," S.u.E., LX, 1940, 89-100.

38. Trials of War Criminals before the Nürnberg Military Tribunals, Vol. VI, The Flick Case, Washington, 1952,
36-39; 179-85.

39. H. Zieliński, "Stanowisko międzynarodowego Kapitału
finansowego i ośrodków międzynarodowej reakcji oraz burżuazji
Polskiej wobec Śląska w latach 1917-1945," Konferencja Śląska,
Wrocław, 1954, II, 9-120.

40. The Flick Case, 448; F. Ryszka and S. Ziemba, " Dwa
dziesięciolecia Huty 'Kościuszko,'" Kwartalnik Historyczny,
LXI, iii, 1954, 3-75.

41. Leopold Wellisz, Foreign Capital in Poland, London,
1938, 148-52.

42. Wacław Obszewicz, "The Economic Structure of Polish Upper Silesia," Baltic and Scandinavian Countries, III,
1937, 256-62.

43. P.G.-H., XIX, 1927, 394.

44. "Les ressources minières de la Pologne," R.d. l'I.M.,
XIII, 1933, Docts., 61-2; Kurt Flegel, Die wirtschaftliche Be-
deutunge der Montanindustrie Russlands und Polens, Osteuropa
Institut, Breslau, 1920.

45. P.G.-H., XIX, 1927, 394.

46. The relative importance of Polish sources of ore is discussed in Tadeusz Szreter, "Rozwój kopalnictwa rudy żelaza w Polsce Ludowej," W.H., X, 1954, 189.

47. P.G.-H., XIX, no. 21; see also, Z.d.O.B.u.H.V., LXV, 1926, 623-36.

48. O. Pszczolka, "Die Bedeutung der inlandischen Erz-vorkommen für die polnische Eisenindustrie," S.u.E., XLVI, 1936, ii, 1558-1560; C. Kuźniar, "Erzbergbau in Polen: I Geologischer Bau und Vorräte der Erzlagerstätten in Polen," Z.d.O.B.u.H.V., LXVIII, 1929, 460-69, 514-18; "Die Erzfrage in der oberschlesischen Eisenindustrie," Z.d.O.B.u.H.V., LXIII, 1924, 119-22; "Iron Ore in Poland," M.B., no. 2379, 4, April 1939.

49. R. Huet, in La Silésie Polonaise, 183.

50. "Gründung eines polnischen Eisensyndikats," M.R., XVI, 1924, 316.

51. F. Pospíšíl, "Über das Ostrau-Karwiner Steinkohlen-revier," M.R., XIII, 1921, 313-18, 333-37, 353-57.

52. J. Blitek, "Aus dem Mährisch-Ostrauer Bergbau," Z.d.O.B.u.H.V., LXV, 1926, 85-88.

53. E. Fanta, "Fünfzig Jahre tschechoslowakischer Stein-kohlenbergbau," M.R., XVIII, 1926, 38-42.

54. The Iron and Steel Industry in Czechoslovakia, Prague, 1930, 105; M.R., XXXIV, 1942, 176.

55. ibid., 151-194; O. Quadrat, "La situation de l'industrie sidérurgique en Tchécoslovaquie," R.d.M.M., XXXII, 1935, 469-481.

56. "Die neue Stahl- und Walzwerksanlage des Eisen-werkes Witkowitz," M.R., XI, 1919, 156-162, 198-202; 228-232; R. Doderer," Geschichte und Entfaltung der tschechoslowaki-schen Eisenindustrie," M.R., XVIII, 1926, 44-47.

57. The Iron and Steel Industry in Czechoslovakia, 105-150; O. Quadrat, op.cit., G. Behagel, op.cit., 99.

58. W. Bruns, "Kontinuierliches Knüppel- und Platinen-walzwerk der Berg- und Hüttenwerkgesellschaft, Eisenwerk Trinec," S.u.E., LI, 1931; i, 547-554.

59. "Die Eisenwirtschaft der Tschecho-Slowakei unter dem Einfluss der Teschener Gebietsabtretung," S.u.E., LVIII, 1939, 1469-70.

60. Gerhard Wende, op.cit., 15.

61. M.B., April 12, 1929.

62. E. Wunderlich, Handbuch von Polen, 423 ff.

63. Jacques de Beylié du Moulin, "Les industries du zinc et du plomb en Haute Silésie," La Silésie Polonaise, 197-210.

64. A. Marcus, Die grossen Eisen- und Metallkonzerne, Leipzig, 1929, 55-64. A. Skelton, in International Control in the Non-Ferrous Metals, 708-10.

65. Śląskie Kopalnie i Cynkownie, Spółka Akcyjna.

66. Pologne 1919-1939, Neuchâtel, no date, vol. II, Vie Économique, 314-16; G. Hirschfeld, "The Zinc Situation in Germany," American Zinc Institute Bulletin, XI, 1928, 17-18, 43; M.B., April 12, 1929; A. Skelton, op.cit., 720.

67. "If Germany loses Silesia," M.B., no. 2963, Jan. 23, 1945; "Upper Silesian Industries," M.B., no. 2971, Feb. 20, 1945; for short accounts of the separate works, see M.B., no. 2359; no. 2362, Feb. 3, 1939; no. 23, April 6, 1939; no. 2418, Aug. 29, 1939.

68. P.G.-H., XIX, 673-75.

69. W. Kondracki, "O produkcji cynku i ołowiu," Gospodarka Planowa, 1949, 50.

70. L. F. Trenczak, "Die Katastrophe und Wiederaufbau der Mathildegrube bei Chrzanów in Polen," B.u.H.J., LXXXV, 1937, 377-383.

71. "Polish Zinc and Lead Industry in 1925," The Mining Journal, CLV, 1926, 817.

72. A. Skelton, op.cit., 710.

73. "Die Versorgung der deutschen Wirtschaft mit Nicht-Eisen Metallen," Ausschuss zur Untersuchung der Erzeugungs- und Absatzbedingungen der deutschen Wirtschaft, Berlin, 1931; Minerals Yearbook, Washington, D.C., 1935, 120-2.

74. A. Skelton, "Lead," in International Control in the Non-Ferrous Metals, 591 ff.

CHAPTER X

THE EAST EUROPEAN REVOLUTION

"An industrial revolution is taking shape in
Europe behind the Iron Curtain... This half-
enforced and half-spontaneous industrialization of the mid-European area is a major
event in European history. The Communist
system may endure or perish, but what has already been done can hardly be undone: Middle
Europe will not return to its pastoral era."
                                    Jan Wszelaki.

On September 30, 1938, the United Kingdom and France
yielded to the bluster and blackmail of the German Führer,
and allowed Germany to occupy the Sudetenland. By this blow
Czechoslovakia lost most of her industrial areas, but, by a
strange chance retained all her more important iron and steel
works,[1] as well as most of her coal mines.[2] At this time Pol-
land chose to revive her earlier claim to the Duchy of Cieszyn.
The line of partition, drawn in 1920, had given Poland the less
industrialized part. She now demanded the rest, including several valuable coal mines and the Třinec iron and steel works.
Czechoslovakia had no alternative but to accede to this demand.
The rest of Cieszyn passed to Poland without a blow, and Poland had just eleven months in which to digest this morsel before she was in turn invaded by the Germans.

The Třinec works had produced about a quarter of Czechoslovakia's iron and steel output.[3] Formerly this had found a
market in the steel mills and processing works of Czechoslovakia. This outlet was closed, and Poland was faced for
these few months with the task of absorbing about half a million tons of steel. The International Steel Cartel permitted
the Polish steel industry to increase its exports, but left Poland to find her own markets. This presented less difficulty
in 1938 and 1939 than it would have done in previous years.
Several European countries were in the throes of re-armament;
Poland herself had embarked a year or two earlier on an ambitious program of industrial development,[4] and the progress

of the Five Year Plans in the Soviet Union offered a market
for steel goods. Early in 1939 Poland received large orders
for rolled goods and ships plates from Italy and the Soviet
Union.[5] But before all these goods could be delivered, the
German army had crossed the Polish border.

The boundary of the German Reich was extended eastwards to include not only those areas which Germany had lost
after the First World War, but also the whole industrial region. Not only the coal basin of Dąbrowa and West Galicia
but also the iron-ore deposits of Częstochowa and the Duchy
of Cieszyn became a part of Germany.[6] A larger part of the
coal-basin and industrial area was gathered under one particular rule than at any previous time. The rest of this region
lay in the "Protectorate" of Moravia, and was no less subject
to the will and whim of the German ruler.

The population of the Moravian sector was almost entirely
Czech in speech and sympathy. Silesia was more Polish than
German, but even in the sector which had been under Polish
rule between the wars, the German minority had retained its
identity and had abused the freedom which had been accorded
it.[7] The establishment of German rule over the whole area
was followed by a thorough going change in both the composi-
tion of the population and the structure of the industry. The
Jewish communities, particularly large in all the cities, were
removed to the extermination camp, which the Germans had
erected at Oświęcim, amid the forests and swamps along the
Vistula.[8] Institutions of Polish culture were suppressed or
destroyed; the Polish population was either driven from the
area or reduced to a condition of helotry within it.[9]

Polish as well as French and other allied holdings in Polish industry were expropriated. Friedrich Flick came into
his own again, and most of what he did not take was incorpor-
ated into the gigantic Reichswerke, presided over by Goering.[10]
The industry of the whole region, both Silesian and Moravian,
was made to serve the military needs of Germany. Mines
and factories were exploited. Transport facilities broke down
under the strain, and Poland which had formerly possessed
more coal than it could sell, was destitute of fuel. On the
other hand, the remoteness of Upper Silesia from the western

margins of the continent, protected it from the attentions of
Allied bombers.

Upper Silesia and Moravia passed through the war years
almost unscathed. And when, in the winter of 1944-5, the Red
Army advanced into western Poland, the area again escaped
heavy destruction. Katowice was occupied in January, 1945
and the German army was forced to evacuate the industrial
area. That they did not destroy the factories and wreck their
mines is to be attributed only to the speed of the Russian ad-
vance and the vigilance of those Poles who remained in the
area. Among the cities, only Bytom and Gliwice suffered
material damage in the fighting.[11]

Nevertheless, the Poles inherited a scene of destruction
and neglect. If the actual buildings had not been leveled, as
they had in Warsaw or Wrocław, they had suffered from years
of neglect. Power-lines, water-mains and gas-pipes had been
broken; plant had been abandoned for lack of repair and maintenance; mine after mine was flooded, and the roads and railways were strewn with wrecked bridges and viaducts. Over
the open country, where the armies, both Russian and German,
had manoeuvred, farm buildings had been been burned and
farm stock slaughtered or driven away.

The New Political Map: At the Teheran Conference of
1943 the matter of the future boundaries of Poland was raised.
It was decided that Poland should be compensated in the west
for the territory she had already lost to Russia in the east,
and, in rather imprecise terms, the line of the river Odra was
adopted as the future limit of Poland.[12] The proposal was
sharpened at subsequent conferences and the boundary took
shape as the course of the western Nysa and the lower Odra,
with the exception of the Szczecin enclave on the west of the
river, which went to Poland.

In this way the whole of Silesia fell to Poland, excepting
only Cieszyn, where the boundary of 1920 was restored. With
the memory of six years of German oppression and misrule
fresh, the Poles were in no mind to tolerate a German minority
in their midst. The Germans were expelled from the Ziemie
Odzyskanie, the "Recovered Lands," east of the Odra and Nysa.

The theory of the new boundaries and population changes
was that Poles from the "lost" territories in the east should

be settled in the "recovered" lands in the west. Not only was
the Polish population of the eastern lands small, but the Polish population as a whole had suffered immense losses estimated at 12 million, during and after the war.[13]

By a law of January 3, 1946, all mines and industrial
works became the property of the Polish State. At the same
time a Four-Year Plan was introduced for the rehabilitation
and development of the country. Much of this plan, and also
of those which have succeeded it, the Six-Year and Five-Year
Plans, was devoted to aspects of Polish economic life with
which we are not concerned. As regards the industries of Upper Silesia the Four-Year Plan foresaw the restoration of the
pre-war levels of production. The restoration of the coal-
mining industry was basic to the Polish plans for industrial
reconstruction, and desirable also for the well-being of many
other European countries. Great Britain's coal export had
shrunk to negligible proportions, and Germany could not supply her own needs. Poland was the only European country
with a surplus of coal, and other European countries needed
this coal as urgently as Poland needed their foreign exchange
to enable her to re-equip her factories.

The task before Poland was a heavy one. German exploitation of mines and factories had been extreme.[14] "They exploited the whole coalfield ruthlessly, concentrating on maximum output without regard to the condition of the workings,
sand filling, or maintenance of the equipment and power plant.
Some indication of the extent of exploitation is the fact that
400 million tons of the best coal were mined between 1940 and
1944.... When the Polish authorities took over the coalfields,
out of a total of 80 mines 42 were on fire and 17 were under
water, the workings of the remainder were seriously in need
of maintenance and would require a large expenditure of effort
to restore them to normal conditions. Sand filling had not
been carried out by the Germans and this backlog had to be
made up; dangerous cavements have in fact, occurred, particularly around the largest iron and steel works 'Huta Pokój'
where the surface sank to a depth of 2 meters...."[15]

Hilary Minc, the Polish Minister of Planning, reported a
year after the war had ended, "our mines have been working
without picks and shovels, without safety lamps and with

breaking transporter bands...our foundries have old and unre-
newed rollers working at the end of their life...."[16] Under
these circumstances the recovery of the Polish coal mining
industry was little short of a miracle.[17]

The Regional Plan for Upper Silesia: The incorporation
into Poland of German Silesia, or Śląsk Opole, raised administrative and social problems. Within the industrial area of
about 200 square miles there lay six cities: Gliwice, Zabrze,
Bytom, Chorzów, Katowice, Sosnowiec, of which the first three
had been under German rule before the war. Around and between them lay a multitude of settlements, some of them urban in appearance and function, which nevertheless had the
status only of gminy, or villages.[18] Between the two wars,
this area had been divided between the German Regierungsbezirk Oppeln (Opole) and the Polish województwo of Katowice.
During the years of the German occupation it was part of the
newly established Regencja of Katowice. In 1945 the old administrative structure was restored, but it corresponded
neither with the economic nor the administrative needs of
the region.

It was not, however, until 1950 that an extensive revision
of administrative structure was undertaken. The województwo
of Katowice was redefined to include the whole of the coalfield
and industrial area, with the exception only of the small sector of the coalfield which continued to lie in the neighboring
Województwo of Kraków. In the following year fundamental
changes were made in the internal organization of the area.
The areas of some of the existing cities was increased by the
inclusion of adjoining gminy, and nine new cities were created:
Ruda, Nowy Bytom, Świętochłowice, Siemianowice, Czeladź,
Będzin, Dąbrowa Górnicze, Szopienice and Mysłowice. The
gminy have disappeared from the industrial area (figures 49
and 50), which now consists of fifteen separate municipalities.
The surrounding rural districts, or powiaty, contain coal
mines and scattered industrial undertakings, but their predominant character is rural.

In June, 1953 the industrial area was placed under a single
planning authority. The Upper Silesian Industrial Region—
Górnośląski Okręg Przemysłowy (G.O.P.)—as defined at this
time, covered 2370 square kilometers (about 915 square miles).[19]

Figure 47: Administrative divisions of the Upper
Silesian region under German occupation. The shaded
area indicates the extent of Zone A of the latter Upper
Silesia Planning Region.

It was divided into two zones, of which Zone A included the industrial cities and Zone B a surrounding belt of predominantly
rural country (figure 49).

   Zone A covers about 700 square kilometers. Its population before the war was about 975,000. This was greatly reduced during the closing stages of the conflict, but by 1946 had
again reached 836,000.[20] By 1955, the population of the area
was 1,395,700.[21] By common consent the population had grown

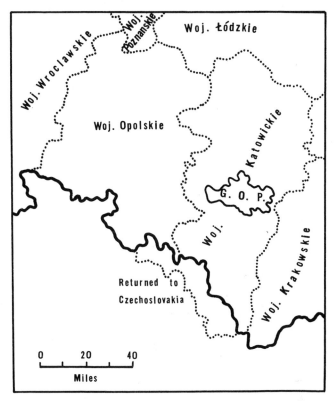

Figure 48: Present day Polish administrative divisions in Upper Silesia.

to be quite large enough. There was very little land available for industrial building; water supply was difficult, and there was every reason for locating future growth in the surrounding rural area. Such a policy had been foreshadowed in the Six-Year Plan of 1950.[22] Zone A was made to include the fifteen cities of the industrial area, together with a few townships and villages,[23] which brought several important industrial undertakings into Zone A, but added relatively little to its population and area.

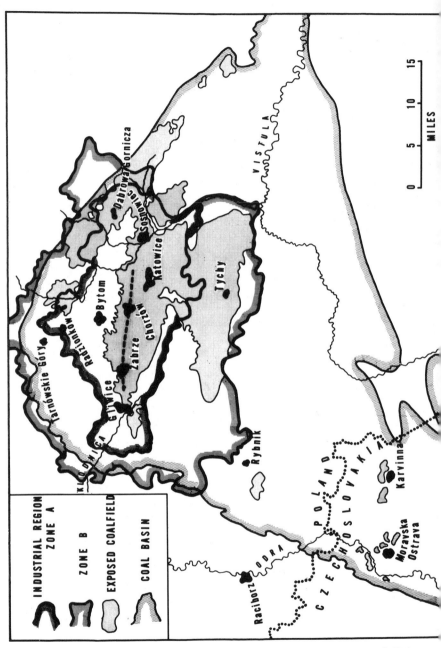

Figure 49: The Upper Silesian Industrial Region (G.O.P.),
as defined for planning purposes.

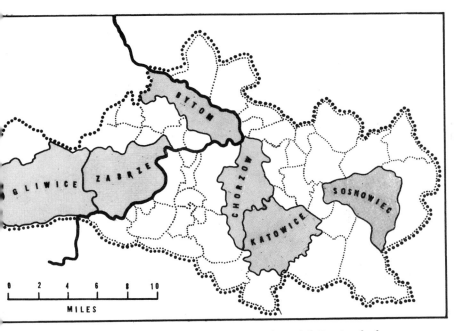

Figure 50: The Upper Silesian Industrial Region before
the administrative changes of 1950. Cities (miasta) are
shaded; rural communities (gminy) are unshaded.

Zone B, which almost completely encircles Zone A, is
more than twice as large—about 1670 kilometers—but has
only about 310,000 inhabitants. The expansion of coal-mining
has inevitably to take place in Zone B, and here it is planned
to establish new industrial works and to build dormitory cities
which will serve the needs of a fraction of the workers in
Zone A.[24]
     The hope that growth in Zone A would be halted has not
been entirely realized. Its population has continued to rise
slowly. It was stated that only industries heavily dependent
on coal, such as zinc-smelting, would be located in Zone A,
but in fact several plants whose consumption of fuel does not

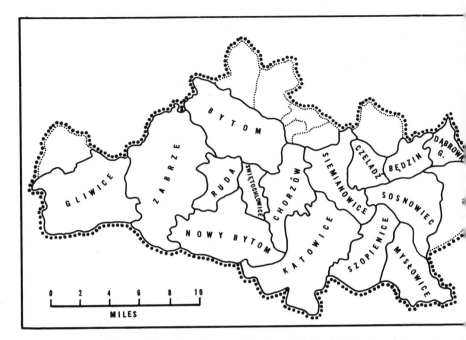

Figure 51: The Upper Silesian Industrial Region (Zone A)
after the changes in administrative districts of 1950. The
fifteen cities (miasta) are shaded.

seem high, have been established here, such as the manufacture of railway signalling equipment and of ball-bearings. It
seems improbable, however, that the scope and size of industry will be greatly extended in Zone A. Already there are
complaints that the plan is lacking in boldness and has too
little regard for the problems of the destruction of land by subsidence and waste heaps within the heavily industrialized area.[25]
Some degree of dispersion of the population from Zone A
also formed part of the plan. The quality of housing over most
of the industrial area leaves much to be desired. Blocks of
flats have been built in recent years, notably in Katowice, but
most of the new housing is around the periphery of Zone A and
in Zone B. New dormitory towns are being built, each consisting

of large, five or six-storied blocks of centrally heated apartments. Largest of these dormitory towns is Tychy, lying about 8 1/2 miles south of Katowice. The site is in Zone B, and the surrounding area is under either crops or forest. A railway, as well as bus services, links Tychy with Katowice and with other cities of the industrial area. The new town of Nowy Tychy adjoins the old village of Tychy, and reinforces the contrast between them. Indeed, the village houses were not disturbed when the new blocks were built, and there are instances of old and tumbledown Silesian cottages completely surrounded and overshadowed by modern apartment blocks.

No other "new town" is as large or its construction as far advanced as Tychy. But great progress has been made in building the "new" Piekary and the "new" Radzionków, which will serve the housing needs of the Bytom area. Other new towns are either planned or under construction at Pyskowice, to the northwest; at Grodziec, Dąbrowa and Mysłowice to the east, and at Halemba to the south-west. Not all these new constructions are in Zone B, but they are at least marginal to Zone A.

The policy of the planning authority for Zone A has been described as "passive deglomeration"—the prevention of growth. The area within the G.O.P. that is suitable for building is small, and there are very good reasons for settling as much of the population as possible at a distance from the G.O.P.'s particular range of industries. But public transport facilities are inadequate for the present needs of the population, and considerable extensions are needed if the population becomes more dispersed.

Water-supply has always been a matter of some difficulty (see page 152). The technical problems resulting from the partition of the industrial area had in large measure been resolved in 1939, but the supply remained inadequate. All sources of water within the industrial area are contaminated, and bore holes in the Shelly Limestone could not be expected to yield a greater supply.[26] The Six-Year Plan has provided for a more radical solution to the problem. Dams have been built on the Vistula at Goczałkowice and on the Brynica at Kozłowa Góra, and further dams are to be constructed on the Biała Przemsza and in the Beskidy. Water from these sources,

supplemented by that from the older wells and catchment
areas, will be fed into a "water-ring," encircling the industrial area. A double pipeline will be laid down to carry puri-
fied water for domestic use, and unpurified for industrial.
At present work has not been begun on the "ring," and the full-
est use is not being made of the new reservoirs. But the completion of the scheme should secure an adequate supply of
water for a long period.

The south-eastern sector of the coal-basin lies in the
neighboring województwo of Kraków, and is not included in
the sphere of planning of G.O.P. A few coal mines are active
in this area, but it is in general thinly populated and has little
industry. The rest of the województwo has, however, long
been notorious for its dense agricultural population and for
the small size of its farm holdings. The solution of this problem has been found in the location here of industrial plant that
might otherwise have been established in G.O.P.[27] The steel
Kombinat of Nowa Huta is a foremost example; others are the
chemical works at Dwory, near Oświęcim; the power station
at Jaworzno and the extension of the coal mining industry.
"New towns" have been built here, as in the Upper Silesian
area, consisting largely of big apartment blocks. Nowa Huta,
with a present population of about 50,000, and a planned population of 100,000, is by far the largest of all the "new towns."[28]

PLANNING IN THE COAL INDUSTRY

The regional plan for the G.O.P. is intended to provide a
social and economic framework within which the coal, iron,
steel and zinc industries may flourish. Foremost among these
is coal. Coal has always been a foremost export of Poland,
and in recent years the need to import equipment for the country's planned development has increased the importance of
the coal exports. In 1949, coal made up 54.5 per cent by value
of Poland's exports. This proportion fell to 41.9 per cent in
1953, but rose again to nearly half the total.[29] Poland has not
experienced difficulty in marketing her coal; the chief problem
has been the excessive demands of the Soviet Union, requited
at a price below the market level. Nor is there any expecta-
tion of a falling off of demand. The future welfare and

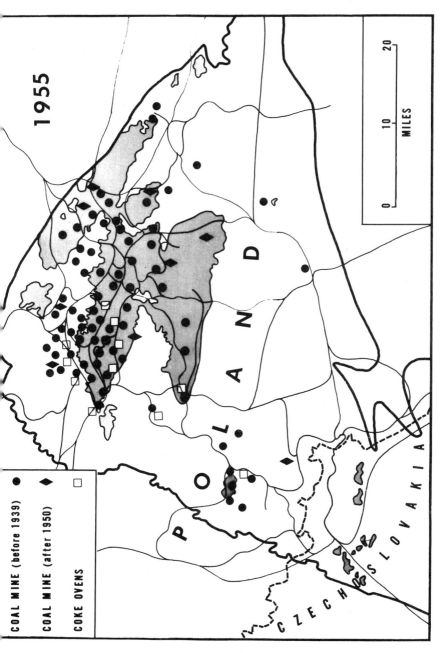

1955

COAL MINE (before 1939) ●
COAL MINE (after 1950) ◆
COKE OVENS □

POLAND

CZECHOSLOVAKIA

MILES
0   10   20

Figure 52: Coal mines in Upper Silesia and adjoining
region, 1955. Data is not available for northern Moravia.

development of Poland are dependent upon coal exports. In consequence, no branch of activity has been more carefully planned or received more encouragement by both direct monetary rewards and expenditure on research. The technical and economic literature is abundant and increasing. No less than four monthly periodicals are devoted to the coal industry and coal trade.

Coal Production: The coal mines were exploited ruthlessly during the period of German occupation; geological work was abandoned, and plant was neither maintained nor replaced. Output rose sharply until 1943, after which, in spite of a labor force of increasing size,[30] the yield of coal began to decline[31]:

	West Upper Silesia (Opole)	East Upper Silesia (Śląsk)	Dąbrowa and Kraków	Total
1940	26,000	33,200	1,500	59,700
1941	24,500	34,000	12,200	70,700
1942	27,000	37,600	12,900	77,500
1943	28,600	41,200	14,500	84,300
1944	28,200	39,800	16,000	84,000
1945	5,200	14,500	4,400	24,100

The purpose of the Four-Year Plan was to restore industrial production to the pre-war level. In this in large measure it succeeded. It ceases to be possible to separate the production of Upper Silesia from that of Lower, or to distinguish the several parts of the Upper Silesian field. The total Polish output rose during these years:

1945	27,366,000 tons
1946	47,288,000 "
1947	59,130,000 "
1948	70,262,000 "
1949	74,081,000 "

Conditions in the Lower Silesian field do not lend themselves to rapid expansion of output. The greatest output from this field, in 1929, only just turned six million tons, and subsequently the highest output was only about 4,700,000 tons. It is unlikely that production in the first post-war period exceeded this total. If 5 million are subtracted from the published totals,

the remainder represents approximately the output from the
Upper Silesian basin. During the period of the Six-Year Plan,
annual targets were set for the coal-mining industry as a
whole, and these were broken down for each mine. Every de-
vice was used to fulfill the plans. Competition was encouraged
between mines; great publicity was given to those which exceeded their quotas, and at the end of each day a bright star
shone above the winding gear of those mines which had fulfilled
their day's quota. Nevertheless, the targets have not been
achieved, though the rate of expansion of the industry shows
how earnestly it strove during these years[32]:

1950	78,001,000 tons
1951	81,992,000 "
1952	84,437,000 "
1953	88,700,000 "
1954	91,600,000 "
1955	94,500,000 "
1956	95,635,000 "
1957	94,096,000 "

The target for 1955, concluding year of the Six-Year Plan was
100 million tons.

The reasons for the non-fulfillment of an exceptionally
ambitious program are easy to discover.[33] In the first place,
the burden of the German occupation still lies heavy on the
industry. Time has been too short in which to replace all the
worn-out equipment. In particular, these years of neglect and
exploitation saw the abandonment of the essential work of
geological prospecting and survey. Some of the recent mine
developments have been costly failures because this prelimi-
nary work could not be completed in the short time available.

The greatly increased output was to be achieved also by
the mechanization of old mines and the construction of new
levels, and by the sinking of new mines. Mechanization of
coal-cutting and loading made very much less progress than
had been anticipated. This was attributed in part to the inadequate supply of machines and spare parts by the factories; in
part to the lack of variety in their design and their unsuitability
for certain conditions met with underground. There was,
furthermore, a shortage of labor competent to instal and
work the newest machines. Machines were far from

fully utilized, and in some mines total production fell sharply after mechanization.   There was some opposition from the miners to using the new equipment, but this resistance is disappearing in the face of a vigorous campaign to familiarize them with modern methods.
It is difficult to estimate the extent of mechanization.   It would appear however that about a third of the coal is cut by machine,[34] but a very much smaller proportion of the coal appears to have been loaded mechanically on to the conveyor belts.[35]
It was anticipated that the planned output of 100 million tons in 1955 would be obtained from[36]:

Old mines	76,500,000
New levels in old mines	14,500,000
New mines	9,000,000
	100,000,000

In fact, however, 93.9 per cent of the coal—about 88,735,000 tons—were obtained from the old mines[37] and only 4,252,500 tons from the new.   The opening of shallow mines, worked by an inclined shaft, and of strip or open-cast mines was not foreseen in the plans, but resort was had to such workings, because they could be developed relatively quickly.[38] In 1955, 1.6 per cent of the coal —about 1,512,000 tons—was obtained in this way.

All the deep coal-mines that had been active before the war, whether in East or West Upper Silesia, were again brought into production. German names were replaced by Polish, and some of the older Polish names were replaced by others more in keeping with the changed climate of political opinion. The Six-Year Plan provided for the opening of eleven new and entirely mechanized mines. But the work was slow in being started, was handicapped by inadequate geological knowledge, by lack of materials and by faulty planning.[39] By 1955 the new mines are said to have been producing only 42.2 per cent of their planned output for that year. Indeed, only five of the new mines were in production at the end of the period, and in each output fell considerably below expectations.

Methods of mining have been modified. A long-wall method has become general, because it not only facilitates the use of mechanical transport of coal, but also enables a higher

proportion of the coal to be extracted. Mining methods had
previously been somewhat wasteful. Large pillars had been
left under cities and factory sites, and elsewhere very thick
seams had not been worked to their total thickness in order to
reduce the subsidence and resulting damage to surface installations. Needless to say, the Germans observed no such precautions during the war, and surface damage was more than usually severe during these years. Today, also, the need for
coal for export is so great that the Polish authorities are obliged to use less wasteful methods.

We have seen earlier that towards the west of the coalfield the seams are numerous but not of great thickness. To
the east some of the intervening beds thin out, leaving seams
of exceptional thickness. Such seams are relatively cheap to
mine. The workings are free of gas, and in some mines it is
the practice merely to break down the coal face with explo-
sives and to load the coal on to a conveyor belt.[40] Such an
operation would normally be disastrous for the ground surface,
and can be used only when accompanied by the process of sand-
filling or podsadzka.

This method has been used for over fifty years (page 69),
but its extension before the war had been hindered by the political division of the area and by the high capital investment
required. In brief, the method consists in enclosing the excavated space, as the mining face moves forward, with wooden
planks, and filling it with sand washed down through a pipe
from the surface. Large concrete coffers are required at the
surface, into which the sand can be tipped from rail-cars and
from which it can be hosed down into the pipes.[41] The supply
of very large quantities of sand has to be assured. In the past
this had been obtained from small alluvial deposits adjoining
the mines. Now it is planned to use the extensive area—over
60 square miles—of sands, known as the Pustynia Błędowska,
lying to the south of the Biała Przemsza, supplemented by
smaller deposits in at Gołonog, in the Kłodnicki valley and
elsewhere. A series of short, narrow gauge lines had previously linked the mines with the sources of their sand supply.
The Six-Year Plan provided for the construction of a railway
from the Błędowa deposits through the industrial area with
branches to the mines. This line is now (1957) nearing

completion. In 1953 there were 57 coffers (zbiorniki), serving 44 mines; it is planned to have altogether 96 such coffers, serving the needs of 65 out of some 85 mines. This great extension of sand-filling is of fundamental importance. It was possible, on the scale on which it is now being carried out, only with a unified control of the whole coalfield. It enables the very large reserves of coal remaining under the cities to be mined as well as the total thickness of the very large seams. In 1950, about 20 per cent of the coal extracted was replaced by sand filling; in 1956 this was increased to 34 per cent, and with the completion of the sand railway much greater use will be made of it.[42]

The use of sand-filling has reduced somewhat the consumption of mine timber. It is not practicable, however, to withdraw roof supports before filling, and the loss of timber is very large. In 1953, about 45 cubic meters of timber were required for each 100 tons of coal extracted.[43] The expansion of the demand for mine timber has strained the forest resources of the country. Economies are being made in the use of timber in the mines, but the alternative, steel girders and supports, are very much more difficult to supply than the wooden.[44]

All the deep mines active before the war are again in production, though reorganization has reduced the number of operating units. The nationalization of the coal mining industry not only facilitated the use of sand-filling, but has permitted several of the older concessions to be either merged or divided according to their technical needs.[45] To the list of older mines are now added the names of a dozen new ones. One of these, the Gottwald mine, near Katowice, was opened before the Six-Year Plan began. About half of the others are now in production.[46] Their sites have been carefully chosen. Poland's chief need is for a greater production of coal of coking quality,[47] found, of course, in Lower Silesia but only in restricted areas of the Upper Silesian field. Foremost among these is the area of Rybnik and the western part of the G.O.P. On the other hand the thick seams and greater ease of mining in the east encourage expansion in this direction to supply the export trade. The map (fig. 52) which shows the position of new mines, shows that the predominant directions of expansion

are south-westwards into Rybnik (for coking coal) and south-
eastwards into the Przemsza valley (for steam coal).
The major developments effected in the Upper Silesian
coal-mining industry have been reviewed. Of lesser importance are the numerous plants, built or extended, for wash-
ing and sorting coal and for improving the ventilation of
mines.[48] Pithead baths have been built at a number of mines,
and, at their best, the amenities at Polish mines compare fa-
vorably with any in Western Europe.

The coal-mining industry of Upper Silesia is keyed into
the industrial structure of the region to a very much smaller
degree in the Ruhr region. Most of the coal comes from the
mines, is washed and graded, and sent out of the area. Relatively little is used in the coke ovens; some goes to the chemical works, such as the Azote (previously Mosicki) works in
Chorzów; there is a large consumption in the thermal electric
power generators at Chorzów, Zabrze, Jaworzno, Łaziska
Górna. In marked contrast with the Ruhr area, very few
mines have coke-ovens.[49] Five of the blast-furnace works
have their own coke-ovens, which use large quantities of coking coal from Lower Silesia. The zinc smelters remain one
of the largest local consumers of Upper Silesian coal.

THE IRON AND STEEL INDUSTRIES

The iron and steel works of Upper Silesia were neither
up-to-date nor in good condition when the war began, and six
years of German rule did nothing to improve their condition.[50]
On the other hand the works were not deliberately destroyed,
and production quickly revived. The Four and Six-Year Plans
have provided for the renewal and repair of plant but for few
major extensions within the older industrial area.

The Six-Year Plan called for the production of 4,600,000
tons of steel in 1955, as against the actual production in 1949
of 2,304,000 tons. The actual output was 4,426,400 tons.[51]

This expansion was achieved in part by modernization and
extension of plant in Upper Silesia, but mainly by the two large
new iron and steel works at Częstochowa and Nowa Huta.[52] The
blast furnaces at the Kościuszko Huta (Königshütte) have been
rebuilt, and a new furnace added.[53] New steel furnaces have

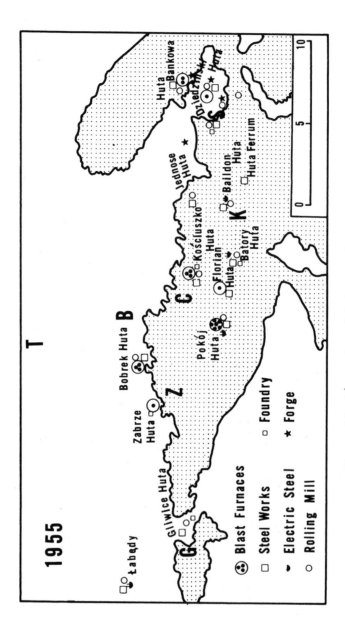

Figure 53: Iron and steel industry of Upper Silesia, 1955.
For symbols, see figure 29.

been constructed at the Pokój Huta (Friedenshütte)[54] and the
Huta Dzierzynskiego (Huta Bankowa), and new rolling mills
set up at the Bobrek Huta (Julienhütte), the Pokój Huta and at
Zawiercie. The Pokój works have been linked by gas pipeline with the coke-ovens at the Walentin-Wavel mine. But the
old industrial area remains a small steel producer. It is
unlikely that the total pig-iron production within the old industrial area can exceed 1, 700, 000 tons, and it is not planned to
increase this total. Steel is made entirely by means of the
open hearth or electric furnace, and of course exceeds the
volume of pig-iron produced.[55] But little iron and steel scrap
is produced in Poland, and the relatively small metal fabricating industry in Upper Silesia restricts the amount of circulat-
ing scrap in the works. There is thus a relatively high pig-
iron charge in the steel furnaces. It is unlikely, therefore,
that steel production within the G.O.P. greatly exceeds two
million tons a year. Considerably more than this is made outside Upper Silesia, at the Warsaw Steelworks; at Stalowa
Wola in south-eastern Poland, and particularly at Nowa Huta
and Częstochowa.

The problems facing the coal-mining industry were seen
to be relatively simple and might reasonably be expected to
be solved in a period of a few years. Obstacles to growth in
the iron and steel industry are less tractable. Poland suffers
from a shortage of ore, of coking coal, of capital and of technically trained personnel.

Ore Supply: Poland is poorly endowed with iron ore. Upper Silesian deposits, of whatever origin, have long been exhausted, and other reserves are small. A recent estimate
gives[56]:

	Proved reserves (in metric tons)	Probable reserves (in metric tons)
"Old" Poland	58,280,000	174,280,000
Recovered Territories	320,000	800,000

These ores occur mainly as bedded deposits of low-grade sid-
erite in the Jura Krakowska, near Częstochowa. Most of the
remainder is farther to the east in Kielce province.[57] In their
wildest flights of imagination the Polish authorities never

dreamed of self-sufficiency in iron-ore, but they have attempted to reduce imports to the smallest volume possible.

It was planned to produce three million tons of ore a
year by 1955, about 30 per cent of needs. In reality, however,
output fell considerably short of this figure, and satisfied only
13 per cent of requirements.[58] About three-quarters of it
came from the Częstochowa district. Attempts are being made
to use the low-grade ferruginous sands, with from 15 to 20
per cent iron, which occur abundantly in the Świętokrzyskie
(Holy Cross) Mountains, but these require a considerable investment in concentrating plant.[59] A methodical survey of the
country is being made for iron-ore, and old slags which contain a usable fraction of iron are being reworked. Nevertheless, output has fallen far short of requirements, and domestic production has risen from about 15 per cent of requirements
only to about 18.

Domestic ores have been extremely costly to mine. It is
true that most of the small mines have been closed and production concentrated at fewer but larger and more efficient
units.[60] But the efficiency of labor in the iron mines has remained extremely low, less than a twelfth of that in the French
mines. In consequence, Polish domestic ore has been extremely expensive[61]:

	Per ton of ore (in Złoty)	Per ton of Fe content (in Złoty)
Poland (average)	325	750
U.S.S.R.	76	152
Sweden	116	194

Clearly, Poland has had to rely heavily on imported ore.
In the years immediately following the war, Sweden was the
chief source of imported ore, but, with the change in the country's political orientation, imports from the Soviet Union began to increase. The failure of domestic ore production to
expand as rapidly as had been planned led to a revival of imports from Sweden, and also to a sharp increase in that of
concentrates from Norway.

The close political association of Poland with the Soviet
Union led to attempts to place the supply of Russian ore on a
more permanent and economical basis. The Bug and Prypeć

rivers were to be canalized and the old Królewski Canal between them enlarged, so that barges would be able to bring ore from Kriwoi Rog to the upper Vistula. But the short cutoff canal from Warsaw to the Bug has not yet been finished and work does not appear to have yet been begun on the Prypeć section of the route. In the meanwhile, the Poles appear to have become less willing to depend heavily on ore from the Soviet Union. Russian ore is brought by rail to Polish iron-smelting centers, but the projected canal from the Odra to the Vistula would appear to facilitate the movement of Scandinavian ore rather than Russian, and the official press has not disguised its hope that more ore may be obtained from the "capitalist" countries.[63]

Location of New Iron and Steel Works: We have already seen that extensions to the iron and steel industry in the G.O.P. have been relatively small, and that most of the new investment has been located elsewhere. Częstochowa and Kraków were chosen. The former site was self-evident. It lies 40 miles north of Katowice, near the northern end of the Krakowska Jura at a site long important for its iron industry. To the east rises the scarp of the limestone plateau in which a low-grade, phosphoric ore is worked. The Huta im. Bieruta was established about a mile to the east of the old Rakow iron works, which remain in production. Two large blast-furnaces were built, with open-hearth and electric steel works and rolling mills. It has coke ovens, and coking coal may be presumed to come from Lower Silesia with some contribution from Upper.

The site of Nowa Huta was a less obvious one. The policy of restricting industrial growth determined that the new works should be outside the G.O.P. On the other hand it would be obliged to draw part at least of its fuel from Upper Silesia, though the market for its rolled steel goods covers all Poland. It is said that the choice of site was narrowed to three: Koźle, on the Odra; Kraków, and Sandomierz, farther down the Vistula. In the final choice, social questions appear to have played an important role—the need to establish industry in the województwo Kraków in order to provide work and raise living standards in a seriously overpopulated region.[64]

The site ultimately chosen lies about six miles east of

Kraków, near, but not on the Vistula. Ultimately the transport of materials by water is envisaged, but the short canal linking the works with the Vistula has not yet been begun. At present the works are dependent entirely on rail transport. At present the Huta im. Lenina has three blast furnaces, open-hearth and electric steel works and a continuous rolling mill, together with coke ovens and by-product works. Another blast-furnace is under construction, and the planned output of the completed works is 1,500,000 tons of rolled steel per year.[65]

The town of Nowa Huta has been built about a mile to the west of the works. It consists of 5- or 6-story blocks of flats, very similar in style and arrangement to the new towns of Upper Silesia. Its population is already some 50,000, and it is planned that this should rise to 100,000 with the completion of the works.

At present, the G.O.P. contributes less than half of the iron and steel made in Poland, and with the completion of plans at Nowa Huta and Częstochowa, as well as at the Huta Warszawa and other lesser centers of industry, the relative importance of the G.O.P. will be diminished yet more.

	Domestic production of iron ore	Approximate percentage of national needs	Pig-iron output	Steel output
1945	102	14*	219	448
1946	395.5	16*	726	1219
1947	544	19*	867	1579
1948	636	16*	1208	1955
1949	684.4	15	1365	2303
1950	732	15*	1488	2515
1951	835	16*	1577	2792
1952	943	16*	1782	3182
1953	1236	16*	2299	3604
1954	1574.5	18*	2598	3949
1955	1856	18	3112	4426
1956	1973	17*	3506	5014

* estimated

The Zinc and Lead Industries: The expansion, which has
characterized the coal, iron and steel industries, has been
less marked in the mining and smelting of lead and zinc. This
is due, at least in part, to the very considerable dependence
of the smelting industry on imported ores, and to the difficulties which Poland at present experiences with foreign exchange. The industry was nationalized in 1946 and organized
in fourteen operating units, consisting each of either a mine
or a smelter.[66] The industry suffered during the war chiefly
from the cutting off of supplies, but was undamaged and recovered relatively quickly.

Mining is now restricted to six large mines, four of them
near Bytom, and the others respectively at Bolesław and
Chrzanów, farther to the east. Ores are now crushed and the
sulphides separated by flotation. Several small smelters active in 1939 have been closed, and smelting is now concentrated at five works[67]: Bolesław, Szopienice, Lipine, Wełnowiec
and Kunigunde. The Bolesław smelter uses only the electrolytic process, and Szopienice uses both electrolytic and muffle
furnaces. At all other furnaces, the old muffle furnaces continue to be used exclusively.

The Six-Year Plan provided for the extension and modernization of the zinc industry, and, in particular, for the replacement of muffle by electrolytic furnaces.[68] This plan has
not been completed; indeed, little progress appears to have
been made with it. Production of metallic zinc increased considerably, but nevertheless fell short of planned objectives[69]:

1945	36,385	1951	
1946	56,614	1952	
1947	71,756	1953	138,400
1948	87,089	1954	142,100
1949	85,300	1955	156,200
1950	86,200	1956	

The production of electrically refined zinc rose, however,
from 10,400 tons in 1946 to 18,800 tons in 1949 and to 50,400
in 1955. The Walter Cronek smelter continues to produce
small quantities of zinc along with lead.[70]

The distribution of zinc and lead smelting remains concentrated in the eastern part of the G.O.P. As long as the muffle furnace, with its extravagant consumption of fuel, remains the chief method of smelting, the industry is likely to remain here. But changes can be foreseen. The focus of ore-mining is expected to move, with the gradual exhaustion of the ores, from the Bytom district to that of Olkusz and Chrzanów, where reserves are greater. This shift coincides with the greater use of electrical methods of refining, and the consequent severance of the smelting industry from its close dependence on coal. Already the Bolesław smelter, near Olkusz, has been wholly electrified. It is not difficult to foresee a time when the whole of this industry will be carried on outside the G.O.P., with electric power generated at the large stations within the coalfield area.

Reserves of ore in the Silesia-Kraków region are large, and were recently estimated to amount to:

Sulphide ores, with 15 per cent zinc and 2 per cent lead	12,000,000 tons
Calcareous ores, with 12-13 per cent zinc and 1.5 per cent lead	4,000,000 "
Old slag heaps, with 6-7 per cent zinc and 0.8 per cent lead	2,000,000 "

This suggests at least 2,400,000 tons of zinc and 316,000 tons of lead, enough, when supplemented by imports of ore and concentrates, to support a smelting industry for a period of many years.

THE EASTERN RUHR

The coal, iron and steel industries of Moravia and Cieszyn have always been politically separated from those of Upper Silesia, and political rivalry had limited economic cooperation between the two parts of the coalfield area. But, with the coming to power of Communist governments in both Poland and Czechoslovakia, plans were prepared for the development as a single unit of the whole coalfield area. As reported in the West, these plans were ambitious indeed. According to

The Metal Bulletin,[71] "The Polish-Czech program for joining
up the economies of the two nations has now been completed
by drawing up detailed plans for incorporation in each of their
next 5-year economic plans. The apparent aim...is to set up
a center of industry which, along with Russian output, can
take over Germany's pre-war role in Eastern Europe. By
far the most important part of the program is the development
scheme for the Silesian basin...an annual steel output target
of at first 5,000,000 metric tons and later 10,000,000. The
industrial center is to be between Bohumin and the Beskidy
mountains, and will employ 25,000. Large integrated steel
works are to be completed within 12 years. Coal for the steel
works is to come from Upper Silesia...." The German, P. H.
Seraphim, has further defined the Russian intention to weld
the industrial potential of this area into a single functional
unit, a Kombinat in Lenin's definition of the term.

These proposals aroused far less speculation in the
countries most directly concerned than outside them.[72] Com-
mittees were established to consider the problems, some
concrete proposals were made,[73] and then the whole project
was forgotten. Indeed, at the very time when the proposals
were made, Poland at least was engaged in the preparation of
other plans that conflicted directly with those for the "Eastern Ruhr." The original agreement belonged to the period of
enforced cooperation among the satellities. One cannot suppose that it had the sincere good will of either Polish or
Czech authorities.

It is difficult to see that more could be achieved by con-
structing a gigantic Kombinat on a virgin site than could be
gained from the autonomous development of two separate, national industries. Scarce materials, especially metallurgical
coke and iron-ore, would remain scarce. Capital, barely adequate for the implementation of national plans, could not have
sufficed for a scheme such as this. Many an ambitious
scheme, sponsored by the Soviet Union, for the development
of water-borne transport between its satellities has foundered,
and there is no reason to suppose that the projected canals between the Odra, Vistula and Danube will be cut in the foresee-
able future.

Commercial relations between the Polish and the Czecho-slovak sectors of the coalfield have been of severely limited extent. Some coking coal from the Karvinná mines has been used in the Polish iron industry, but it has been asserted repeatedly in Poland that the quantities involved were very small. Exchange of half-finished and finished goods between the two countries has also been on a very small scale. Despite the blanket of Russian-inspired planning, the development of both Polish and Czechoslovak industrial regions has been along strictly national lines.

Ostrava-Karvinná: The Czechoslovak industrial area, no less than the Polish, has been subject to economic planning, though industrial growth has been much less fully documented than in Poland. Coal production has been increased, though less spectacularly than in Poland. Until recently there appears to have been little attempt to extend mining, though under the present plan six new mines are being opened. [74]

It is impossible to separate from the total coal production of Czechoslovakia the share contributed by Morava–Karvinná, though there can be little room for doubt that the latter has expanded more rapidly than the output of other coalfields. The total output of coal [75] from Czechoslovak mines has been:

	Total production of Czechoslovakia (thousands of tons)	Approximate production of Morava-Karvinná (thousands of tons)
1945	11,424	9,144
1946	14,136	11,306
1947	16,212	12,972
1948	17,746	14,195
1949	17,002	13,621
1950	18,456	14,767
1951	18,392	15,348
1952	20,270	14,900 (est.)
1953	20,341	16,500 (est.)
1954	21,605	17,500 (est.)
1955	22,136	18,000 (est.)
1956	23,411	19,000 (est.)

(Statistická Ročenka Republiky Československé, 1957)

We have seen already that the Morava-Karvinná sector of the Upper Silesian coalfield is relatively rich in coking coal.

Production of metallurgical coke has expanded more sharply than that of coal as a whole.[76]

1947	3,337	1952	6,138
1948	4,281	1953	6,500
1949	5,225	1954	6,789
1950	5,399	1955	7,000
1951	5,469	1956	7,327

(In thousands of tons)

Small quantities of coke have been exported to Poland and also to Austria, Hungary and other central and south-east European countries.

The iron-smelting and steel-making industries of Czechoslovakia were at the beginning of the period of planned development very much larger than those of Poland. But their rate of growth has been less rapid[76]:

	Pig iron	Crude Steel
1937	1,675	2,301
1946	960	1,668
1947	1,428	2,280
1948	1,645	2,621
1949	1,885	2,806
1950	1,951	3,122
1951	2,057	3,455
1952	2,306	3,754
1953	2,781	4,366
1954	2,790	4,270
1955	2,982	4,474
1956	3,282	4,882
1960 (plan)	4,780	6,540

(In thousands of tons)

Czechoslovakia has a number of rather old iron and steel works in Bohemia.[77] It is probable that modernization and additions have been effected here, but the only significant extention of the industry has been the Gottwald Huta at Kunčice, near Vítkovice.[78] A similar project at Kosice in Slovakia appears to have been abandoned. The Gottwald works are similar in scale and scope to the Huta im. Bieruta at Częstochowa. It has two large blast-furnaces, and is expected to produce about a million tons of steel a year. The Morava-Karvinná region produced about 90 per cent of the pig-iron smelted in Czechoslovakia and, before the recent expansion, contributed about two-thirds of the steel. Its steel-making capacity is now between 80 and 90 per cent of the national total. The site of the newest Czechoslovak iron and steel works, unlike those of the Polish, appears to have been chosen with regard mainly to fuel supplies. Of the adequacy of the reserves of coking coal there can be no question. The Czechoslovak iron ore reserves are larger than those of Poland, but still do not in themselves justify the establishment of a major iron and steel industry. Ores mined in Bohemia are supplemented by imports, chiefly from Sweden, and smelted at Beroun and Kladno. The Ostrava-Karvinná district draws upon the ores of Slovakia, but uses also large quantities of Swedish and Russian ores. In the years immediately following the Second World War heavy reliance was placed on Swedish ores; then ores from the Soviet Ukraine came to be used increasingly. More recently there has been a great expansion in domestic ore production.

1948	1,428	1953	2,255
1949	1,469	1954	2,193
1950	1,604	1955	2,490
1951	1,762	1956	2,542
1952	2,098		

(In thousands of tons)

CONCLUSION

The Industrial Region of Upper Silesia bears on its scarred landscape the marks of its two hundred years of history. Its few, small and scattered farms and villages of the eighteenth century have grown into sprawling industrial cities and suburbs. Of the 217 square miles of the G.O.P., perhaps a quarter may be said to be built up, in the sense that farmland has been replaced entirely by the bricks and concrete of streets, factories and buildings. Over most of the remaining area, farms have been reduced to minute proportions, affording only a part-time occupation. In the areas which have

not been built up, the imprint of industrialization shows, on
the one hand, in the accumulations of slag and mine waste,
and, on the other, in the hollows formed by subsidence.[79]
No estimate is available of the extent of the land withdrawn
from both agricultural and industrial use in these two ways.
The morphological maps of the region, now being prepared at
the University of Kraków under the direction of Professor
Klimaszewski, will show the extent of these human modifications of the terrain. Very few parts of the industrial area are
free of them.

Waste or spoil heaps are less extensive than might be
supposed, owing mainly to the fact that the coal seams are
thick and little waste is obtained with the coal.[80] Waste tips
are most numerous at the mines in the west of the coalfield,
where, of course, the coal seams are thinner than to the east.
Heaps of furnace slag mark the sites of the older iron and
steel works, and in Chorzów (Kościuszko Huta) and Sosnowiec
these slag heaps are of enormous size.

Land-forms produced by subsidence cover a larger area
than those due to the accumulation of waste. No part of the
central industrial area is free from them, except the city
areas where mining is only now beginning. Elsewhere may be
seen houses tilting as a result of subsidence or bound with
steel rods to hold them rigid. The landscape is dotted with
small depressions, many of them filled with water. Where
lakes have not actually been formed, the water-table has often
been raised so high in the soil as a result of the subsidence,
that crop-husbandry is impossible.

Other negative forms have been produced where limestone, clay and, particularly, sand have been extracted. Sand-
digging is of increasing importance with the extension of
sand-filling in the coal mines. The most extensive sand deposits used in this way lie to the east of the Przemsza river,
but sand deposits along each of the small river valleys of the
industrial area have been used at some time for this purpose.
The hollows thus formed sometimes form lakes or are sometimes used for the dumping of factory waste and the fines
from the zinc separating plant.[81]

These circumstances clearly prevent the extension within the central industrial area of factories and other industrial

installations, and afford one more reason for the policy of "deglomeration" that has already been examined. Indeed, as is so often the case within an industrial area, it is difficult to discover a profitable use for much of the land. Consider-able areas have been very tastefully laid out as public parks, and some have been planted with trees.

Areas lying between the built-up centers of the cities are dotted with cottages, many with kitchen gardens, some with farm buildings. Despite the losses of soil through subsidence, quarrying and the encroachments of spoil heaps, agriculture continues to be practiced, though its importance is small and probably diminishing.

North of the industrial area, on the rolling hills of Trias-sic limestone, the opposite trend is found. Here agriculture is vigorously pursued, and villages, once centers of lead and zinc mining, are now predominantly agricultural, though the cultivated fields are often interrupted by the scars left by the shallow, open mines of earlier times.

Notes

1. "Die Eisenwirtschaft der Tschecho-Slowakei unter dem Einfluss der Teschener Gebietsabtretung," S.u.E., LVIII, 1938, 1469-1470.

2. That is, bituminous or black coal; she lost heavily in her brown coal holdings.

3. M.B., No. 2410, July 28, 1939.

4. F. Zweig, Poland Between the Wars, London, 1944, 77-82.

5. M.B., No. 2412, Aug. 4, 1939.

6. E. Wiskemann, Germany's Eastern Neighbors, Oxford, 1956, 262.

7. W. J. Rose, The Drama of Upper Silesia, London, 1936, 318-329.

8. Simon Segal, Nazi Rule in Poland, London, 1943.

9. Edmund Osmańczyk, Śląsk w Polsce Ludowej, Konferencja Śląska Instytutu Historii Polskiej Akademii Nauk, Wrocław, 1954, II, 189-291.

10. Trials of War Criminals before the Nurnberg Military Tribunals, VI, The Flick Case, Washington, 1952, 895-8; S. Segal, op.cit., 89 ff.

11. E. Osmańczyk, op.cit., 189-195; also The Tragedy of Silesia, 1945-46, ed. Johannes Kaps, trans. G. H. Hartinger, Munich, 1952-3, 43-56.

12. Winston S. Churchill, The Second World War, V, 1952, 350-1.

13. The Population of Poland, U.S. Department of Commerce, Washington, 1954, I.

14. Alfred Hornig, Przemysł węglowy w Polsce podczas wojny 1939-1945, Diss., unpublished, 1948.

15. Industrial Rehabilitation in Poland, Operational Analysis Paper no. 35, UNRRA., London, 1947, 26.

16. Quoted in D. W. Douglas, Transitional Economic Systems: the Polish-Czech Example, London, 1953, 59, from Information on Poland, Ministry of Foreign Affairs, Warsaw, 1948.

17. La transformation du bassin industriel de Haute-Silésie, Bulletin du Bureau d'Information Polonaise, June 4, 1955.

18. Wacław Kaczorowski, "Studium podziału administracyjnego Górnego Śląska," in Górny Śląsk: Prace i Materiały Geograficzne, Kraków, 1955, 559-589.

19. Janusz Ziołkowski, "Z problematyki przestrzennej i gospodarczej górnośląskiego okręgu przemysłowego," Przegląd Zachodni, XIII, 1957, 257-279.

20. Based on figures in Dokumentacja Geograficzna, zeszyt 5, Liczba ludności miast i osiedli w Polsce w latach 1810-1955, Instytut Geografii, P.A.N., Warsaw, 1956.

21. Ibid., and Rocznik Statystyczny, 1956, 58.

22. M. Ziomek, "Województwo Katowickie w planie 6-letnim," G.P., V, 1950, 534-540; W. Buch, "Lokalizacja

przemysłu w planie sześcioletnim, " G.P., IV, 1949, Jan., 25-30; M. J. Ziomek, "Problem deglomeracji Górno-Śląskiego Zagłębia Węglowego, " Ż.G., III, 1948, 497-7.

23. K. Szwabowicz, "Teoria i praktyka deglomeracji Śląska, " G.P., XI, 1956, 64-4.

24. Miasta niewydzielone and gminy.

25. Tadeusz Mrzygłod, "Potrzebna jest śmiała koncepcja deglomeracji GOP, " Ż.G., 24 Nov., 1927; G.P., XI, 1956, 64-6.

26. K. Nowakowski, "Zagadnienie zaopatrywania w wode zakładów hutniczych w górno-śląskim okręgu przemysłowym, " Hutnik, XV, 1948, 118-124; W. Zukowski, "Żaopatrzenie Zagłębia Węglowego w wodę, " Ż.G., III, 1948, 515-6.

27. K. Kisielewski, "Województwo Krakowskie w perspektywie planu 6-letniego, " G.P., VII, 1952, No. 8, 27-31.

28. N. J. G. Pounds, "Nova Huta, " Geography, XLIII, 1958, 54-56; M. Gardner Clark, Report on the Nova Huta Iron and Steel Plant named after Lenin, near Cracow, Poland, Cornell University, 1957, privately circulated.

29. Rocznik Statystyczny, 1956, 248.

30. Output per miner declined from 1940:
      1940   1430 kgm. per day
      1941   1335   "   "   "
      1942   1322   "   "   "
      1943   1279   "   "   "
      1944   1210   "   "   "
      See also: Ż. G., II, 1947, 84-5.

31. Alfred Hornig, Przemysł węglowy w Polsce podczas wojny 1939-1945, Diss., unpublished, 1948; "Produkcja i zbyt przemysłu węglowego w 1947 roku, " Ż.G., 84-5.

32. Quarterly Bulletin of Coal Statistics, United Nations Economic Commission for Europe.

33. J. Dzierżyński, "Zadania przemysłu węglowego w pierwszym roku planu pięcioletniego, " G.P., XI, 1956, no. 2, 1-5; T. Musziet, "Główne problemy rozwoju górnictwa węglowego w planie 5-letnim, " G.P., X, 1955, no. 4, 1-8; "Mechanizacja robót górniczych jako środek realizacji tez IX Plenum KC PZPR w przemyśle węglowym, " W.G., V, 1954, Feb., 33-8.

34. I. Blauth, "Aktualne zagadnienia mechanizacji górnictwa węglowego, " G.P., X, 1955, no. 3, 5-10.

35. M. Lesz, "Techniczno-organizacyjne zadania mechanizacji kopalń węgla, " G.P., VI, no. 10, 1951, 7-11.

36. Jozef Kokot, "Przebudowa gospodarcza Ślaska, " in Górny Śląsk, 481-4.

37. This includes production from new levels; see J. Dzierżyński, op.cit.

38. M. Lesz, "Zadania przemysłu węglowego w dwu ostatnich latach sześciolatki, " G.P., VIII, 1953, 12-16.

39. T. Muszkiet, "Kierunek obniżenia kosztów inwestycji w górnictwie węglowym, " G.P., XI, 1956, no. 11, 11-19.

40. In one mine visited, General Zawadzki at Będzin, it is the practice to use the three daily shifts for:
   a. boring, setting charges and blasting,
   b. loading the coal,
   c. extending the timbering and moving forward the conveyor belt preparatory to blasting again.

41. Most of the issue of Wiadomości Górnicze for October 1954 (IV, no. 10), was devoted to sand-filling, with articles on: "Podsadzka—podstawowym zagadnieniem przemysłu węglowego, " "Magistrala piaskowa—jedna z głównych inwestycji przemysłu węglowego w Polsce."

42. J. Dzierżyński, in G.P., XI, 1956, no. 2, 1-5.

43. "Jak zaoszczędzić drewno kopalniene?" W.G., IV, 1953, 139-142.

44. J. Ryszka and B. Zyska, "Problem zmniejszenia zużycia drewna w przemyśle węglowym, " G.P., XI, 1956, Jan., 16-20.

45. T. Muszkiet, op.cit., G.P., XI, 1956, Nov., 11-19.

46. W.G., IV, 1953, 344-9; "Budujemy nowe kopalnie, " W.G., IV, 1953, Sept. 240-1.

47. Types 33 to 37 according to the Polish scale: F. Byrtus, "Baza węglowa Polski jako podstawa rozwoju przemysłu hutniczego, " W.H., X, 1954, 207-212.

48. J. Dzierzynski, G.P., XI, 1956, Feb., 1-5; T. Musz-kiet, G.P., XI, Nov., 11-19.

49. This includes the Dębieńsko coke ovens which came into production in 1955; see W.H., XI, 1955, 64.

50. Polish Iron and Steel Industry Progress, M.B., 3263, Feb. 3, 1948; N. Gąsiorowska, "Górnictwo i hutnictwo w Polsce współczesnej," Myśl Współczesna, 1948, 19-47.

51. Rocznik Statystyczny, 1956, 89; W. Kuczewski, "Rozwój wielkopiecownictwa w Polsce Ludowej," W.H., X, 1954, 163.

52. S. Łowiński and Zalewski, "Perspektywy rozwoju hutnictwa żelaza," G.P., IX, 1954, May, 12-16.

53. F. Ryszka and S. Ziemba, "Dwa dziesięciolecia Huty Kościuszko," Kwartalnik Historyczny, LXI, iii, 1954, 3-75.

54. A. Szklarski, "Z wędrowek po naszych hutach: Huta Pokój," W.H., XI, 1955, 398.

55. Steel Developments in Poland, Monthly Statistical Bulletin, British Iron and Steel Federation, XXVIII, Oct. 1953.

56. R. Krajewski, "Przegląd polskich złóż rudnych z uwagi na ich znaczenie gospodarcze," H., XIV, 1947, 348-353.

57. A valuable list of Polish iron ore deposits is given in K. Bohdanowicz, "Rudy żelazne," Ż.G., II, 1947, 70-1.

58. A. Adamczyk, "Niektóre problemy efektywności rozwoju krajowego kopalnictwa rud żelaza," G.P., XI, 1956, Nov., 4-11.

59. S. Kawiński, "Problemy postępu technicznego w hutnictwie żelaza," G.P., X, 1955, Dec., 12-18.

60. A. Adamczyk, op.cit.

61. Ibid., 6.

62. V. H. Winston, Mining, MS, Mid-European Studies Center, New York, 1956.

63. Notably G.P., XI, 1956, Nov., 5.

64. K. Kisielewski, "Województwo Krakowskie w perspektywie planu 6-letniego," G.P., VIII, 1952, August, 27-31.

65. The building of Huta im. Lenina was a matter of great national pride, with the result that its progress and achievements are unusually well documented. See particularly J. Aniola, "Rola Nowej Huty w postępie technicznym hutnictwa," G.P., VI, 1951, July, 25-9; "Nowa Huta— stalowy fundament budownictwa socjalizmu," G.P., VIII, 1953, 57-60.

66. Minerals Yearbook, 1945, U.S. Department of the Interior, 198-9.

67. M.B., no. 2963, Jan. 23, 1945; M.B., no. 2971, Feb. 20, 1945.

68. B. Churzio, "Metale nieżelazne w Planie 6-letnim," H., XVII, 1950, 406-10.

69. Minerals Yearbook, U.S. Department of the Interior: Rocznik Statystyczny, 1956, 88.

70. Figures for metallic lead production are not quoted in the Rocznik Statystyczny, 1956.

71. M.B., No. 3318, Aug. 24, 1948, 7.

72. W. Jastrzebowski, "Polsko-czechosłowacka współpraca gospodarcza," Myśl Współczesna, 1948, 48-76.

73. Particularly in the coalfield area, for power and chemicals: "Polska i Czechosłowacja przystąpiły do budowy elektrowni w Dworach," Ż.G., III, 1948, 768; "Obrady polsko-czeskich komisji przemysłowych," ibid.

74. Prague News Letter, March 2, 1957.

75. Statistická Ročenka Republiky Československé, 1957, Prague 84. This refers to bituminous coal—both "hard and soft" in the American terminology. The Czechoslovak production of brown-coal is very much larger.

76. Ibid., 85.

77. Notably at Kladno and Beroun.

78. The European Steel Industry and the Wide-Strip Mill, Economic Commission for Europe, U.N., Geneva, 1953, 27.

79. Alfred Hornig, "Formy powierzchni ziemi stworzone przez człowieka na obszarze wyżyny śląskiej," in Górny Śląsk: Prace i Materiały Geograficzne, Kraków, 1955, 123, 149.

80. A. Hornig, op.cit., 138-43.

81. A. Hornig, op.cit., 136.

ALTERNATIVE FORMS OF PLACE-NAMES

Polish	Czech	German	English
Bogumin	Bohumín	Oderburg	
Będzin		Bendzin	
Biały Szarlej		Bleischarley	
Bytom		Beuthen	
Brynica river		Brinitza	
Brytomka river		Beuthener Wasser	
Budkowiczanka		Budkowitz	
Biskupice		Biskupitz	
Byczyna		Pitschen	
Chorzów (Król. Huta)	Královská huť	Königshütte	
Cieszyn	Těšín	Teschen	
Chrzanów		Chrzanow	
Czeladź		Czeladz	
Częstochowa		Tschenstochau	
Dąbrowa Górnicza		Dombrowa	
Dębiensko		Dubensko	
Dębska Kuźnica		Dembiohammer	

Polish	Czech	German	English
Gliwice	Hlivice	Gleiwitz	
Głubczyce	Hlubcice	Leobschutz	
Góra Świętej Anny		Annaberg	
Gdańsk	Gdansko	Danzig	
Gniezno	Hnězdno	Gnesen	
Głogówek		Glogau	
Gdynia	Gdyně	Gdingen	
Hulczyn	Hlučín	Hultschin	
	Karlova Huta	Karlshütte	
Katowice	Katovice	Kattowitz	
Kłodnica river		Klodnitz	
Kraków	Krakov	Krakau	Cracow
Kłodzko	Kladsko	Glatz	
Krasiejów		Krascheow	
Kluczbork		Kreuzburg	
Koźle	Kozle	Cosel	
Karwina	Karvinná	Karwin	
Królewska Huta (Chorzów)	Královská hut	Königshütte	

Polish	Czech	German	English
	Kunčice	Kunschau	
Lubliniec		Lublinitz	
Łabędy		Laband	
Odra river	Odra	Oder	
Olza river	Olsa		
Otmuchów		Ottmachau	
Morawska Ostrawa	Moravská Ostrava	Mährisch Ostrau	
Morawa	Morava	Mähren	Moravia
Miechowice		Miechowitz	
Małapanew		Malapane	
Mikołów		Nikolai	
Mysłowice		Myslowitz	
Namysłów		Namslau	
Niemodlin		Falkenberg	
Nysa river	Nisa	Neisse	
Opawa	Opava	Oppau	
Olesno	Olešno	Rosenberg	
Orłowa	Orlová	Orlau	
Opole	Opolé	Oppeln	

Polish	Czech	German	English
Ostrawa	Ostrava	Ostrau	
Oświęcim	Osvietim	Auschwitz	
Orzesze		Orzesche	
Polska Ostrawa	Polská Ostrava	Polnisch Ostrau	
Pszczyna	Pština	Pless	
Poznań		Posen	
Poręba		Poremba	
Racibórz	Ratiboř	Ratibor	
Radzionków		Radzionkau	
Rawa river			
Rybnik			
Śląsk	Slezsko	Schlesien	Silesia
Stobrawa river		Stober	
Siemianowice		Siemianowitz	
Szarlej		Scharley	
Sosnowiec		Sosnowice	
Szczecin	Štětín	Stettin	
Sucha Góra	Suchá hora	Trockenberg	
Strzelce Opolskie		Gross Strehlitz	

Polish	Czech	German	English
Świętochłowice		Schwientochlowitz	
Szopienice		Schoppinitz	
Tarnowskie Góry		Tarnowitz	
Trzyniec	Třinec		
Toszek		Tost	
Tychy		Tichau	
Witkowice	Vítkovice	Witkowitz	
Warszawa	Varsava	Warschau	Warsaw
Wałbrzych		Waldenburg	
Wisła river	Visla	Weichsel	Vistula
Wesoła		Wessola	
Wrocław	Vratislav	Breslau	
Wiedeń	Videň	Wien	Vienna
Zawiercie		Warthenau	
Zabrze	Zábřeh	Hindenburg	

INDEX

242